THE MUM'S GUIDE TO HAVING YOUR BABY IN IRELAND

Tips, Tricks and Survival Tactics

MM

THE MUM'S GUIDE TO HAVING YOUR BABY IN IRELAND

Tips, Tricks and Survival Tactics

LUCY TAYLOR ∽

Gill & Macmillan

Gill & Macmillan Ltd
Hume Avenue, Park West, Dublin 12
with associated companies throughout the world
www.gillmacmillan.ie

978 07171 4736 6

Index compiled by Cover to Cover
Typography design by Make Communication
Print origination by O'K Graphic Design, Dublin
Printed by GraphyCems, Spain

This book is typeset in 12/15 pt Minion.

The paper used in this book comes from the wood pulp
of managed forests. For every tree felled, at least one
tree is planted, thereby renewing natural resources.

A CIP catalogue record for this book is available from
the British Library.

5 4 3 2 1

The extracts from *The Bad's Dad's Survival Guide* by Adam Brophy, published
by Gill & Macmillan, 2009, are used by permission.

The extract from *Feed Your Child Well* by Valerie Kelly, Phyllis Farrell and
Therese Dunne, published by A & A Farmar, 2008, is used by permission.

The extract from *You and Your Baby* by Mary Maher, published by Torc/Gill &
Macmillan, 1973, is used by permission.

CONTENTS

ACKNOWLEDGMENTS

A big thank you goes out to a toddler who asked her mum to write a book 'with me in it' — I want to dedicate this book to my curious and loving daughter who has given me so much inspiration, and to her dad who encouraged me every step of the way. Also I couldn't write a book about becoming a parent without thanking my parents, Jane and Mike — for all the trouble I have caused them over the years.

My thanks go to my agent, Ita O'Driscoll, and the team at Gill & Macmillan — Sarah Liddy, Fergal Tobin, Deirdre Rennison Kunz, Nicki Howard, Ciara O'Connor, Teresa Daly, Tony Hetherington, and to Alison Walsh. Also to Jim Kelleher, Louise O'Conor and Rose Kervick at eumom.com.

A big thank you to all the women who generously shared their pregnancy and birth stories with me, and to friends who listened to me throughout the process — Emma Cullinan for her patience and Aifric Aiken for reading the book and providing a great sounding board.

My thanks to those who generously gave their advice and expertise including Krysia Lynch at AIMS Ireland and the Home Birth Association; Niamh Healy and Anne-Marie O'Dowd of Cuidiú (Irish Childbirth Trust); Tracy Donegan at Doula Ireland; Marguerite Hannon, Home Birth Association; Ciara O'Neill, Multiple Births Association; the Miscarriage Association of Ireland; Anne Rogers at Pet Central; Madge Fogarty, PND Ireland; Dr Joan Lalor, TCD; Dr Anne Matthews, DCU; Professor Fergal Malone. Thanks also to Marianne Hartigan and Barry McCall, Coinneach Shanks, David O'Brien, Sara Burke, Peter Orford and Camilla Galli da Bino.

INTRODUCTION

Whether you're planning a baby or have just found out that you are pregnant, welcome to *The Mum's Guide to Having Your Baby in Ireland*. For me, having a baby in Ireland was a unique experience and it has inspired me to write about pregnancy, birth and parenting.

Ireland today is in the midst of a baby boom, with a whopping 74,278 babies born here in 2009 (Central Statistics Office). There's no shortage of other new mums and more experienced parents ready to welcome you into the parenthood community with open arms.

Pregnancy is a wonderful journey that you will remember for the rest of your life. It does bring questions, concerns and decisions that have to be made, which is why I have written this uniquely Irish book.

I hope to give you a woman's perspective on pregnancy and birth in Ireland, and some of my own experiences, too, although I don't intend to bore you with too much of that. Instead, I have included lots of pregnancy and birth stories from Irish women. They will bring you their take on pregnancy and a whole host of different birthing experiences, all of which took place in Ireland.

I won't be overly medical, preachy or scary. And even though you may not agree with everything I say, I hope you find this book a balanced guide to every step of your pregnancy journey, written in a way that helps you feel like we're just having a friendly chat in a café over a sinful hot chocolate or latté. My book aims to help you find the best model of care for you and your baby, and I've packed it with tons of tips on how to enjoy every stage of pregnancy and childbirth, right through to you and your baby's six-week check. In *The Mum's Guide to Having Your Baby in Ireland* you will find information on all aspects of your pregnancy, including healthy eating and exercise, how your baby is developing during each trimester, what to expect during labour, and how to cope with the exhilarating, but sometimes exhausting, days and weeks after your baby is born.

For most women pregnancy and childbirth is a perfectly normal experience, but that doesn't mean you won't have niggling discomfort and normal fears and anxieties along the way. In writing this book I have tried to represent the everyday experience. It is not a medical 'bible' with every possible complication and medical term included.

My experience as a journalist has led me to interview many pregnant women and new mums about their experiences — something most women are more than happy to share. What I've found out is that women in Ireland have a broad range of experiences of pregnancy and birth, but we all think it's well worth it when we hold our new baby in our arms.

I first had the idea of writing this book after my daughter was born in 2005 — because, believe it or not, there wasn't a single Irish pregnancy or childbirth book on the market. Thankfully, since then, that has changed. A number of other things have changed, too, including the way some hospitals in Ireland offer services.

If you've never had a baby before you would be forgiven for finding the way maternity services work in Ireland today a little complicated — Domino, community midwives, public, semi-private, home birth — this is a minefield for the uninitiated, and I wish I knew what I have since learned through writing this book before my daughter was born!

The aim of my book is to give you the information you need to empower you to have the pregnancy and birth you want, in so far as you possibly can: of course, nothing is perfect. In fact, there's a whole chapter (Chapter 2) dedicated to this subject where I have laid out your care options in the simplest way I can, with information on how they work and how much they cost. The research from Cuidiú (Irish Childbirth Trust) in Chapter 9, who kindly allowed me to include it in the book, also paints a picture of how different hospitals and maternity-led units operate across the country. For your information, when I refer to babies, doctors, midwives and other people along your pregnancy journey I have used both 'she' and 'he' throughout.

I hope you enjoy *The Mum's Guide to Having Your Baby in Ireland*. I'll be thinking of you when your beautiful baby is born, a big smile plastered across your overjoyed face.

All the very best,
Lucy

Chapter 1 ∽

PREPARING FOR PREGNANCY

Once you decide to try for a baby, suddenly nothing else seems very important. It's on your mind all the time and you and your partner will be walking around thinking, 'We might be parents soon', while the rest of the world is more concerned with catching the bus. This is a very special time, not least because the result of all that loving will be an all-giggling baby that looks just like you and your partner and whom you will love more than you can imagine. So relax and enjoy it.

You might want to read this chapter, which is all about how to give your baby the best chance in life, while he's still a twinkle in his father's and his mother's eye.

You know how pregnant women are so well behaved — no smoking, no drinking and only eating healthy stuff, at least until the cravings kick in? Well, I hate to say it but this is how you should aim to act in the weeks before you get pregnant because, basically, the fewer toxins you put into your body at this time, the better — and the same goes for your partner. After all, you both want to give your baby the best chance of a good start in life.

A quick note, however, on unplanned pregnancies — even if you were getting drunk and swinging from the chandeliers before you found out you were expecting, the likelihood is that your baby will be absolutely fine. So don't beat yourself up about that drink you had at a wedding, or other behaviour this chapter is going to say you should avoid. It *is* important to follow medical advice, but you can't change the past so agonising over what may have happened won't change anything. If you are concerned, talk to your GP, who should be able to allay your fears.

THINGS TO TALK TO YOUR GP ABOUT

Once you and your partner have decided to try for a baby, your first port of call should be your GP. Even if you have no specific medical concerns, it's a good idea to talk to your GP and to tell her that you are planning a baby. She may decide to prescribe a multivitamin supplement that is suitable for you and will give you advice based on your medical history.

Your GP may advise you to be cautious about taking over-the-counter drugs as some of them contain ingredients such as aspirin that will work against a pregnancy establishing itself in your body.

Folic Acid

A pre-pregnancy and pregnancy must. I have read in various publications that women should take 0.4 mcg folic acid every day once they get pregnant, or for up to 14 weeks before they get pregnant and for varying lengths of time after they know they are pregnant. A bit confusing, eh?

What we do know is that folic acid reduces the risk of neural tube defects such as spina bifida. This mostly occurs during the first two months of pregnancy, and in many cases before some women know they are expecting, so the sooner you start taking it, the better. And remember, your diet will probably contain some folic acid, if you eat fortified breakfast cereals and green leafy veg.

When you see your GP or have your booking appointment in the hospital or community clinic, talk to them about it. The best way to ensure you get enough folic acid is to take a folic-acid-only supplement rather than one that is part of a multivitamin. For further information take a look at *www.folicacid.ie*.

Rubella Protection/Immunisation

Rubella or German measles, if contracted in the first 16 weeks of pregnancy, can be extremely damaging to an unborn baby, so before conception you may want to check whether you were immunised at school. If you think you weren't, you could opt for a booster shot, but it's important not to get pregnant too quickly after having this and your GP should be able to advise you on how long to leave it before trying for a baby: it's usually around three months. You cannot have the vaccination once you are pregnant, for obvious reasons. If you're worried about catching Rubella, you might want to break your pregnancy news to parents of children who might catch it at school or in childcare so that you can reduce your risk of being exposed.

The good news is that the Economic and Social Research Institute (ESRI) Perinatal Statistics Report (for 2007) found that 92.4% of women who had babies in Ireland that year were immune to Rubella, so there's a very good chance you will be too.

Smear Test

Having regular cervical smear tests should be a part of your normal healthcare programme and your GP will tell you how often this should be done. If you're planning on trying for a baby in a few months and haven't been tested in a few years, ask your GP whether you should be tested now to ensure you are up to date with all your medical checks. However, if any abnormalities are discovered and you become pregnant soon after a smear test, your doctor may recommend that treatment takes place after your baby is born. Cervical cancer is a slow-developing disease in most cases and it's also important to bear in mind that the cervix changes during pregnancy. Your GP will give you the best advice on this, but it's not a problem for the vast majority of women.

Unknown Infections

If you're serious about having a baby and suspect that you may have been exposed to a sexually transmitted infection in the past, get it checked out now. Don't be embarrassed — an infection such as chlamydia can cause scarring to your fallopian tubes and you may not even know you have it. It may be treatable and you wouldn't want to lose months of baby-making opportunities because you were too embarrassed to get tested.

Other Conditions

Another condition that can affect fertility is Polycystic Ovary

Syndrome (PCOS) — the symptoms are irregular periods, excessive body hair, haywire hormones, acne and weight gain. Once diagnosed it can be successfully treated.

Women who have painful or irregular periods and general pelvic pain may have *endometriosis,* where tissue that normally grows in the lining of the womb is found in other parts of the body, such as the ovaries and fallopian tubes, making it difficult to conceive. If you have pelvic pain, see your GP and explain that you're trying for a baby — endometriosis is usually treated in a variety of ways, with pain killers, hormones or surgery.

Pelvic inflammatory disease (PID) is another disorder that can affect fertility — it leads to inflammation of the uterus, fallopian tubes and sometimes ovaries, leading to the formation of scar tissue.

Stopping Oral Contraception

This may seem obvious, but before you get too excited and think, 'This is it!' many doctors will recommend you give your body a break from contraceptive hormones before conceiving, in order to allow it to get back to normal. You may be keen to get started, but medical experts often recommend using alternative contraception for around three menstrual cycles before taking the plunge.

Your Menstrual Cycle

Start marking in your diary when your period starts: that way you can work out how long your average menstrual cycle is. A normal cycle is anything between 21 and 42 days from the start of one period to the start of the next, and most women hit their most fertile time 14 days before their next period. This fertility gap is pretty narrow — despite what your mother told you when you were a teenager — because your egg, once released, only lives for about a day during which time your partner's feisty sperm can make you pregnant.

If you have regular periods, you should be able to work out roughly your most fertile days and make sure your partner and you try to conceive at this time. If your periods tend to be chaotic this can be more of a challenge.

Many women swear by ovulation predictor kits which can be bought from pharmacies. These kits can test for hormones that signal ovulation and identify your best days for getting pregnant. If you get the green light, it's time to go for it.

It's also a good idea to talk to your GP if you think your cycle is making it hard for you to fall pregnant as he may be able to prescribe some medication that will help to regulate your periods.

Having regular and enjoyable sex right through your cycle, rather than only pressurised sex when you hit your most fertile time, is thought to increase your chances of getting pregnant. I'm not sure why this is, but it certainly helps to keep your relationship happy too.

ACT PREGNANT BEFORE YOU ARE

Some of the recommendations below will be easier to follow than others, but they are all included because if you follow them in the weeks before conception, your body will be less exposed to anything that can harm your baby.

It's also worth pointing out that many women don't really believe they are pregnant until they miss a period, making them about two weeks pregnant, but four weeks gone in medical terms. Your baby will have already formed some of his organs by this point, so if you don't want to take any chances, then this section is for you.

Watch your Diet

Most of this advice about eating and drinking is common sense really — put good things in and keep your body in tip-top condition to conceive a much-wanted baby, and avoid other foods in case you become pregnant more quickly than you think (see pages 89–92). So here we go:

- Eat a healthy balanced diet.

- Eat five portions of fruit and vegetables every day.

- Cut down on fat and sugar in your diet.

- Cut down on caffeine by drinking fewer cups of coffee, tea and cans of fizzy drinks.

- Drink lots of water.

- Cut down on saturated fats, convenience foods and anything with lots of additives and preservatives.

- Choose the high-fibre versions of foods.

- Eat protein such as chicken, meat, fish, eggs, beans and pulses every day.

- Eat oily fish once or twice a week.

- Eat little and often to keep your blood-sugar levels steady — and always eat breakfast.

Your Weight

Being a normal weight and physically active will help you to get pregnant and to have a healthy pregnancy. The ideal to aim for here is a BMI (body mass index) of 20–25, considered a healthy body weight. This is because fat cells regulate the amount of oestrogen in your body, which can affect your menstrual cycle and ability to produce eggs. If you are over- or underweight, talk to your GP as it might affect the maternity care options open to you.

Your Lifestyle

This section might not be all that welcome to you — after all, you're not pregnant yet — however, some activities can make it more difficult for you to conceive, and you may want to moderate your lifestyle while you're in the baby-making zone.

Both you and your partner should cut down on alcohol. Drinking has been shown to affect a woman's ability to conceive and has been linked to lower fertility rates in men.

Smoking is a no-no, too. It can affect your partner's sperm count and make it harder for you to become pregnant. Cutting down now may make it easier to give up completely once you are expecting — and that means both of you. Smoking while pregnant can lead your new baby to have a lower birth weight because the chemicals cross the placenta, so he may suffer birth complications. He will also be more likely to suffer from asthma and chest infections, and there is now evidence that maternal smoking plays a role in Sudden Infant Death Syndrome (SIDS or cot death).

Illegal drugs also affect fertility and unborn babies and should be cut out completely. There are a couple of other lifestyle factors that can affect a man's fertility, too — your partner should avoid driving for long hours or taking hot baths at this time as both affect his sperm-making equipment.

Have a Dental Check-up

In order to avoid having x-rays, anaesthetics or medications while you are pregnant, go to see your dentist now. x-rays in particular are not always recommended during the first 14 weeks of a pregnancy as this is the time when your baby's organs are forming. Your dentist will give you more information on x-ray safety.

Avoid Toxic Baddies

This is not something we think about all that much in our daily lives, but it becomes more important once you consider bringing a little life into the world. Toxins are all around us and you can protect your baby by taking some simple steps:

- Avoid heavily polluted air from smoke or car fumes. Lay off the bleach and anything that is used to clean the house that has a strong smell, such as oven cleaner. Substances used for house renovations such as paints, paint thinners and strippers should be avoided, as well as pesticides and petrol.

- At work, talk to your safety officer if you have any worries — if you work near chemicals, you could be putting your pregnancy at risk and may need to make changes.

- If you have an old boiler, gas fire or appliances such as a cooker or microwave, you may want to have them serviced to ensure nothing dangerous is leaking.

- Avoid heating up food in plastic or under cling film as chemicals can leach into the food, according to recent health advice.

Mentally Prepare

You don't need to have the whole nine months of your pregnancy planned out in advance, but giving some thought to a number of issues will help you to take every stage in your stride.

- Reading about pregnancy and how the maternity services work in Ireland will help you to be informed about the decisions you will have to make along the way.

- Giving some thought to how your finances will change when you have a baby will help you both to make sensible spending decisions over the coming months.

- Spending time with a friend who has a small baby can be a good idea, and she will probably welcome the help, too. A ten-minute visit doesn't count, though: you will need to be there for several hours in order to get a real idea of what's involved.

Relax

Take it easy — this is not the time to be stressed and have too much on your plate. Mums have told me that when they worried about whether they could get pregnant, nothing happened. When they gave up on the idea and stopped obsessing about it, they miraculously got pregnant. Finding ways to manage work stress such as exercise, quality sleep and treating yourself, can all help you to relax.

WHEN TO SEEK FURTHER ADVICE

It's hard to know whether you and your partner will get pregnant the first time you try for a baby or will still be waiting a year down the line. According to the Human Fertilisation and Embryology Authority (HFEA) in the UK, when couples have regular sex:

20% of couples conceive within a month of starting to try for a baby;
70% of couples get pregnant within six months;
85% of couples get pregnant within a year;
95% of couples conceive within two years.

So, in the majority of cases, patience is the answer, but if you think something might be wrong and have been trying for a baby for a year, it may be time to seek some medical advice. Your GP should be able to refer you to a specialist who can test your fertility and recommend treatment or lifestyle changes. If you're over 35 and worried about your ability to conceive, don't wait as long as a year — time is of the essence and prompt action can give you a better chance of becoming pregnant.

In September 2009 the Women's Health Council (WHC) published two reports about infertility and its treatment in Ireland. The reports concluded that fertility problems have been ranked as one of the great stressors in life, comparable to those of divorce and death in the family. However, it is not an issue that is widely discussed. The most common infertility treatment in Ireland is IVF which has undergone a rise from 135 babies born in 2000 to 301 in 2005. The WHC found that the average cost of one IVF cycle is €4,000, with fertility drugs costing €2,000–€3,000. Sperm donation can cost around €800 and egg donation costs €5,000–€12,000.

According to reports, a couple's chance of having a healthy baby as a result of fertility treatment depends largely on patient age, weight, pregnancy history, the number of embryos transferred and the method of embryo transfer (in the case of IVF treatment). Statistics for 2005 reveal that the percentage of deliveries per IVF cycle is 21.15% for a fresh cycle and 11.3% for a frozen cycle.

What Infertility Help is Available in Ireland?
Your first port of call is to talk to your GP. If he is a man and you're too embarrassed to talk to him, ask to see a female doctor or go to a different practice. She will ask you about your menstrual cycle, about previous pregnancies and miscarriages, about infections, including sexually transmitted diseases, and about your sex life and what kind of contraception you have been using. She won't be judgmental, but you will need to be open and honest in order to give her the full story. She may then refer you to a specialist for investigations and treatment.

You may benefit from the help and advice of a support group such as the National Infertility Support and Information Group, which offers a confidential listening ear to couples and individuals (*www.nisig.ie*).

I would also recommend the following book: *Trying to Conceive: The*

Irish Couple's Guide by Fiona McPhillips (Liberties Press). This is a guidebook for anyone trying to conceive, taking readers from the stage of recognising fertility signs and timing intercourse, to looking for help, finding a fertility clinic, right through to IVF and beyond. It's full of facts and figures and advice.

The following websites are also a good source of information on the subject of infertility:
www.eumom.com
www.fertilityfriend.com

SIGNS YOU MIGHT BE PREGNANT

Feeling sick, going to the loo a lot, sensitivity to smell, feeling light-headed and weepy, having a raised body temperature and missing a period are all classic signs of very early pregnancy, and some women claim that they just 'know'. However, don't start celebrating yet as your pregnancy will have to be confirmed first.

This can be done using a number of different tests, but the most commonly used one is the home-pregnancy testing kit available in pharmacies. Some of these come in double packs and many excited women like to test a couple of times just to make sure.

These tests are designed to look for the pregnancy-related hormone hCG (human chorionic gonadotropin) which is made by the embryo soon after conception. You get the results in minutes and they are pretty accurate.

While you can use one of these tests from the first day of your missed period, it's a good idea not to get your hopes up too much and tell everyone you know at this stage. Do the test again a week later to make sure. I'm advising caution here because sometimes a fertilised egg may not implant successfully in the womb, and you will get a late period.

By contrast some women will actually get light bleeding when they should have had their period and then discover they are pregnant.

After a positive test your next step is to see your GP (although this is not necessarily required) — mine asked me to pee into a cup then put a coloured paper stick in it and said, 'You're pregnant'. He then asked when my last period had been and told me my due date. Some doctors will take a blood test instead.

Next, my GP asked me where I wanted to have my baby — I hadn't a clue. He made some suggestions and after I agreed that combined care sounded ideal (more on this in Chapter 2) he wrote a letter to my local maternity hospital in order to get a date for my 'booking' appointment (see page 51), the first hospital appointment at which a detailed history is taken and scans or other checks booked. However, a lot of other pregnant women have told me that they had to book themselves into their maternity hospital of choice, so it varies quite a bit. Whoever does it, it's important to organise your booking appointment quite early in your pregnancy in order to ensure you get the best antenatal care. Maternity hospitals, especially the three main ones in Dublin, are very busy so the sooner you contact them, the sooner you can be seen and have all the necessary checks done.

Congratulations, you are expecting a baby — get ready for the rollercoaster ride to follow!

SOME WORDS FOR DAD-TO-BE

In the words of Adam Brophy in his book *The Bad Dad's Survival Guide* (Gill & Macmillan), 'No matter how much we desire to have a child, no matter how secure we are, financially, emotionally, physically even, when the words "I'm pregnant" are uttered to us for the first time, we have something of a tremor.

'…The sense of relief kicks in immediately afterwards. You're not shooting blanks, you're all man, there's ammo in your cannon, you're a big blue-balled stallion… Note the swagger of the prospective new father's walk.

'It doesn't matter how you got to this point, whether it was through a military operation of astutely-timed precision or from a head-aching drink- and drug-fuelled recovery fumble, the fact is that you are here now. At the starter's blocks, about to set out on a long trudge of a race without a map or a manual to your name.'

Chapter 2 ∾

PRACTICAL
CONSIDERATIONS

This chapter will look at your choices for antenatal care, where you can have your baby and the care you will receive after he is born. My aim in this chapter is to make it easier for you to find out what is available in your area, to choose the most ideal care for you and to negotiate the system to get the best pregnancy and birth you can.

I'm not going to say that one service is better than another, only to lay out the options that are generally available and then let you decide what's best for you. However, if you want to have your baby in hospital, I would advise you to make an informed decision and act on it as soon as you know you are pregnant. This is because your first 'booking' appointment in hospital, which tests for various treatable pregnancy-related conditions (see page 51 for more on this), should happen at around 12–16 weeks of pregnancy. However, because there is great demand, especially for public care, in some hospitals you may have to wait longer — if you feel the wait is very long, ask your GP to help you contact the hospital or phone up at regular intervals and ask about cancellations.

In recent years there have been changes in the way the maternity system works in Ireland, in terms of antenatal care, how long you get to stay in hospital after you have your baby and your postnatal care. Many of these changes have been woman-friendly, such as the introduction of community midwife schemes from some hospitals, which means that pregnant women categorised as low risk can have most of their antenatal and postnatal care closer to home. This, of course, saves on queues in hospitals and makes total sense to both hospitals and mums-to-be.

When you're thinking about antenatal care and where you will have your baby, bear in mind that some GPs can be a mine of information and some are less up to date about what's on offer in your area, or may even favour one type of care over another.

Friends who live close by and have recently had babies can share their experiences with you, but beware: they may have wanted a different birth from you and may value certain facilities and conditions more or less than you do. But you can still glean some useful information from them. Try to find out how they were treated in labour: Were they continuously monitored by machine? Was the midwife willing to consider a birth plan? Was the woman encouraged to move around and be upright during labour? Were her wishes taken into account and was she asked to consent to minor procedures? The answers to these questions, especially if given by women with different birth experiences, will help you to get a picture of how labour is managed in different circumstances.

Looking over the Cuidiú research into maternity services in Ireland in Chapter 9 will also help you to find out more about the policies and practices used in different hospitals. This research will allow you to compare the numbers of caesarean sections, inductions, epidurals and so on in each hospital and to draw conclusions of your own. Some hospitals practise 'active management' of labour, which means that the person caring for you during labour will move things along using drugs or other interventions if they are progressing slowly. Many women say they are unhappy with this policy as it can lead them to feel they are losing control and in greater need of pain relief. Other women are quite happy with this approach. All labour experiences are different.

In Mary Maher's book *You and Your Baby* (Torc/Gill & Macmillan), which was published in 1973, she says, 'Any hospital with a reputation for heavy reliance on drugs should be regarded warily… when it seems to be routine policy it suggests that the staff for one reason or another want to keep maternity patients as manageable as possible by the simplest method known, rather than teaching them how to make their own labours progress more smoothly.' In many cases this still holds true in Ireland today, over 35 years later.

Before I start looking at each of the options available in Ireland, I'd like to make a point about the best person to give you antenatal care and to help you to give birth to your baby. The Irish system is currently largely obstetric-led, which means that most pregnancies and births are managed by an obstetrician and his or her team, some of whom are midwives. An obstetrician is a medical doctor who specialises in abnormal, assisted and dangerous pregnancies and births, and yet the majority of women in Ireland having normal pregnancies believe that it is necessary to see an obstetrician at every antenatal visit and that s/he should be there for the birth.

Whilst this is certainly true in the case of complicated or high-risk pregnancies — if you are expecting twins, for example, or develop medical conditions such as obstetric cholestasis, gestational diabetes, placenta praevia, pre-eclampsia or are carrying a breech baby (these terms will be explained in Chapter 3, You and Your Pregnancy) — the vast majority of women have a completely normal pregnancy, with only minor health issues that are not dangerous for either mum or baby. For these women, the midwife is their most suitable lead caregiver — because midwives are trained in every aspect of normal pregnancy and birth. Not many women realise that if you choose to hire a private consultant but experience a normal labour, the chances are that you will give birth attended by midwives, although your doctor is likely to appear at some point if he is available.

However, you should be reassured that if at any point during your pregnancy or delivery your midwife is concerned about you or your baby, you will be immediately referred back to the care of an obstetrician, whatever type of care you have chosen.

Obviously the model of care you choose is totally up to you, but if you can't afford semi-private or private care, or would prefer to spend the money on your baby once he is born, there is no reason to be concerned. You will not receive inferior care by going through the public system; however, it is likely to be more crowded and may have longer queues due to the levels of demand.

Here are facts and figures from the Economic and Social Research Institute (ESRI) Perinatal Statistics Report for 2007:

- The average age of women who gave birth was 31 years.

- 14% of first births were to women aged 35 or older, which has been increasing each year and was 9% in 1999.

- The average age of first-time mothers was 28.8 years.

- 31.84% of mothers were single.

- 1.6% had a multiple pregnancy.

- 77.45% of women chose hospital and GP combined antenatal care. (Deliveries under Domino schemes and midwifery-led maternity units within some hospitals were included under combined care.)

- Hospital/obstetrician care accounted for 20.8% of total births with booked hospital admissions at 99.01%.

- The average amount of time spent in hospital was 3.58 days.

- The percentage of spontaneous singleton births (i.e. without forceps or ventouse) decreased from 65.35% in 1999 to 58.41% in 2007.

- The rate of caesarean sections for singleton births increased from 19.69% in 1999 to 25% in 2007.

- In terms of multiple births, the number of spontaneous births dropped from 32.33% in 1999 to 21.86% in 2007, while caesarean rates for multiple births were at 47.23% in 1999 and rose to 63.66% in 2007.

- There were 2,185 twin births, 83 triplet births and 3 quadruplet births.

- Figures show an increase in the percentage of mothers breastfeeding, with age. 44.1% of women aged 25–29 years breastfed in 2007, 49.4% at age 35–39, 51.2% age 40–44, with a small drop at age 45 plus, to 49.5%.

The ESRI Perinatal Statistics Report for 2008 was not published at the time of going to press. You can find a link to it on *www.havingyourbabyinireland.com*.

PUBLIC CARE

If you live in Ireland, and fulfil residency criteria 'ordinarily resident' in Ireland, you are entitled to free maternity care, whether you have health insurance or not. Public care covers all the medical and accommodation costs of your antenatal care, pregnancy and labour, whatever happens. If you choose public hospital care, you will attend the hospital, or in some cases a local antenatal midwife clinic, for your antenatal appointments and may choose combined care and see your GP for some of your visits. If the hospital runs a midwives clinic and you are suitable because your pregnancy is considered low risk, you may be transferred to the care of the midwives, which means that they will be familiar to you right through your pregnancy. It is not guaranteed that you will see the same doctor/obstetrician at every antenatal hospital visit.

Hospitals have different practices and policies when it comes to giving patients ultrasound scans during pregnancy (see page 52), and public hospitals in particular may not be able to afford to offer you as many as you would like. You can visit a private clinic for additional scans, which cost from €145 to €190, depending on the type, available from a number of centres in Dublin, Cork and Co. Wicklow. (See page 54 for more information.)

When you come into the hospital to give birth, the hospital midwives will help you to deliver your baby. You may not know these midwives, and if you are having a normal labour with no complications, you may not see a doctor at all.

If your labour becomes more complicated and you need forceps, ventouse or a caesarean section, you will be aided by an obstetrician and his or her team. If you choose to have an epidural, the hospital anaesthetist will attend you.

After your baby is born, you will be moved to a public ward, which generally has around eight beds and can be a busy place at visiting times. You might like to check whether your hospital offers an Early Transfer Home Scheme (ETHS) with postnatal visits at home.

There are a number of options available to you in the public system:

COMBINED CARE

When your GP (or hospital staff) confirms your pregnancy, she may suggest that you opt for *combined care*. This means that you will see your GP for about half your antenatal check-ups and attend the hospital or midwife clinic for the rest.

Your GP will be paid for this by the HSE, including the appointment where she/he confirmed that you were pregnant, so you don't have to pay them.

You can go for combined care whether you are choosing community midwives, public, semi-private or private care. Fewer visits to see your obstetrician may mean a smaller fee for you if you are having private care.

Your GP and hospital will provide you and your baby with postnatal care up to and including the six-week check under this free scheme.

MIDWIFERY-LED UNITS

In a hospital Midwifery-Led Unit (MLU), a team of two to six experienced midwives look after a pregnant woman from her initial booking right through to the birth of her baby and for her postnatal care. This is a free service that is available in two locations in Ireland and accessible to women who have no risk factors in their pregnancy.

The environment in which women labour and deliver their babies is a homely birth room that is more like a hotel room than a hospital room with no medical instruments and harsh lighting. There are birthing balls, bean bags etc. as well as music and a water pool. The Entonox mask (gas and air) is available too.

MLUs support active birth and encourage women to find their own preferred positions for birthing. There are less inductions and less interference in the natural course of your labour. This means that women who attend MLUs are less likely to have epidurals and caesarean sections.

Women who have their babies in MLUs can go home from six to 48 hours after the birth, and one of the members of the midwife team will visit them at home every day until their baby is around seven days old. From this point the public health nurse will take over the care of mum and baby.

If at any point during pregnancy or labour a woman experiences a problem or the midwives are concerned for her or her baby, she will be transferred to the care of the obstetrician in the hospital and his team.

There are two MLUs in Ireland, in Cavan General Hospital and Our Lady of Lourdes Hospital, Drogheda, Co. Louth.

Cavan General Maternity Hospital
Phone 049 4376000

Our Lady of Lourdes Hospital, Drogheda
Phone 041 9837601

COMMUNITY MIDWIVES SCHEMES
In community midwives schemes, care is provided in the community through a combination of pregnancy, labour and postnatal care by a team of midwives attached to one of the maternity hospitals. There are a number of different schemes in operation in Ireland.

Community Midwives Home Birth Schemes
This scheme means that a pregnant woman will see a team of midwives for her antenatal care and give birth at home. The service is free of charge.

Only women categorised as having a low-risk pregnancy may avail of this service. According to the World Health Organisation (WHO) 80% of all pregnant women have a low-risk pregnancy, but you can discuss this with your midwife. Women availing of this scheme do not have to have their booking appointment at the hospital, although they may wish to — it can be in a local health clinic with a community midwife.

Women who are being cared for on a Community Midwives Home Birth scheme will be offered a scan at 18–22 weeks to confirm the pregnancy is low risk. If any problems develop they are immediately transferred back to full hospital obstetric care. Also, if a mum-to-be feels the scheme is not for her she can ask to transfer to hospital care.

Antenatal appointments take place in a midwives clinic or local health centre, making it easier for many women to attend.

After the birth mum and baby will be visited at home by a member of the midwife team until the baby is seven days old (on some schemes this can be up to ten days old) when the care of mum and baby is transferred to the public health nurse. Women who take up this scheme can choose combined care with their GP, who will give their baby a six-week check.

You will need to contact your hospital to find out whether they run a Community Midwives Home Birth Scheme, and if so whether you are in the catchment area.

There are presently a number of Community Midwives Home Birth Schemes running in Ireland:

National Maternity Hospital (NMH), Holles Street, Dublin.

The community midwives team consists of 14 experienced midwives (who provide home birth and Domino scheme) working in two teams. These services are available to women living in South Dublin and certain parts of Bray. Local midwife clinics are run by NMH in Ballinteer, Dun Laoghaire, Bray, Greystones and Carrickmines. The Community Midwives service at the NMH takes only low-risk pregnant women who haven't previously had caesarean sections. If you wish to consider this service, contact the hospital on the number below, ask whether you are in the catchment area, and request a booklet:
Central Booking Office
Phone 01 637 3288

Waterford Regional Hospital

Covers some of Kilkenny and some of Wexford
Valerie Cosgrave
Phone 087 9080391

Wexford General Hospital

Wexford Maternity Unit
Phone 053 9153000

Carlow/Kilkenny/South Tipperary (SEHB)

Eithne Coen
Phone 056 7785619

The HSE Southern Health Area provides a free home birth service covering women who live in Cork and Kerry.
Joan Delaney
Phone 021 4923483

Community Midwives Domino Schemes

With the Domino Schemes the mother gives birth in hospital — DOMINO stands for DOMiciliary IN and OUT. Women have their antenatal care in conjunction with their GP in pregnancy, have their baby 'IN' hospital with a community midwife caring for them, then transfer 'OUT' — home 6–12 hours following the birth.

Only women categorised as having a low-risk pregnancy may avail of this service. Women availing of this scheme do not have to have their booking appointment at the hospital, although they may wish to — it can be in a local health clinic with a community midwife.

Women who are being cared for on a Community Midwives Domino scheme will be offered a scan at 18–22 weeks to confirm that the pregnancy is low risk. If any problems develop they are immediately transferred back to full hospital obstetric care. Also, if a mum-to-be feels the scheme is not for her, she can ask to transfer to obstetric hospital care.

Antenatal appointments take place in midwives clinics or at the local health centre, making it easier for many women to attend.

After the birth mum and baby can be discharged early from hospital and be visited at home by a member of the midwife team until the baby is around ten days old, when the care of mum and baby is transferred to the public health nurse.

You will need to contact your hospital to find out whether they run a Domino Midwives Scheme, and if so, whether you are in the catchment area.

There are presently a number of Domino Midwives Schemes running in Ireland:

National Maternity Hospital (NMH), Holles Street, Dublin
This service is available to women living in South Dublin, Bray and North Wicklow. Local midwife clinics are run by NMH in Ballinteer,

Dun Laoghaire, Bray, Greystones and Carrickmines. Contact the hospital on the numbers below, ask whether you are in the catchment area, and request a booklet.
Central Booking Office
Phone 01 637 3288
Wicklow
Phone 01 274 4163

Rotunda Hospital, Dublin
The Domino Midwives scheme in the Rotunda operates principally in the Dublin 7 and Dublin 11 areas.
Phone 01 8171700

Coombe Women and Infants University Hospital, Dublin
At the time of writing there was no Domino scheme in operation in the Coombe Women and Infants University Hospital, however there are plans to introduce a scheme in 2011.
Phone 01 408 5200 for more information.

Hospital Midwives and Local Antenatal Midwife Clinics
Whatever hospital care you decide to have, you can choose to see midwives for your antenatal care instead of an obstetrician. Some hospitals run midwife clinics in hospital and community midwife clinics in local health centres even though they do not yet have a Domino scheme in operation. This means less travel for you, especially if you live far from the hospital. Ask for leaflets and up-to-date information.

Coombe Women and Infants University Hospital, Dublin
The hospital midwife clinic (staffed by hospital midwives) has been expanded to Monday–Friday mornings. To attend this clinic you need to be referred by a Coombe doctor after your first booking appointment at the hospital. The Coombe also offers midwife clinics in the community as well as antenatal and parentcraft classes:
Wednesday mornings in Clondalkin — for appointments, phone 087 7986453.

Tuesday mornings in Tallaght — for appointments, phone 087 7986453.
For the Tallaght Hospital Clinic, phone 086 7809354.
Wednesdays in Naas — for appointments, phone 087 7977159.

The National Maternity Hospital (NMH), Holles Street, Dublin

Runs local midwife clinics in Ballinteer, Dun Laoghaire, Bray, Greystones and Carrickmines.
Central Booking Office
Phone 01 637 3288

University College Hospital (UCH) Galway

Antenatal midwife clinics (outreach service), available in Health Centre, Oughterard; Dental Centre, Gort. Book through the hospital under consultant. Hospital midwife clinic also available, alongside consultant clinics, mornings and afternoons.
Phone 091 544 661 for information.

The Rotunda, Dublin

Holds midwife clinics in the following places:
Evening clinic — Blanchardstown and Swords
Afternoon clinic — Coolock and Ballymun
Phone 01 817 1700

EARLY TRANSFER HOME SCHEME

This scheme means that healthy women and babies can go home as early as six hours after the birth as long as they are assessed as ready by the hospital. Women whose babies are born during the night can go home in the morning.

After you have gone home you will receive daily midwife visits to ensure that you and your baby are doing well and will be given advice on feeding, the Guthrie/PKU or heel-prick test (see page 185) and your baby will be weighed — the midwife will usually make up to five visits.

The Early Transfer Home Scheme is available to women irrespective of who their caregivers have been. Many hospitals run an ETH scheme, even if they don't offer a Community Midwives or Domino Scheme, so it is worth checking with your hospital.

Coombe Women and Infants University Hospital, Dublin
Early Transfer Home Scheme now covers D8 Dolphins Barn/Rialto, D10 Ballyfermot, D12 Crumlin, D20 Palmerstown, D22 Clondalkin, D24 Tallaght, Lucan, Naas, Urban, Sallins, Newbridge, Johnstown and Kill, Co. Kildare.
For more information, phone 01 408 5616.

National Maternity Hospital (NMH), Holles Street, Dublin
Central Booking Office
Phone 01 637 3288

Rotunda Hospital, Dublin
Phone 01 817 6850

University College Galway
Phone 091 544 661

SEMI-PRIVATE CARE
This type of antenatal, labour and postnatal care is subject to the policies and practices of different hospitals, and can mean different things. Usually it means that you attend a semi-private clinic for your antenatal appointments, and will see a consultant or member of his team when you visit. You may not see the same person for every hospital visit.

When you arrive at the hospital to have your baby you will be looked after by midwives, but a member of the consultant's team should be available for your baby's birth in case there are complications.

After your baby is born you will be put in a semi-private ward if there is a bed available. These wards usually have between four and six beds, but this depends on how many babies are being born at the same time in the hospital.

Costs of semi-private care vary and are subject to change, but to give you a rough idea, the semi-private fee totals approximately €4,000. This fee covers the cost of accommodation in a semi-private room, antenatal clinics, delivery, anaesthesia and a certain number of scans. If you have private health insurance, it will cover some of these costs, such as accommodation, for example, but others, e.g. scans or antenatal visits, you may have to pay for yourself. For information on hospital charges, contact your hospital, who will be able to provide you with an itemised list. Your health insurer will also tell you what services are covered by your policy.

PRIVATE CARE

The main difference between semi-private and private care is that you will see your own consultant for every antenatal visit at the hospital and that he or she will usually attend your baby's birth. Of course, circumstances change and if your consultant cannot be there he/she will arrange for another consultant to attend your baby's birth.

After your baby's birth you will be moved to a private room, but if one is not available because the hospital is extremely busy, you may spend some time in a semi-private or public ward. This is becoming increasingly common in busy maternity hospitals.

Most private care takes place in public hospitals because at the moment there is only one private hospital offering maternity services — Mount Carmel in Dublin. Private health insurance usually covers the cost of private accommodation in public hospitals and the cost of delivery. Some insurers will pay a contribution to consultant's fees, which cost from €3,500 to €5,000 in Dublin and from around €2,500 to €4,000 in the rest of the country.

For those who choose to have their baby in Mount Carmel, three nights' stay is currently approximately €6,000, with consultant's fees of €3,200–€3,800. You can check with your insurer to see what is covered by your policy.

HOME BIRTH WITH A SELF-EMPLOYED COMMUNITY MIDWIFE (SECM)

About 1% of all births in Ireland take place at home. According to some studies in countries where home birth is more common, for mothers whose pregnancies are considered low-risk, home birth has been demonstrated to be as safe as hospital delivery; however reports vary and the safety of home birth remains a contested issue. In Ireland, there are not enough home births to confirm these findings, but the Home Birth Association of Ireland (*www.homebirth.ie*) outlines the current research into safety on its website and have been helpful in providing information for this section.

Your suitability for a home birth will be assessed by a midwife. Home birth is available to all women experiencing a low-risk pregnancy, although in reality there are very few Self-Employed Community Midwives in Ireland. Home births are not considered safe if you are carrying twins, a baby in breech or transverse presentation, or have a serious medical condition such as placenta praevia or high blood pressure (pre-eclampsia). Women are carefully screened to ensure they are low risk before being accepted for a home birth.

In September 2008 a Memorandum of Understanding (MOU) agreed between the Self-Employed Community Midwives (SECMS) and the Health Service Executive (HSE) led to slightly different practices being required by the HSE of home-birth midwives. In effect, this means that there are stricter criteria for women to be considered for a home birth. The most significant is that women who have had a previous caesarean section, even if they have had a subsequent vaginal birth after caesarean (VBAC) in hospital, or even a previous home birth, are extremely unlikely to be able to find a care provider for a home birth. Also, the rules governing transfer to hospital before, during and after labour are more extensive. Women who go past their Expected Due Date (EDD) will be expected to attend hospital to have their baby monitored sooner than previously.

Self-Employed Community Midwives (SECMS) are registered with the HSE but practise independently. They can provide full antenatal care by visiting you at home; during labour and delivery where they stay with you throughout, in your home; and postnatal care in your home up to and including a six-week check-up. Your midwife may also conduct the regular paediatric newborn checks and the Guthrie/PKU (heel-prick test) on your baby. She will provide breastfeeding encouragement and support.

Booking a Midwife

There is a severe shortage of Self-Employed Community Midwives (SECMS) in Ireland, and the best advice is to act as soon as you know you are pregnant. Contact the *Home Birth Association* (*www.homebirth.ie*) for information on how to arrange a home birth and the names of midwives working in your area. Once your midwife accepts you, she will need to fill out a Form of Application for Maternity Care to be sent to the director of public health nursing in your local area. This will entitle you to a grant for your care from the HSE, which goes directly to the midwife. The HSE will also provide you with a 'maternity pack', with waterproof sheets, scissors to cut the cord, cord clamps, sterile pads etc. Sometimes these come in a handy plastic 'toolbox'.

Blood Tests and Scans

Your midwife will require you to have blood tests taken at 12–18 weeks. You could ask your GP to refer you to a non-maternity hospital for your blood tests, however it is more likely that your midwife will suggest that you open a file with your local maternity hospital and go through the standard public booking route in case you need to be transferred to hospital care at a later stage. The number of appointments you will attend varies, but will usually involve a booking visit in hospital, a scan if you want it and one or two visits in the late antenatal period.

Pain Relief

Midwives carry gas and air (the Entonox mask) and Pethidine. You can hire a birthing pool if your midwife is trained in water birth, or labour in your own bath if they are not — discuss this with your midwife. Many women giving birth at home choose to hire a Transcutaneous Electrical Nerve Stimulation (TENS) machine — see page 140 — which can be hired from pharmacies.

Transfer to Hospital

Even though most home births go to plan, your midwife may decide that you and your baby need extra care and will transfer you to hospital care. Be prepared for the possibility that this may happen while you are pregnant, during labour or after your baby is born. Discuss this possibility with your midwife during one of your antenatal visits.

Costs

If your midwife has made a minimum of 11 visits in total (both antenatal and postnatal) and attended the birth at home, then she is paid €2,400 directly from the HSE. However, the cost of hiring a SECM for a home birth currently can be between €2,500 and €5,000. If you have private health insurance you may receive a grant from your insurer towards the cost of a home birth. Employees and spouses of certain companies with group health insurance such as An Garda Síochána, ESB, prison officers etc., may also be eligible to claim for midwifery service fees. You will need to research this yourself.

WHAT IS A DOULA?

A *doula* provides continuous emotional and physical support to a couple before, during and after the birth of their baby. A birth doula will provide support and information during pregnancy and labour and a postpartum doula provides help with the overwhelming experience of being a new mum, although the role is a flexible one. A doula is generally not medically trained: she is usually a mother herself and works with the couple to help them have the best birth possible, as determined by the couple. Unlike the midwife, the doula has no clinical responsibilities — she is completely focused on the needs of the mother. The doula's care complements the care mum is already receiving from her midwife. Studies have shown that women who use the services of a doula increase the likelihood of having a normal birth, with less intervention and greater satisfaction.

There are approximately 30–40 trained doulas in Ireland; about ten are actively working in the Irish maternity system. They mostly work in hospitals but will also attend home births.

Not all hospitals are 'doula friendly'. In some hospitals a second birth partner is not permitted, nor is swapping the birth partner during labour. Hospitals that support the mother's wishes to have a doula present are: Our Lady of Lourdes Drogheda, the Coombe Women and Infants University Hospital, Cork University Maternity Hospital (CUMH), Galway University Hospital, Portiuncula Hospital, Letterkenny Hospital, Waterford Regional Hospital and Wexford General Hospital. To get the most up-to-date information, contact your maternity unit (a list of numbers is provided in Chapter 11). If a mother is refused access to a doula she should contact the Director of Midwifery in her hospital and AIMS Ireland (Association for Improvements in Maternity Services). Doulas are welcome at home births by either community midwives or self-employed community midwives.

Doulas are self employed and offer different services so their rates vary from €600 to €1,200. Some health insurers provide partial reimbursement for doula services. Most Irish doulas volunteer their services or provide services for a reduced fee for teen mums or mums with financial difficulties.

Doulas are on call from 38 weeks, which can potentially go on until 42 weeks, so it's a significant commitment for a doula to be on call and she can be with a woman and her partner for up to two days.

A postpartum doula can help if you are recovering from the birth, trying to establish breastfeeding and getting little sleep. The idea behind a doula is that she 'mothers' the mother and helps you to adjust to the demands of a newborn baby, and she will help with any household chores so that you can concentrate on yourself and your baby.

For more information on doulas, check out *www.doulaIreland.com* or *www.doula.ie*.

MATERNITY BENEFIT — YOUR ENTITLEMENTS AND HOW TO GET THEM

The information in this section, on maternity benefit and maternity leave, parental leave and antenatal visits comes from *www.citizens information.ie*.

Maternity Leave

Working women in Ireland are entitled to 26 weeks' maternity leave plus an additional 16 weeks' unpaid maternity leave.

- You must take at least two weeks of this leave before the end of the week of your baby's expected birth and at least four weeks after.

- You must give your employer at least four weeks' written notice of your intention to take maternity leave and provide a medical certificate confirming the pregnancy.

- You must give your employer four weeks' written notice of your intention to take the additional 16 weeks unpaid maternity leave.

- You must give your employer four weeks' written notice of the date you intend to return to work.

Maternity Benefit

Maternity Benefit is payable to all women who have paid a certain amount of PRSI during a relevant tax period. It is paid on a weekly basis into your bank or building society account for 26 weeks.

The amount you receive each week will depend on your earnings and is subject to an upper and lower limit.

- PAYE workers receive 80% of their gross income divided by the number of weeks they actually worked in the second to last complete income tax year before the year in which their maternity leave starts.

- Self-employed women receive 80% of their gross income divided by 52 weeks in the same relevant tax year.

- You will need to apply at least six weeks before you go on maternity leave (twelve weeks if you are self-employed).

- For information on the minimum and maximum payments for Maternity Benefit, check *www.citizensinformation.ie*.

- Women who are already on certain social welfare payments will receive half-rate Maternity Benefit.

- Some employers will pay your full salary while you are on maternity leave and ask you to pass on the social welfare payment to them. Others may top up the difference between Maternity Benefit and your salary, and some may not pay anything at all. Check your contract of employment to see what applies to you.

To apply, log onto *www.citizensinformation.ie*, download and complete a MB10 form and send it to: Maternity Benefit Section, Department of Social Protection, Inner Relief Road, Ardarvan, Buncrana, Co. Donegal. LoCall 1890 690 690 E-mail: *maternityben@welfare.ie*. You can also apply for a form by post from this address.

WORKING THROUGH PREGNANCY

Many women are reluctant to tell their boss their great news, for fear they may be judged differently by their employer and colleagues. Others are keen to keep it a personal matter for as long as possible or until the first trimester has passed, but may find that colleagues suss them out and they have to reveal all sooner than they'd like. Those tell-tale signs of early pregnancy such as having to go to the toilet more frequently and turning up for work looking peaky due to morning sickness may not go unnoticed by colleagues who have been through it themselves.

It's a good idea to check out your rights by reading your contract of employment before breaking the news so that you are armed with the information you need. Thinking about what your boss will ask you when he or she is given the news will also help you to stay calm about it. Issues such as how long you plan to be off work, how you think your work should be covered in your absence etc. may be considered. You won't need to have answers to these questions now, but being as helpful about the situation as you can will be appreciated. You may need to train someone in to cover for you or to brief colleagues, for example.

It's a good idea to plan for a possible drop in income as soon as you can. You may be entitled to less in maternity pay than you are currently earning and you may decide to take additional unpaid leave. Any savings you have will help cushion the blow. If you return to work full time you will need to consider childcare options and costs — the more you plan and save for now, the easier it will be to cope later.

When you go on leave make sure everything is easy to find for the person covering your work, inform clients of your plans and change your e-mail and voicemail to redirect work to colleagues. Having a plan and keeping your boss informed will make the transition go as smoothly as possible.

Some women are not totally honest about their predicted due date, so that they can spend less time waiting to go into labour and more time with their new baby. However, there's a good reason why maternity leave start two weeks before your due date. The idea is to give mum-to-be a chance to relax and get ready for the birth. If you are worn out from working too much, the whole experience will be more difficult.

Returning to Work

This is a subject that, understandably, is of great concern to many women when they discover they are pregnant, but bear in mind that you do have some employment protection under law. If you are unhappy about the way you have been treated by your employer, you can seek trade union representation or get legal advice. Here's what the government website *www.citizensinformation.ie* says about this subject:

'Under *Section 26 of the Maternity Protection Act 1994* you are entitled to return to work to the same job with the same contract of employment. *Section 27 of the Act* states that if it is not reasonably practicable for your employer to allow you to return to your job, then they must provide you with suitable alternative work. This new position should not be on terms substantially less favourable than those of your previous job.

'Otherwise, you are entitled to be treated as if you had been at work during your maternity leave. Your employment conditions cannot be worsened by the fact that you have taken maternity leave, and if pay or other conditions have improved while you have been on maternity leave, then you are entitled to these benefits when you return to work.'

- You cannot be made redundant while you are on maternity leave. According to the Department of Trade and Enterprise, 'Notice of redundancy cannot issue when a person is on maternity leave'. If you're worried that you may face discrimination because you are pregnant and your job may be at risk, call The Equality Authority for advice on 1890 245 545, *www.equality.ie*.

Antenatal Visits

- You are entitled to as much paid time off as is necessary to attend hospital and medical visits, including travelling time. There is no upper limit on the time allowed for medical visits.

- You should give your employer medical evidence confirming your pregnancy and two weeks' notice of any medical visits.

Antenatal Classes

- You are entitled to take paid time off work to attend one set of antenatal classes, not including the last three that normally take place once your maternity leave has started. This set of antenatal classes covers all pregnancies you may have while in employment.

Paternity Leave

- By law, employers in Ireland do not have to give new fathers special paternity leave, however, they may take annual leave following the birth of their baby.

- Some employers, such as the civil service, give fathers three days' paternity leave following the birth or adoption of their child.

- Expectant fathers have a once-off right to paid time off work to attend the two antenatal classes immediately prior to the birth. Fathers are not entitled to paid time off for antenatal classes during every pregnancy — it's just a once-off right only.

Parental Leave

- Each parent of a child can take up to 14 weeks' unpaid leave for each child up to the age of eight.

- You can take the 14 weeks in one continuous period or in separate blocks of a minimum of six weeks. If your employer agrees you can separate your leave into periods of days or even hours.

- You will need to apply to your employer for this leave and there may be some negotiation before the time and conditions are agreed.

- If both parents work for the same employer and your employer agrees, you may transfer your parental leave entitlement to each other.

IF YOU WILL BE A SINGLE PARENT

There are many reasons why you may find yourself facing parenthood alone, including being single, divorced or bereaved or widowed, and Irish society is more open and supportive of single parents than in the past. There is also greater recognition that single parents need help and support.

One of the first things you will need to think about is ensuring that you have enough support during pregnancy, labour and after your baby is born. You should make an appointment to see your GP and get registered for antenatal care — like all other pregnant women you are entitled to free maternity care in a public hospital should you wish to have it.

As your due date draws near you will need to decide on who will accompany you during labour, as this is not an experience any woman should go through alone. Sisters and friends can make very good labour partners. Having someone stay with you, or staying with a friend or family member, in the last few weeks before your baby is due is a good idea so that you have their support when you go into labour. And you will need all the help on offer after you return home with your baby.

Whether you are keen to do so or not, you should tell the father of your baby that you are expecting and discuss maintenance payments. This is important as it can affect your ability to claim any relevant benefits you may need down the line.

For information and advice on any aspect of being a single parent contact Treoir, the National Information Centre for Unmarried Parents, on 1890 252 084, *www.treoir.ie*.

Single-parent Benefits

- Before your baby is born, find out what state benefits you might be entitled to. Like all pregnant women you can apply for maternity benefit — phone 1890 690 690 to find out how to do this or see page 29.

- Once your baby's birth has been registered you will automatically be entitled to claim Child Benefit (phone 1890 400 400) or see page 200.

- You may also qualify for:

  One-Parent Family Payment (phone 1890 500 000)

  Family Income Supplement (phone 01 704 3000)

- It's also a good idea to contact the Community Welfare Officer (cwo) at your local health centre as you may be able to claim:

  Exceptional Needs Payment

  Rent Supplement

  Supplementary Welfare Allowance

- Some single parents may qualify for a medical card or GP visit card — phone the HSE National Information Line on 1850 241 850 for more information.

- The Citizen's Information Phone Service on 1890 777 121 is also a good source of information and advice.

MUMS OVER 35

The number of women over 35 having babies for the first time has massively increased in Ireland during the last two decades, with many women waiting until they are more settled at work and home before deciding to start a family. However, there are some risks involved in leaving motherhood until later in life. The biggest risk is that fertility decreases as we age, so older women may find it difficult to become pregnant and are more likely to suffer early miscarriage.

Most women know that the risk of having a baby with a chromosomal abnormality such as Down's syndrome increases as we age (see page 53), but the vast majority of older mums (we're not ancient, just older in fertility terms!) have perfectly healthy babies. The risks of developing diabetes in pregnancy and having problems with the placenta also increase with mum's age, leading to a higher chance of needing a caesarean section, but with the right care, outcomes for both mum and baby are overwhelmingly positive.

There are a number of screening tests that can help older women gain peace of mind and enjoy their pregnancy. A Nuchal Translucency scan, at 11–13 weeks, is when the fluid at the back of the baby's neck is measured. More fluid than usual can be an indication of Down's syndrome. However, this scan can only estimate your risk of having a baby with Down's syndrome. You will then need to have a diagnostic test, such as amniocentesis or cvs (see below and pages 54 and 65). The

Nuchal Translucency scan may not be offered in your hospital, or your booking-in appointment may take place after this window has closed, but it is possible to have it done privately (see page 54).

Mums to be can also avail of other diagnostic tests:

- from weeks 8–11—cvs (chorionic villus sampling) where a sample of placenta is analysed.

- at 14 weeks—maternal serum testing, a blood test that measures for specific proteins.

- at 15–18 weeks—amniocentesis, where a thin needle is inserted through the abdomen and amniotic fluid is withdrawn from the womb.

You should be made aware that some of the diagnostic tests carry a small risk of miscarriage. Your doctor will advise you on which, if any, of these tests are recommended depending on how your pregnancy is progressing. Currently, most of these tests are only available privately, or on medical indication, and only in selected units.

At 18–22 weeks a head-to-toe 'fetal anomaly survey' or 'big' ultrasound scan is performed to assess the functioning of vital organs and map detailed measurements of the spine, skull, arms and legs. Most parents find this scan an amazing experience. If any problems are found, special care can be planned with specialists. If you are not offered the big scan, but you would like to have one, talk to your doctor or midwife about it.

On the positive side, women over 35 can bring a different perspective to parenting. Being more mature means that you may have more patience with a demanding newborn, you are more likely to be in a stable and supportive relationship, are less likely to resent being tied down by a baby and may have more work flexibility.

IF YOU'RE HAVING TWINS OR MORE

Finding that you are carrying more than one baby at your first ultrasound can be something of a shock. Not surprisingly, this news will have implications for how you look after yourself during pregnancy and your childbirth options (see pages 50–51).

You will need to eat a diet that is higher in calories and protein than other pregnancies with a particular emphasis on slow-release carbohydrates, dairy products for calcium, eggs for protein, meat, fish, fruit and vegetables and iron-rich foods. Try to avoid eating bigger meals as the day goes on as this will mean you going to bed with a full stomach, which can be uncomfortable. Carry around a bottle of water and drink at least a glass every hour to stave off constipation.

You will get bigger earlier in the pregnancy than other mums-to-be and may suffer more pregnancy ailments such as indigestion, heartburn and piles (see pages 104–16).

You will be tired as your body copes with growing not just one but two or more babies, and will need to take plenty of rest. When you do have energy try to take mild exercise such as walking and swimming. Take your partner or a friend if you find it hard to get in and out of the pool as you get bigger. You may be advised to take it easy by your doctor and want to cut your working hours.

Your doctor is likely to advise you to have your babies in a hospital in case of complications and you will receive more hospital consultations and scans during your pregnancy than other mums-to-be.

You may be induced at 38 weeks if labour hasn't started. Depending on the position your babies are lying in, you may be able to have a vaginal birth. If your babies are in difficult positions such as transverse (lying sideways across your abdomen), or breech (with bottom facing down), you may be advised to have an elective caesarean section.

There are some increased medical risks associated with having two or more babies, namely gestational diabetes, premature birth, pre-eclampsia and placental abruption (where the placenta comes away from the uterus), but most of these are successfully dealt with by your care team.

You may want to talk to other parents of multiples to find out how they cope. The Irish Multiple Births Association is run by volunteers, parents of multiples, and provides information and support to parents of multiples. Their patron is President Mary McAleese, who is also the mother of twins. *www.imba.ie*

HEALTH INSURANCE

Each of the health insurers in Ireland offers different benefits and levels of grant towards maternity services. Benefits also depend on which plan you are paying into. Depending on which plan you are currently in (if you are already pregnant it's generally too late to upgrade your payments in order to get a better pregnancy package) you can get money towards the following:

- Antenatal hospital cover

- Consultant fees

- Three nights in a semi- or private room in a public hospital, or private hospital

- A grant-in-aid allowance which can be used to cover home-birth medical expenses

- Doula birthing assistant

- 4D scanning (not routinely available in hospitals)

- Cord blood stem cell preservation (see page 150)

- Postnatal home help

- Breastfeeding consultancy sessions with a qualified lactation consultant

- Newborn's free cover until your next renewal

- Baby massage classes

- Fees for approved complementary therapies—acupuncture, homeopathy, chiropractic, osteopathy and reflexology

- The cost of dental examination

- The cost of optical test

- Charges for physiotherapy by a participating therapist

- Charges for chiropody by a participating therapist

- Nutritionist services provided by a member of the Irish Nutrition and Dietetic Institute (INDI)

- Counselling by a participating therapist for postnatal depression

- Midwifery services provided by a qualified midwife

- A maternity bra

If you are taking out private medical insurance for the first time, or it has been more than 13 weeks since you last had private cover, a 52-week waiting period for maternity benefits usually applies. If you upgrade your package, you will usually have to wait a year until your insurer will offer you the additional benefits.

ANTENATAL CLASSES

For first-time mums antenatal classes are a must. When it comes to childbirth, knowing what's in store can only help you to cope with such a life-altering experience. In general it's best to ignore 'helpful' advice from others and to get the latest and most accurate information from the experts. If you know what to expect, you are more likely to enjoy the challenge of labour rather than panic when you don't understand what is happening. This is why antenatal classes have an important role to play.

When choosing your antenatal classes think about the convenience of attending them — are they held at a practical time and place for you? Will your partner be welcome? Is there a charge for classes? What will the classes cover?

Broadly speaking, there are two types of antenatal classes — information-based, where you are told about the basic physiology of labour and how it is managed and what may happen to you and your baby. These classes are very useful for finding out more if this is your first baby. The second type of class is more focused on your body and helping you get to know what positions, breathing and coping techniques might work well for you. These classes usually include some aspect of relaxation. I have included information on both.

Information-based classes can be very useful in helping you to make decisions about how you would like your birth to be; if you want to be actively involved in the physical birthing of your baby, then body-based classes are important.

If you want to attend the antenatal classes run by your hospital, book early, as places may be limited. You may have to pay for some of them, especially if they are for couples or at premium times. Hospital classes explain how to birth your baby in the hospital setting, instruct you on the model of birth followed in the hospital and help you navigate your way round the way birth is managed in hospital. Some hospitals run an early antenatal class before 16 weeks, where they talk about diet, exercise and concentrate on your pregnancy rather than solely on your baby's birth.

One of the most useful things that most antenatal classes teach is how to recognise that labour has started — this can be crucial if you want to avoid dashing to the hospital at the slightest twinge and being sent home again. You will also be given information about the pros and cons of different methods of pain relief as well as techniques for breathing through contractions in order to conserve your energy. Learning about the three stages of labour will help you to understand what is happening to your body during labour.

Many antenatal classes focus on labour and delivery alone, but others include practical advice on how to care for your baby and adjust to parenthood. Some antenatal classes include a child safety talk with some really helpful information about the type of cot, car seat and buggy you will need to keep your precious bundle safe.

Antenatal and childbirth-preparation classes can be beneficial to pregnant women because they can make you focus on your body and your baby amidst the rush to get everything sorted before going on maternity leave.

You may decide to take some private classes. These are often run by organisations such as Cuidiú (Irish Childbirth Trust), public health nurses or by midwives and can vary in price. Some can be intensive weekend courses, others can be arranged to suit you.

Cuidiú antenatal classes are popular because they tend to be small and informal (usually with three to six couples), making it easy to ask questions and to get individual assistance with your own issues and concerns. Partners are also included in all classes. Classes look at practical coping skills, such as breathing, relaxation, massage, exercises and birthing positions with an opportunity to try them out in the class.

You can take a full course of six to eight classes with an additional 'reunion' gathering after all the babies are born, a short course of four classes, an all-day Saturday course that focuses on just the birth and your questions around it, 'one-to-one' courses of one to four sessions to suit individual needs for first-time couples, or a refresher course. There's also a course which deals with caesarean-section births.

Cuidiú antenatal instructors are accredited through the UK National Childbirth Trust after completing a two- to three-year training programme in Antenatal Education. This programme has recently been accredited by Luton University in the UK. All instructors are mothers themselves.

Check out *www.cuidiu-ict.ie* or phone 01 8724501 for a full list of teachers.

Check out these websites for more information on antenatal classes:

www.doulaireland.com
www.antenatal.ie
www.2as1.ie
www.tots2teens.ie
www.gentlebirth.ie
www.hypnobirthingireland.com
www.birthingfromwithin.com

Chapter 3

YOU AND YOUR
PREGNANCY

Congratulations — you are pregnant! Seeing that blue line appear on the pregnancy testing kit is a moment like no other. Whether this is your first time or you have been pregnant before, and whether you were planning a baby or not, finding out that you are expecting is nearly always a shock to the system. Your mind does its best to process what this means for your life as you know it and questions come flooding out:

Who should I tell and when?
How will we afford a baby?
What kind of antenatal care do I want to have?
How will my career cope with the change?
Will I be a good mum?

Then just as you are taking in your exciting news, in the next breath you start to worry:

What about that drink I had last week?
Have I eaten anything I shouldn't?
How can I protect myself from miscarriage?

But don't race ahead. Try to enjoy the moment you found out about your precious baby and if your partner is there, celebrate it together.

While it's true that pregnancy brings with it a number of decisions that have to be made, and your lifestyle, home and work life will all have to adapt to a new life, try to remember that nine months is a long enough period of time to organise what you have to and to get used to the idea of being parents.

Reading this book will help you along this wonderful journey towards parenthood and many pregnant women find it very useful to join an online community of other pregnant women — you'll be surprised how much support is out there from women in the same position as you.

REAL STORY

'I couldn't believe it as my husband and I had been trying for nearly three years. I was on fertility treatment at the time — tablets and a hcg injection. It was my first month to take the injection and as I had been doing pregnancy tests with no success for nearly three years, I was expecting a negative result. I couldn't believe it when the result was positive. I must have bought at least five more tests as I was afraid to even dream it might be true.'
Lorraine

Telling Other People

While you may be bursting to share your exciting news, many mums- and dads-to-be decide to wait until the 12-week mark before shouting from the rooftops because there is a greater chance of miscarriage (see page 48) in the first trimester of pregnancy. Telling people at this later stage means that the pregnancy is more established and you can relax and not worry. It also gives you and your partner a chance to discuss maternity care and get used to the idea before telling others.

However, other couples wish to celebrate this new life even in the very early stages and tell close family members soon after they find out. Whatever you decide to do, it's totally up to you.

One advantage of being open about your condition is that you won't have to explain why you're suddenly not drinking alcohol if you drink, have become the chauffeur in your relationship, are making frequent trips to the toilet, suffering from morning sickness, spending 12 hours a night in bed and generally look a bit exhausted and rough. Close friends who have had babies themselves will be understanding of your condition — they won't offer you raw seafood, home-made desserts made with raw eggs, or other pregnancy no-nos.

Telling friends who have had babies recently also has the added advantage that you may be offered maternity clothes, baby gear and so on that they have used and want to give away now that their home has become a toy shop. Baby equipment is expensive and will only be used for a few short months, or even weeks, so say yes to any offers. The same goes for maternity clothes.

A tricky situation may arise where you have a good friend who has suffered a miscarriage or is going through fertility problems, and you may feel awkward about sharing your good news with her. A friend who has had a miscarriage will need lots of support and to know that you are there for her as she goes through the grieving process. She may prefer to retreat for a while to come to terms which her loss, but it's important to keep the lines of communication open by phoning or texting so that she knows you are there if she needs you. A friend who has been trying unsuccessfully for a baby may be understandably upset by your news, and announcing the news for example at a party or family get-together may make it even more difficult for her as she has to hide the fact that she is upset and may feel that others feel sorry for her. Similarly, don't try to hide it from her because that's insensitive, too. Better to tell her yourself, either in person or the over the phone.

Telling your boss and work colleagues is another matter. Your absence from work will have consequences for others and so you will need to be professional in your approach to your boss. See page 30 for more on this.

Once you have absorbed the news and told friends and grandparents-to-be, and basked in their congratulations, your thoughts will turn to your pregnancy. As your baby grows and your body changes to accommodate this new life inside you, you will need to know what is happening at each stage for both of you. The next section of the book details what you can expect at each stage.

THE FIRST TRIMESTER

WEEKS 1–13

Your nine-month pregnancy is split into *trimesters* — three sets of three months in other words — and the first lasts for 12 or 13 weeks. It's a time when your pregnancy will only be known to you and your partner because your shape will not significantly change and it's up to you to decide when to share the news with others.

When working out how many weeks' pregnant you are, doctors count from the first day of your last period. So if you miss a period, you will be four weeks' pregnant, even though your baby was conceived two weeks ago. So the average pregnancy actually lasts 38 weeks, even though we all think of it in terms of 40 weeks with a two week head-start.

What is Happening to your Baby

A lot happens to your baby in the first trimester, although you won't be able to see much change from the outside. In the first six weeks of her life your baby starts to develop a brain, blood, blood vessels, bones, muscles and major internal organs. By six weeks she is 8 mm long — that's a tiny but perfect human being.

She is working really hard during the first trimester to develop a digestive system, kidneys and liver and will be growing arms and legs by week eight. From ten weeks an ultrasound scan should be able to hear a heartbeat (although not always) and her bones are forming. It's a rapid miniature process that takes her from 2.5 cm long at 8 weeks to 6.5 cm at 12 weeks — no wonder you need to rest.

By week 12 your baby's reproductive organs have formed as well as her head, eyes, arms — and amazingly, her nails have started to grow. She weighs around 18 g.

How You will Feel

You might be one of the lucky ones who doesn't suffer from many pregnancy conditions, and this is by no means an exhaustive list, but it will give you an idea of what you might commonly expect in the first trimester.

You may experience any combination of the following:

- breast changes and sensitivity

- frequent visits to the loo, often in the night, which means you lose sleep

- increase in vaginal mucus

- moodiness

- morning sickness

- sensitivity to some smells, which may make you want to be sick

- sore teeth and swelling gums

- tiredness and exhaustion

- weepiness

For more information on how to ease these conditions and why you may suffer from them, see Chapter 4, Your Health During Pregnancy.

What is Antenatal Depression?

In a small number of cases pregnancy news can lead to what is known as antenatal depression. Not as well known as postnatal depression, this condition can lead to a number of psychological issues during pregnancy as women go through the process of adjusting to the enormous changes that a baby brings.

Feelings of guilt over alcohol you drank or cigarettes you smoked before you knew you were pregnant can start to torture you. You may burst into tears without being able to say why, you may lack energy or enthusiasm for anything in your life and your fears for the health of your unborn baby may become overwhelming. Your partner may wonder where the real you has gone, and why you are not ecstatic at the great news. Neither of you may realise that you are suffering from antenatal depression.

Other symptoms of antenatal depression include a loss of self-confidence, feeling isolated and alone with your feelings, conflict with your own mother and a growing fear that as the pregnancy progresses and your bump grows, your partner will no longer find you attractive and will leave you. This can lead you to become possessive and jealous at a time when you should both be looking forward to becoming parents.

Whilst every pregnancy is different, hormonal changes and in particular a dramatic rise in oestrogen and progesterone in the body can lead to tearfulness and other symptoms of antenatal depression. Suffering from morning sickness can also affect your emotions, especially if it continues past the first trimester, and being sick on a regular basis can leave you deficient in minerals such as iron and zinc, which can affect your mood.

If you think this sounds like you talk to your partner or GP about how you feel. Your doctor won't be able to prescribe anti-depressants because you are pregnant, but might advise you to take a 'talking cure', in other words, counselling, to resolve any emotional or psychological difficulties you may have before you give birth.

RISKS TO YOUR PREGNANCY

The first 12 weeks of pregnancy is a crucial period in your baby's development, and it's wise to be as careful as possible. In Chapter 1, Preparing for Pregnancy, I outlined a number of things you can do to ensure your baby gets as much protection as possible, but in addition to this, you should also be aware that any illness you develop that gives you a temperature of 39°C/102°F will require treatment. Sustained high fever can result in potential developmental problems for your baby. So keep a thermometer at home just in case. If you do get a fever and think it is more than a headcold, take advice from your GP.

Vaginal bleeding in the first trimester will send most women in a panic to their doctor or midwife as they fear it may be the start of a miscarriage, but in fact, many women suffer from this and still have healthy babies. For more detailed information on how to recognise a miscarriage and what to do, see page 48.

Swine Flu — H1N1 Influenza

A big concern for pregnant women in late 2009 was swine flu, characterised by a sudden fever of 39°C/102°F with some or all of the following symptoms: cough, sore throat, runny or blocked nose, muscle pain, exhaustion and perhaps vomiting and diarrhoea.

The World Health Organisation (WHO) advised that pregnant women were at higher risk of complications from the virus and were a high priority for the H1N1 vaccine, after fourteen weeks of pregnancy, up to six weeks after delivery. This is still the case even though the vaccination programme ended in March 2010.

According to the HSE, the biggest risk from H1N1 influenza in your first trimester is from a temperature because if your body temperature goes above 38°C in the first 12 weeks this could be dangerous for your baby. Women are advised to contact their GP if they have flu-like symptoms.

Other risks from H1N1 are more prominent in the second and third trimester and can include early labour or possibly severe pneumonia, therefore prevention is best. Be scrupulous about washing your hands, covering your nose and mouth while sneezing or coughing and binning used tissues. Avoid contact with sick people if you can.

If you are unwell, stay hydrated with plenty of fluids, rest and do not take any over-the-counter medications without checking with your GP, midwife or obstetrician.

Stay at home for seven days and try to limit your contact with others. Contact your GP or the HSE Flu Freephone line on 1800 94 11 00 for more instructions.

The Health Service Executive website is kept updated with the latest information and advice. *http://www.swineflu.ie.*

Lambing and Livestock

If you live on a farm and are exposed to sheep and other pregnant livestock, you would be wise to take precautions around these animals until your baby is born. This is because exposure during your pregnancy could put you at risk of contracting toxoplasmosis, listeria and and an organism called Chlamydiphila abortus. All of these can have a damaging effect on you and your baby.

Emergency!
If you have any of these symptoms, contact your doctor right away:

- Shortness of breath at rest or while doing very little

- Painful or difficult breathing

- Coughing up bloody sputum

- Drowsiness, disorientation or confusion

- Sudden dizziness

- Severe or persistent vomiting

- Fever for 4–5 days and not starting to get better (or getting worse)

- Starting to feel better then developing high fever and feeling unwell again
- Pains or bleeding suggesting early labour

Miscarriage

The 'M' word that most pregnant women fear, miscarriage can sometimes happen so early in the pregnancy that you might not even know you are pregnant, and nearly always occurs in the first 12 weeks. About one in every five pregnancies in Ireland ends in miscarriage, so if it happens to you, you will not be alone.

If you do suffer from bleeding in the first trimester, this does not automatically mean that you are having a miscarriage. Many women will have light bleeds or 'spotting' in early pregnancy and go on to have healthy babies. If you bleed heavily, or if the blood is bright red and has clots in it, contact your caregiver or go to the hospital immediately. The same goes for severe stomach cramps. Your midwife or doctor can check your baby's heartbeat or give you an ultrasound scan to ensure everything is well. You may be advised to take some bed rest for a certain period of time.

Not all miscarriages happen quickly — of course it can happen this way, but can also be slow and steady, which makes the process even harder for many women to go through. Some women experience a 'missed miscarriage' where they have no symptoms of miscarriage, but when they have a scan no heartbeat is detected. If you have concerns don't hesitate to get a second opinion. Depending on her caregiver and her medical condition, a woman may be offered to let nature take its course, to take medication to bring on a form of labour, or, a doctor may recommend D&C (dilation and curettage) or ERPC (evacuation of retained products of conception) which is a small operation under general anaesthetic.

A woman who has already started bleeding may find that it can take days or even some weeks before it stops. Some women take a pregnancy test after the bleeding has stopped to confirm that the pregnancy has passed and there is no need for a D&C. However it happens, a woman who has had a miscarriage will find that her hormones are upside down for some time as her body adjusts to no longer being pregnant.

Many women, whether they are aware of it or not, will blame themselves for a miscarriage, but doctors agree that miscarriages do not happen because of anything the expectant mum did or didn't do. The most common reason for miscarriages in the first trimester is chromosomal abnormality.

While some women recover quite quickly physically and emotionally from a miscarriage, others find that they are not truly able to move on and look to the future or try for another baby, until their due date has passed. Losing a baby, however early in the pregnancy, is a tragedy and both you and your partner will be grieving and devastated by the loss. You should both take things slowly and not try to rush to get everything back to normal — grieving is a very real process that takes time and patience.

If you're keen to try for a baby straight away, it's a good idea to see your GP, midwife or obstetrician first to discuss what happened and see whether he or she might recommend you have tests or further investigations.

The Miscarriage Association of Ireland (*miscarriage.ie*) holds support meetings once a month in Dublin, where people can meet in a supportive environment and if they wish they can share their experiences with others who have had similar experiences. They also have a telephone line for those in need of support, understanding and a listening ear.

If you decide to tell close family and friends about a miscarriage, because you had already announced your pregnancy, you should receive lots of love and sympathy.

At times like these, when you are so upset, your partner may feel left out and it's important to involve him in your grieving process, even if that means attending counselling together.

Looking at it from a dad's point of view, Adam Brophy in *The Bad Dad's Survival Guide* says, 'When a child dies at this premature stage, everybody still grieves. Unfortunately, there are few support systems in place to comfort parents who have to deal with this scenario; instead they are shoved back out into the world and encouraged to have another shot at it.'

A book about the experience of miscarriage, written by an Irish couple, is *We Lost our Baby* by Siobhán O'Neill-White and David White (Liffey Press). They wrote the book in 2007 after they lost their baby and found there were no books to help them with what they were going through.

TWINS

There are two different types of twins: non-identical twins are conceived from two separate eggs fertilised by two separate sperm. They have their own amniotic sacs and own placentas. They can be two boys, two girls or a girl and a boy. Identical twins are conceived from one egg and one sperm and are always of the same sex.

Whether you are carrying identical or non-identical twins shouldn't affect your pregnancy significantly, but carrying two babies instead of one can put an added strain on your body and from a medical point of view you are likely to be viewed as 'high risk' right from the beginning, even if you are as healthy as a horse.

You may not know you are having twins until your first scan, and it can be something of a (mostly nice) shock for many parents-to-be. One minute you are lying on a bed with gel on your tummy and the next you are looking at double the expense and double the work — but double the love. There's no doubt that it might take you some time to adjust to a twin diagnosis, and talking to the Irish Multiple Births Association can help (see page 36).

Ways in which a twin pregnancy may differ from a singleton include:

- You will gain weight and show your pregnancy earlier than a mum of one.

- You may suffer more from pregnancy conditions such as back pain, indigestion and heartburn, leg-swelling and breathlessness due to the extra weight you are carrying.

- You may suffer from anaemia due to your body having to create enough blood to support both you and two babies. You will be tested for anaemia at hospital visits and may be advised to take a supplement.

- You will be monitored more closely by your caregivers during pregnancy because of the higher risk of gestational diabetes and preterm labour.

- You will need to really look after yourself and get as much rest as you can.

- You may need to go on maternity leave from work earlier than for a single-baby pregnancy, or to limit your work hours in order to rest.

- You will not be allowed to have a home birth.

- Your labour is likely to be more medicalised than if you were having one baby because of the risk of complications.

- Different hospitals have different policies for twin births. Twins may be delivered by caesarean section from 37 weeks, or a vaginal birth may be possible, if the first baby is in the correct position. You will need to discuss this with your doctor or midwife and to check your hospital's policy.

The Hospital 'Booking' Appointment

This usually takes place between 10 and 12 weeks, but in practice in busy hospitals can happen later. If you feel the wait is very long, ask your GP to help you contact the hospital or phone up at regular intervals and ask about cancellations. The booking appointment can last for several hours, so take a drink, snack, something to read and a willing partner, mum, sister or friend.

- You will be asked detailed questions about your pregnancy and medical history, some which you may find personal, and will have urine and blood tests.

- You will be weighed, your blood pressure will be checked.

- You will be asked to give a urine sample which will be tested for protein and glucose levels. This test is used to indicate conditions such as gestational diabetes, pre-eclampsia and kidney infections.

- What seems like a lot of blood will be taken and sent away to be tested for anaemia, immunity to rubella and chicken pox, hepatitis B, HIV and other sexually transmitted diseases.

After this marathon visit, you will be scheduled in for subsequent visits — these will not take anywhere near as long. Initially, the visits will be roughly every month, but more frequent in the final few weeks. At later appointments you will be asked to lie down and the doctor or midwife will check the fundal height — the length of your bump from the top of your uterus to the pubic bone — which will tell them if your baby is growing at a good rate for his age.

If your doctor or midwife detects any complications in your pregnancy he/she will see you more often and you may require more tests or ultrasound scans. He or she will also check your medical history and you may have additional tests if you have a family history of a genetic disorder or a previous baby with Down's syndrome or spina bifida.

How do Ultrasound Scans Work?

Ultrasound scanners use high-frequency sound waves, like a ship's sonar, which are transmitted through a clear water-based conducting gel spread across your abdomen. The scanner is passed over the gel in order to locate the fetus and placenta and the sound waves are reflected back and converted into a detailed image on a monitor that you and the sonographer can see.

Ultrasound scanning gives expectant mums and dads a chance to see their growing baby before he or she is born and to be reassured that the pregnancy is progressing healthily. Scanning is now available in every maternity unit and many consultants' rooms. Many parents feel reassured by the experience and their midwife or obstetrician can glean crucial information about the pregnancy. If problems are detected, special care can be planned.

Scans in the first trimester confirm that the baby is growing at the appropriate rate. They can also give you a fairly reliable due date; a second-trimester scan gives a detailed developmental check of your baby; and a third trimester scan is often done when clinically indicated because a doctor suspects your baby may be a small size, may be lying in the breech position or you may have a low-lying placenta.

The number of scans you will get depends on several factors, including the hospital you attend, whether you choose public or private care and medical indications. Some hospitals offer patients a 'booking scan' or 'early pregnancy assessment scan' sometime between 10 and 13 weeks and then a 'fetal anomaly scan' at about 18–22 weeks in the pregnancy. Some just offer the later scan and early scans are done for obstetric reasons such as previous miscarriage or carrying multiples, for example.

Additional scans may be recommended by your midwife or doctor, for a number of reasons. Some scans or tests may only be available privately.

The 'Dating' Scan or 'Early Pregnancy Assessment'

Done between weeks 10 and 13, this ultrasound scan will give you a more accurate expected due date (EDD) which is why it is often called the 'dating' scan.

Even at this early stage the sonographer should be able to tell you how many babies you are expecting and whether your baby's vital organs are developing properly.

Women with a history of miscarriage may feel reassured by this scan as their baby's heartbeat will be detected.

Because your baby is so small at this stage, you may need to drink several glasses of water to push him closer to the ultrasound scanning equipment so that he can be seen more clearly.

Additional Tests

In most cases tests and scans will reassure you and your partner that everything is going well, but if your doctor is concerned, he may ask for additional tests to be done. If your doctor does not recommend additional tests, but you want them, you may have to pay for them privately. You might want to have extra tests if you are over 35 and concerned about the likelihood of your baby having Down's syndrome or another abnormality.

In general, the risk of a baby having Down's syndrome rises according to the age of the mother. The figures are:

- Mum aged 21 — 1 in 1,520 births

- Age 35 — 1 in 355

- Age 40 — 1 in 95

- Age 43 — 1 in 40

Additional tests for the first trimester are:

Chorionic Villus Sampling (CVS)

Between weeks 8 and 11 a sample of placenta is removed from the uterus using a fine needle and sent to be analysed. This test will give a definitive diagnosis of Down's syndrome and other chromosomal abnormalities or genetic disorders, so it may bring moral issues into question. You may want to ask yourself what you will do and how you will cope if you are told that you are definitely carrying a Down's-syndrome baby. Statistics vary, but there is an average 1% risk of miscarriage with this test, although it's hard to tell definitively as first-trimester miscarriages are more common. It takes around two weeks to get the result. You may or may not be offered this test.

Nuchal Translucency Scan

By measuring the amount of fluid at the back of the baby's neck during an ultrasound scan at around 11 or 12 weeks, the risk of having an abnormality such as Down's syndrome or a genetic condition can be calculated. The result is available straight away, and if your risk is high, your doctor may discuss additional tests with you such as chorionic villus sampling (CVS) or amniocentesis (see page 65).

You may be offered this scan in hospital, but if not, you could contact the following:

Ultrasound Dimensions — *www.ultrasounddimensions.ie*
The Irish Maternal Foetal Foundation — *www.imff.ie*
Landscape Clinic — *www.landscapeclinic.ie*
Mount Carmel Hospital — *www.mcm.ie*
Cork Women's Clinic — *www.corkwomensclinic.com*
The Ultrasound Suite — *www.theultrasoundsuite.ie*

WHAT QUESTIONS SHOULD I ASK THE HOSPITAL?

It might seem very early to be asking these questions, but in my experience the more you know about how the hospital operates and the earlier you know it, the better. Having the information early on gives you time to consider your options and make alternative arrangements should you wish to.

- Do you run antenatal classes?

- Do you encourage birth plans?

- What are your policies on pain relief, electronic fetal monitoring (see page 142), episiotomy and forceps delivery?

- Are fathers, relatives and friends welcome in the delivery room? (Hospitals have different policies on how many birth partners are allowed.)

- Do you encourage women to move around in labour?

- How long do new mums usually stay in the hospital after their baby is born?

YOUR PARTNER'S REACTION

If your partner doesn't seem as enthusiastic as you would like when you give him the brilliant news that you are pregnant, don't worry. It may take him some time to really believe he is going to be a father, and he may be worried about how you will both cope with such a big change to your lives.

Just because he doesn't want to sing to your tummy, spend hours talking about what the baby is doing this week and go shopping for baby gear doesn't mean he won't make a fantastic father.

He may be concerned about all the medical tests you are likely to have and what they might reveal, and it's not unusual for both parents-to-be to find their lives taken over by medical appointments and the worry they can bring. On the plus side an ultrasound scan in the second trimester allows expectant parents to see their baby for the first time which can be incredibly exciting, and if any problems are detected they may be treated or planned for.

> *Eumom Tip*
> *Try to avoid contact with anyone who has a high fever, especially at this early stage of pregnancy. A virulent flu virus can cause miscarriage, so avoid contact with anyone who has influenza, chicken pox or other infections.*

Eumom Tip

Urinary tract infections are common in pregnancy. Protect against them by drinking plenty of fluids, particularly water and cranberry juice, which has been shown to help prevent recurrent infections and is also rich in vitamins.

Lucy's Tip

Book your antenatal classes now, even if your doctor says there is no hurry. A friend of mine found that hers were nearly booked out before the end of her first trimester, so make that call today. For more information on what antenatal classes cover and where you can have them, see Chapter 2.

REAL STORIES

'In the early days when we hadn't told anyone, I used to drive if we went out and then say I couldn't drink because I was driving. Also, we went through the whole of Christmas with me telling people I had "gone off" wine and paté — maybe I should have just come clean, but I thought it would be bad luck.'
Lucy

'I didn't mind not being able to drink when pregnant, but having to stop eating soft cheeses and shellfish really annoyed me. I felt you should be able to eat what you want when pregnant, but that's obviously not the case.'
Name withheld

'At about 12 weeks my teeth were in agony — my whole head seemed to ache and I just couldn't understand it. I went to the dentist and he had a look and said there was absolutely nothing wrong — it was just "growing pains". The pain went away a few days later.'
Jane

HOW DAD FEELS AND HOW HE CAN HELP

Many women find the first trimester difficult due to morning sickness, hormonal changes and sheer exhaustion. Your job is to keep your cool, be supportive and most of all, to talk. Most couples still manage to enjoy sex at this time although it's wise to avoid vigorous penetration and remember that her breasts may be tender. Don't be surprised, however, if she would prefer some sleep as exhaustion sets in.

Adam Brophy, in *The Bad Dad's Survival Guide,* counsels to beware the pregnancy demon. 'There aren't three of you involved here, your brood has grown to a minimum of four. You, her, it or them (please God not twins — go on, chant it for safety) and the pregnancy demon. Many people know this creature but none will acknowledge it.

'You must spend your time with the beast. Your woman remains, in fact because of the baby growing in her she will appear, despite some physical maladies, even more buoyant and physical than ever. Her possession is subtle and intangible and her possessor's sole purpose is to use her as a vessel to attack you…

'This time is hard for guys. Without any real, outward, physical signs that much change is afoot we struggle to come to terms with a very definitely, suddenly skewed playing field.'

THE SECOND TRIMESTER

WEEKS 14–27
This is the trimester when your pregnancy starts to show and your baby is learning how to suck and smile — and in the later weeks you will be amazed by kicks and somersaults in your tummy. In general, most women find this is their best trimester as morning sickness abates and they start to 'glow'. You will also get a fetal anomaly (big) scan during this trimester which is incredibly exciting as you can see your baby in great detail and will most likely get the reassurance that everything is going well.

WHAT IS HAPPENING TO YOUR BABY
By week 14 your baby's hair is starting to grow and he measures 8 cm long. Just two weeks later he is 16 cm long, is fully formed and can even smile. Kicking can start from as early as week 18, with sucking his thumb the following week and he can hear now, which includes your voice. He's making an amazing journey but is still too small at this stage to survive outside your body.

From around week 20 your baby will be covered in vernix, a whitish greasy substance that will keep his skin from drying out in its watery environment. He is 28 cm long and weighs around 16 oz at the end of week 21 and is moving around a lot.

At week 23 your baby will respond to sounds and he may move in response to sudden noise. Week 24 is the earliest babies have been reported to have survived outside the womb with specialist medical help, but his lungs are not developed enough to support him yet. He weighs over 1 lb and is 32 cm long.

At around week 26 your baby's skin, which up until now has been transparent, starts to fully develop, his eyes are open and he may get hiccups, which you may feel. At 28 weeks he will fill up all of the space in your uterus so you may get less somersault movements and more kicks and jerks. He is now 38 cm long.

WHAT IS HAPPENING TO YOU

You might be one of the lucky ones who doesn't suffer from many pregnancy conditions, and this is by no means an exhaustive list, but it will give you an idea of what you might commonly expect in the second trimester.

You may experience any combination of the following:

* back pain

* breast changes

* constipation and piles

* fluid retention

* heartburn and indigestion

* itchy skin

* pelvic pain

* skin changes including hyperpigmentation and *linea nigra,* 'pregnancy mask' and spots

* stretch marks

For more information on these conditions and why you may suffer from them, see Chapter 4, Your Health During Pregnancy.

For most pregnant woman (but not all) morning sickness will stop during this trimester and you will start to look a bit more pregnant. It's a time to enjoy telling people your great news as you have come through the anxious period of pregnancy in the first trimester.

Don't be surprised, too, if people tell you that you look great and have a pregnancy 'glow'. Mums-to-be who suffer from sickness earlier on can look exhausted and pale, and then when they reach the second trimester they get their energy back. All of a sudden their skin, hair and nails look fabulous and they start to enjoy the pregnancy.

You might find at this time that going without food for more than a couple of hours leaves you ready to eat everything in sight — and right now! When a pregnant woman needs to eat, she's not kidding. So to avoid being caught out without food, carry healthy snacks with you to munch on.

A little word of warning, though. Just because you don't need to spend every morning with your head over the toilet bowl doesn't mean you can carry on your working and social life just as before — remind yourself that you are pregnant and need to think about both you and your baby. Your body is working very hard to sustain and grow your little one, and generally slowing down and having a daily nap will help you to get enough rest.

From as early as week 18 it's possible to feel butterflies in your tummy, which is the first sign of movement from your baby, but in many cases this can take longer. Within weeks you will get big prodding movements as arms and legs jut out in odd places — it can feel very strange at first but you will grow to enjoy the reassurance it gives you that your baby is active.

After week 20 you will find that your weight gain starts to take on a momentum of its own and this can feel very strange for most pregnant women, especially if you haven't experienced it before. My advice is to try not to worry about your weight — you should be gaining pounds at this time and if your doctor or midwife thinks you are gaining too much or not enough, she will tell you.

Risks to your Pregnancy

Obstetric Cholestasis

This is a liver condition that is characterised by extremely itchy skin and most commonly affects women in the second and third trimester of pregnancy. While it's normal to have slightly itchy skin during pregnancy because of the stretching skin needs to do, intense itching on the arms, legs, hands and feet is not normal. If it gets worse at night, if you cannot sleep, eat and feel sick, see your midwife or doctor straight away. Obstetric cholestasis is rare but prompt action is important. In some cases, the baby can become distressed and will have to be born early. After the baby is born the liver returns to normal and the itching stops.

Rhesus Incompatibility

When mum's blood is Rhesus (Rh) negative and her baby's is Rh positive, mum develops antibodies to her baby. This is not normally a problem with a first baby, but the antibodies developed while the baby is being born can cause danger to any subsequent babies. This is why all mums-to-be are blood tested at their booking-in appointment. If your blood group is found to be negative, you may be asked for the blood group of your baby's father so that appropriate medical care can be taken. You may be offered an Anti-D injection at 28 and 34 weeks to avoid problems for subsequent babies.

Unwanted Advice

You are starting to show now, so take a deep breath because all sorts of people you've never met will give you unwanted advice (They will also stare at your bump like they've never seen a pregnant woman before and stretch out their hand to touch it, which can be disconcerting).

In contrast, others may be able to give you valuable inside information about pregnancy and birth, such as friends who have recently had babies or your mum who went through it all with you. Bear in mind that rose-tinted spectacles can cloud even the most clear memories and things may have changed since your mother went through the experience, so you may need to take some of her advice with a pinch of salt. Don't worry if people say your baby should be kicking or you should be slowing down, for example — every pregnancy is different. If persistent comments are upsetting you, ask your partner to support you when he can.

DRESSING FOR PREGNANCY

There's no getting away from it, you will need to get your hands on some maternity clothes at some point during this trimester. The good news is that these no longer consist of tents that fall unflatteringly from your bump and make you look even bigger than you are. Now maternity wear can be bought in your normal size from most high-street fashion stores.

Up until now you have probably managed to wear your roomiest normal clothes — the ones you slip on when you have your period. From the start of your second trimester you may not feel big enough to wear official maternity gear, but your existing clothes cut you in half — so now is the time to buy some normal clothes in bigger sizes. This might seem like a waste of money, but in fact is a good idea because you will need something to wear for a few weeks after your baby is born and you definitely won't want to wear those maternity jeans again.

Before you invest a fortune in your maternity wardrobe, though, ask around friends or family who have been pregnant and see what clothes you can borrow. Charity shops are a great source of maternity jeans which didn't see much wear first time round and factory outlet sales often sell maternity wear too. E-bay is also a good source of maternity gear as people sell it in bundles.

One new item you won't be able to do without is a good bra as your boobs will need plenty of support and will grow, too, so it's a good idea to get fitted in a proper lingerie shop or department store. If you're thinking about breastfeeding it's a good idea to get fitted for a feeding bra (with a clip-down front) as this will save you having to do it later. Nowadays these bras are less utilitarian and more beautiful than before. But don't get measured for a feeding bra too early, as your assets will grow when your milk comes in, and your ribs, which widened to accommodate your growing baby, will narrow again.

Another item of your wardrobe that can elicit some debate is what kind of knickers to wear. You can buy massive maternity knickers that go over your bump and look like the kind your granny might wear, or alternatively buy the low-slung kind that you wear under jeans in a bigger size and wear them under your bump. Whichever you find most comfortable, make sure they have a cotton crotch.

When you're out of the public eye and relaxing at home, why not raid your partner's wardrobe to see what you can find. Loose T-shirts and white shirts can look great, jogging trousers will be comfy for relaxing in and depending on his size, you might be able to find a jacket you can wear to work.

By buying a few basics you can still look stylish throughout your pregnancy. Here are a few ideas:

- Dresses are good and some non-maternity ones, such as wrap-over styles, will expand with your waist size.

- Vest tops are good for layering at times when you are likely to get hot.

- Maternity jeans are comfy, most of them have a waist that you can adjust as you grow and they make you feel like a normal person. Most mums find that jeans with a high waist that goes over their bump are ideal because they don't keep falling down! I resorted to braces to keep my favourite maternity jeans up!

For work, invest in a few key pieces such as:

- A long jacket

- A long cardigan

- A plain black skirt or lighter colour for summer

- A pair of maternity trousers

- A couple of long tops that completely cover your bump

- A pair of flattish slip-on shoes — you will be glad of these when you can no longer get past your bump to tie your laces. Shoes with a good arch support are essential.

Throughout your pregnancy have fun using accessories to accentuate your best features, namely your bust, which has never been as fulsome. Great shoes, a bag and jewellery do not have to be expensive but can give you a better overall look.

Eumom Tip

Various types of tights and stockings are now available to give your legs support during your pregnancy. If you would rather wear socks, try to stick to loose cotton ones so that they are comfortable and prevent your feet from sweating. Remember to avoid tight knee-high socks, which can restrict your blood flow and encourage varicose veins.

BABY'S KICKING

It's usually from around week 18 that you feel your baby's first kick — which can be a strange experience. Some babies make your stomach ripple and flutter, others feel like they are trying to kick their way out and give you a few internal bruises in the process.

Feeling regular kicks is a sure fire way of knowing that your baby is doing well and it can help to allay any fears you may have. Kicks often happen when you are lying down at the end of a busy day and settling down to sleep — this is because stretching out gives your baby more space to move. Also, during the day your moving body will often rock your baby to sleep so you may feel less activity. Think of this as preparation for looking after a newborn who doesn't recognise day from night.

Every baby is different and will move around and kick as much or as little as he likes. I remember being asked whether I was counting my baby's kicks, as some say that babies should kick a certain number of times in a day, but this seemed like a recipe for inducing even more stress to me. I didn't worry too much as long as my baby moved at a regular time every day. Lo and behold, when I stretched out on the sofa to watch TV in the evening, my daughter saw it as a sign to get moving. On the few occasions this didn't happen and I was concerned about it, I'd find eating a few squares of chocolate soon got her kicking away — no wonder she likes chocolate now!

It's hard to say how much every individual baby should kick, but from around 20 weeks, 10 kicks in a 12-hour period can be considered roughly normal. Your intuition will also help you to judge whether your baby is acting normally for him. If your baby was very active then suddenly stops moving for 24 hours, contact your doctor or midwife straight away, who may want to monitor your baby's heart rate. Reduced movements from your baby can be associated with your baby being anaemic or your placenta failing, so it's important to get it checked out.

In the last few weeks before your due date your baby will have less space to move around, but he should still be kicking right up to birth, so again if he stops, contact your midwife or doctor.

Don't forget to tell your partner when you feel a kick — he may want to have a feel and it will make your pregnancy seem more real to him.

CONSULTATIONS: WHAT TO EXPECT

During the second trimester you will continue to have regular consultations with your midwife, doctor or GP and can look forward to the 'big' scan and the excitement it can bring. These checks will give your doctor or midwife an opportunity to check your blood pressure, weight, take a urine sample and look out for swelling or oedema. You will be asked to lie on the bed with your tummy exposed and your doctor or midwife will check by feeling your bump that your baby is growing properly for his age. You may also get the opportunity to listen to your baby's heartbeat as the doctor or midwife listens in. This is a good time for you to ask about anything that is concerning you.

The 'Big' Scan

An exciting if nerve-wracking event in any pregnant woman's life, the 'fetal anomaly survey' ultrasound scan will let you get a good look at your baby. This head-to-toe scan is undertaken at 18 to 22 weeks and the sonographer will take lots of measurements to check that everything is well with your baby's spine, skull, arms and legs. The sonographer will also be able to see whether your baby's organs are working properly and look for abnormalities such as spina bifida, cleft lip or palate. If any problems are found, special care can be planned with specialists.

The scan will also show the position of the placenta and how much amniotic fluid surrounds your baby, both of which are important for sustaining your baby throughout pregnancy.

This amazing scan may reveal your baby doing somersaults and sucking his thumb and you may stare in wonder or burst out crying. It's a big event, you will both remember being there, but when you show other people the pictures of your precious little one, don't be surprised if they can't work out what is what.

If you already had a scan in your first trimester and are attending a public hospital, you may not be offered a routine anomaly scan unless you ask for one or have a particular medical indication. This depends on which hospital you are attending.

Amniocentesis

If recommended by your doctor, you may have an amniocentesis, which takes place at 15 to 18 weeks. Only used when indicated by the results of a screening test, amniocentesis can give you a diagnosis of Down's syndrome, spina bifida or other abnormalities and also tell the sex of your baby. A thin needle is inserted through your abdomen and amniotic fluid is taken from your womb. This test carries an approximate 1% risk of miscarriage.

FINDING OUT THE SEX OF YOUR BABY

'Do you know what you're having?' A fairly common question that you may be asked during the latter months of your pregnancy, and it is possible to find out if you are expecting a boy or girl, but do you want to?

Many couples decide not to find out so that they can enjoy the lovely surprise when their precious baby is born. Others are dying to know in advance — they choose a name for their baby while still pregnant, paint the nursery and buy girl- or boy-specific clothes. In some cases your doctor may recommend that you find out the sex of your baby, because if you or your partner carry a genetic condition that is passed down to one sex or the other, knowing could help your doctor ascertain the risk of your baby carrying the same gene.

Ultrasound scans later in pregnancy can detect the sex of your baby, but he or she will need to be lying in a position that enables the sonographer to make a judgment. Sometimes a boy's penis can look like a girl's labia, so it's not surprising that sometimes even the experts get it wrong.

Some hospitals have a policy of not revealing the sex of babies and are not willing to reveal this information, even if you ask for it.

REAL STORY

'If any one is finding out the sex of their baby ask for more then one scan as, as it was with me it could be wrong. We wanted to find out what sex we were having as I like to prepare myself as much as possible, like the room, first outfit and especially the most important, the name. So when I was told I was having a boy I asked twice and the midwife reassured me that she was certain. So after that we were so happy we were having a boy. I got everything prepared: I even got three baby name books and it took us three months to finally agree on a name. I was in the operating theatre drugged up to the nines and the obstetrician held up my baby; there was a long pause. The midwives were looking at each other, whispering. I didn't know what was happening until my obstetrician said "It's a girl!". I said "Are you sure it's a girl?" and the whole room went quiet until I burst out laughing. I couldn't believe what a day I'd had and to be surprised like that was lovely, especially when I held my healthy daughter for the first time, even though she was dressed in blue. Amazingly it only took me and my partner Ian two days to find her a name — Mia Zoe.'
Natasha

Eumom Tip

The effects of hormones can alter the moisture of your eyes, making them drier, so some women may find that they are unable to wear contact lenses during their pregnancy. Why not invest in a new and trendy pair of glasses?

Eumom Tip

Research has shown that babies can hear music in the womb and remember it 12 months after they are born. Why not start playing your baby music, or get your partner to sing to your bump?

Eumom Tip

If you are having difficulty sleeping, catnapping whenever possible may help. You can also try various ways to relax before you go to bed: for example, have a warm bath or a massage, listen to some calming music, read, watch TV or carry out some simple relaxation exercises. Having a hot milky drink and finding a suitable sleeping position that is more comfortable may also help. Lying on your side and using extra pillows behind your back, between your knees and under your stomach may be one way to get comfortable.

REAL STORIES

'I had read about leg cramps but didn't believe they could be so awful until I was woken up by one in the dead of night — screaming! My poor hubby thought I was being attacked. The only way to make the awful cramps go away was to pound away at my leg until it went away — at which point we were both wide awake. I read that cramps may be caused by not eating enough calcium so I upped my yogurt and milk intake.'
Lucy

'I had heartburn, so I ate little and often. Big meals with big gaps in between just made it worse. I needed to eat every two hours as my blood sugar levels would go down. For heartburn I took Acidex (on prescription) which I kept beside the bed, and carried Rennies in my bag.'
Suzanne

'During the fifth month my back became extremely painful, due to pregnancy hormones loosening the ligaments. And then I developed Symphysis Pubis Dysfunction, a severe pelvic joint pain where the bones in your pelvis have moved due to the pregnancy and are grinding together. I couldn't really walk, had to wear a special belt and saw a physiotherapist. You can't take any strong painkillers because you are pregnant, so it really is miserable. The only good news is that the pain goes away as soon as the baby is born.'
Louise

HOW DAD FEELS AND HOW HE CAN HELP

The second trimester is often a good time for a pregnant woman as morning sickness has usually gone and she glows with pregnancy. You may find your partner very attractive at this point, but your libido can be affected by impending fatherhood. It's not uncommon for a dad-to-be to be afraid of having sex with his partner in case he harms the baby, and your partner may fear that you no longer find her attractive. These challenges can be overcome if you talk and if you are caring and generous with hugs and kisses, but it's quite normal for some couples to be sexually incompatible for a short time during pregnancy. The good news is that sex cannot harm the baby as he or she is protected in mum's uterus.

If you are feeling left out of the pregnancy, talk to your partner about how you are feeling, attend doctor's and midwife's appointments and antenatal classes, talk, read and sing to your unborn baby (he can hear from about six months), feel kicks with your hand, go shopping for baby gear and decorate the nursery.

Both you and your partner should remind yourselves that pregnancy is not permanent, even though it can sometimes feel like it. A few months down the line things will go back to something more like normal and you will have a beautiful baby to show for it.

According to Adam Brophy in *The Bad Dad's Survival Guide*, 'All pregnancies place great strain on relationships. This interim period where, for a short while, you actually like each other again was probably designed in evolutionary terms so that mother and father would have some idea as to why they got together in the first place, and therefore might have some designs on staying together after the child is born.'

THE THIRD TRIMESTER

WEEKS 28–40

You may feel heavy and ungainly during the third trimester and it's no surprise when you consider what you are carrying around with you 24 hours a day. This trimester is a time to really look after yourself and avoid overdoing it. You are nearly there and will see your beautiful baby's face for the first time soon.

Your baby is putting on weight and becoming more baby-like during these weeks. He can hear you and will give you jabs to remind you that he is there — as if you could forget.

WHAT IS HAPPENING TO YOUR BABY

Your baby is becoming more baby-like with every passing week as his skin fills out and becomes more smooth. At week 29 he will weigh around 2–3 lb and is set to gain much more. At week 32 your baby has a good chance of survival on his own as his lungs have developed.

From week 35 he will put on 8 oz a week until he is born, may move into the head-down position ready for birth and can hear as well as he can when he is born. He will weigh around 5 lb and will be 31 cm long at 36 weeks and you should feel regular kicks and other movements.

Your baby can tell the difference between light and dark from around week 37 and if his head is engaged at roughly week 38, you may only feel jabs higher up your abdomen from legs and arms shooting out. Your baby should keep moving until he is born, so if you think he's gone very quiet, and eating something sweet doesn't wake him up, go straight into the hospital or call your midwife.

By week 39 your baby is getting ready to be born and may weigh around 6–8 lb. His lungs are maturing ready for birth and his intestine is filled with meconium, a thick greeny-black waste that will fill his first nappy.

What is Happening to your Body

You might be one of the lucky ones who doesn't suffer from many pregnancy conditions, and this is by no means an exhaustive list, but it will give you an idea of what you might commonly expect in the third trimester.

You may experience any combination of the following:

- back pain
- blocked nose
- breast changes and leaking colostrum
- breathlessness
- constipation and piles
- dizziness
- fluid retention
- frequent visits to the loo
- heartburn and indigestion
- itchy skin
- leg cramps

- hot and sweaty

- sciatica

- sore ribs

- varicose veins

For more information on how to ease these conditions and why you may suffer from them, see Chapter 4, Your Health During Pregnancy.

I'M AN ELEPHANT!

From week 30 you wonder can you get any bigger — you can! You will be starting to think about labour and childbirth and wondering how you can survive another ten weeks when you cannot breathe, eat properly or get comfortable.

Eating little and often is a good idea in this trimester as your stomach is squashed by your growing baby and heartburn and indigestion start to get worse. You will feel hot and sweaty all the time and be making umpteen trips to the loo as baby presses on your bladder.

Your belly sticks out way in front of you and you will be forced to walk like a waddling duck to maintain any sense of balance. A massive shift in your centre of gravity means that you may fall over and lose your balance if you have to move fast and may bang into furniture as you underestimate how big you have become. An uninterrupted view of your feet is a thing of the past and you may have to ask a friend or put on hold activities such as cutting your toenails and shaving your legs. Slip-on shoes become a god-send.

Getting out of bed is not just a case of sitting upright then putting your feet on the floor — you will have to roll onto your side with your legs together and get up from there by pushing up with your arms. You may also find it an effort to do things like housework that you previously flew through.

It's difficult to breathe as there is not much space in your body for both baby and your internal organs. An uninterrupted night's sleep may be a thing of the past as you contemplate your baby's birth combined with not being able to get comfortable.

All in all, the last trimester is fairly tough going for mum-to-be and a time for slowing down and contemplating your baby's birth and beyond.

As your due date draws near you may start to feel anxious about the birth of your baby. If you've never had a baby before, going into labour can resemble heading off into the great unknown — without a map. If you have questions or concerns make sure to talk to your midwife or doctor about them as he/she may be able to calm your fears.

WHY AM I FINDING IT DIFFICULT TO SLEEP AND HAVING WEIRD DREAMS?

Physical reasons for insomnia during the third trimester include difficulty getting comfortable when your bump is taking up loads of space in the bed, the need to go to the toilet more often, muscle cramps, heartburn and restless legs.

Something strange can happen to your mind when you are pregnant and you can have unusual and sometimes quite distressing dreams. At times when you think you are switching off and resting your tired body, your mind is working overtime. When you are asleep, your subconscious mind is dealing with the many changes you are experiencing now you are pregnant and trying to get ready for the changes to come when your baby is born.

Don't worry about strange dreams, they are just a coping mechanism during this amazing time in your life and will pass when the baby is born. Talking about them with your partner will help to put your mind at rest. I used to sit bolt upright in the middle of the night and get up to answer the door because I had heard the bell ring, but my husband said I was imagining it. I seemed very real to me!

To improve your chances of a good night's sleep don't drink or eat too close to going to bed, make sure your bedroom is not too hot, listen to a relaxing CD, have a bath and read a book as part of your bedtime routine. Sleep on your left side with a pillow between your knees and another one beneath your bump as this helps digestion and improves circulation.

WHEN SHOULD I STOP WORKING?

This depends on the kind of work you do and whether there are any facilities for you to rest during the day. Most experts advise finishing work at around 36 weeks so that you are not overdoing it in the last weeks before your baby's birth, and Irish law states that you must finish two weeks before the last day of the week of your due date. In the last few weeks of pregnancy before you go on maternity leave it is perfectly normal to become more interested in babies than in your job and you should avoid any long car journeys, eat proper meals and try to take breaks when you can.

CHOOSING A NAME FOR YOUR BABY

If you haven't done it yet, it might be time to start thinking about baby names. Some couples decide to find out the sex of their baby and then choose a name and refer to the bump by this name for the rest of the pregnancy, but remember that not all scan results can be 100% accurate and you may end up with a Charlotte instead of a Charlie, so it's a good idea to think of names for both boys and girls.

The best advice I can give you is not to talk to anyone else about your name deliberations — it is a private matter between mum- and dad-to-be and you don't want any (well-meaning) friends or family members putting in an opinion because it just leads to confusion and arguments. Most parents are quite capable of choosing a name for their baby that will fit nicely with their surname and will not lead them to be teased in the school playground.

Choosing a name for your baby is something special you and your partner can share. When you announce the healthy arrival of your baby, everyone will be too thrilled to be worried about the name.

CONSULTATIONS

During your third trimester you will find yourself in your GP's surgery and the hospital more often as routine checks now happen roughly every two weeks. Home-birth mums will be visited more often by their midwife. After week 37 your visits will become weekly as your caregivers keep a closer eye on you and your baby. During these appointments your midwife or doctor will check the size of your baby, check how much fluid surrounds your baby in the uterus and your blood pressure. This is a good opportunity to ask about when you should come into hospital or when you should call your midwife once labour sets in. You can also discuss what happens if you go past your estimated due date (EDD).

RISKS TO YOUR PREGNANCY

Gestational Diabetes

If your doctor or midwife suspects you have gestational diabetes, an oral glucose challenge/tolerance test (OGCT/OGTT), which involves testing blood sugar levels before and after a glucose drink, will confirm it. Common symptoms are going to the toilet a lot and being thirsty all the time.

Gestational diabetes is more common in women who have a BMI of more than 30, women from ethnic minorities and women carrying two or more babies. It means that your body is less able to process sugars from the foods you eat and your baby may gain excessive weight, which can be dangerous.

It is treated with a healthy diet and light exercise, and in a small number of cases women may need insulin injections.

After your baby is born your blood-sugar levels should go back to normal, but you may be more prone to developing type-2 diabetes later in life.

Placenta Praevia

Placenta praevia is a rare condition where the placenta is lying close to or over the opening of the womb instead of at the top of the womb, which could make a vaginal birth dangerous. These days this condition is spotted on an ultrasound scan and your caregiver will make a judgement on whether a vaginal birth is possible or your baby will be delivered by caesarean section.

Symptoms of placenta praevia are bleeding, and if you bleed after week 28 you should always see your doctor. You may be admitted to hospital for monitoring and bed rest.

Pre-eclampsia

Pre-eclampsia is a rare condition and symptoms are high blood pressure, protein in the urine, sudden weight gain, headaches, dizziness and stomach pain. Your hands and feet may also swell up.

Pre-eclampsia is usually diagnosed after week 20 and the only cure is for your baby to be born. It is more common in first pregnancies, women over 40 and women with a body mass index of 35 or over.

If you experience any of these symptoms contact your GP or midwife ASAP. Eclampsia, if it develops, can be very dangerous for both mum and baby as the baby's supply of nutrients and oxygen is restricted by narrowed blood vessels.

Your doctor may prescribe bed rest, medication and even staying in hospital until your baby is born. Pre-eclampsia is obviously more dangerous if it is diagnosed earlier in the pregnancy before your baby is big enough to survive outside the womb, and in cases where your doctor recommends delivering your baby before term you may be given a steroid injection to help your baby's lungs mature.

Premature Labour

If your baby is born early due to induction under medical recommendation and he is over 30 weeks' gestation, then the likelihood is that he will be absolutely healthy after some special care.

If your doctor suspects that your baby may have to be born early he may try to delay it by 24 hours so that you can be given steroids to mature your baby's lungs or transferred to a hospital that has a neonatal unit so that your baby can be given the best care after he is born.

Any baby born before 37 weeks is considered premature, and this applies to many twin births where a bigger medical team will be available to give you whatever specialist care you need.

If you haven't reached 37 weeks and your waters break, or if you experience bleeding, or back pain that goes on for several hours, you should contact your midwife or go straight to the hospital.

If you go into early labour your baby will receive extra care from a specialist doctor once he is born. He may need to spend some time in an incubator and be fed through a tube. Breast milk is tremendously beneficial to premature babies as is skin-to-skin contact and the sound of his mum's voice.

Thrush in Pregnancy

The rise in oestrogen levels during pregnancy can lead to thrush, or vaginal candidiasis, especially during the third trimester. Thrush is characterised by a thick white curd-like discharge from the vagina, itching and irritation in the vaginal area, pain during sexual intercourse and burning when passing urine.

One cause of embarrassment may be due to the misapprehension that thrush is a sexually transmitted disease — this is not true. Yeast, or candida, is a fungus that lives in the vagina and thrush is the result of yeast over-growth caused by an imbalance in good and bad bacteria.

The good news is that thrush during pregnancy will not affect your unborn baby, but if you still have it when you give birth, your baby may develop thrush in her mouth. However this is easy to treat.

If you think you have thrush, see your GP for advice on which treatments are suitable at this time. Whichever treatment you use, you should have some relief of symptoms within 48 hours. You may also find that applying natural yogurt to the affected area and eating yogurts that contain *lactobacillus acidophilus* can help to reestablish your levels of friendly bacteria.

To prevent recurring thrush it's best to wear cotton underwear, to avoid tight trousers and not use scented soaps.

REAL STORIES

'My advice to any new mum is to have some idea of what is happening in your tummy at each stage and what could happen during the delivery, take rest when you can in the run-up to your due date (if you have no other children), go to your antenatal classes, take all offers of help in the first couple of weeks with cleaning (hire a cleaner if you can afford it), offers of cooked meals etc., keep a diary of your pregnancy and after your baby is born and above all enjoy every minute of it!'
Ruth

'Don't spend your pregnancy fearing the labour part. The truth is that by the time your nine months are up, you are so dying to see your little baby, that you can handle going through labour. Fair play to all who manage it without pain relief. I didn't and certainly didn't want to... The important thing is to make sure that wherever you are, you feel safe and comfortable. For me, that meant hospital, for others it might be at home. Just do what suits you and try your best not to be too influenced by others.'
Sinead

Eumom Tip

You may find it is becoming uncomfortable to wear a seat belt in the car. The most comfortable and the correct way to position the belt is by fitting the belt's diagonal shoulder strap over your shoulder and between your breasts. The lap strap should fit comfortably below your tummy. For added comfort, you may want to invest in a back support cushion available from car shops or department stores.

Eumom Tip

To help prevent back pain make sure that you sit properly. The ideal posture is one where your neck is long, your chest is lifted and your pelvis is tilted so that your bottom is tucked under. If you sit for long periods, try to get up and stretch frequently. When sitting in a car, adjust the seat so that it is at a comfortable distance from the controls to suit you.

Preparing a First Child for a New Baby

It's normal for parents to feel a little nervous about introducing a new brother or sister into the family mix, especially if their older child is a toddler and can be rough and prone to jealousy. However, most parents are finely tuned to their children's moods and feelings and instinctively know how to talk about the new baby to their older child before he or she is born.

Saying this, there are a few tricks you can have up your sleeve to help prepare your firstborn for such a momentous event. Visiting family or friends who have a newborn will help your child to see how small, delicate and demanding new babies are. Looking at pictures of your oldest child as a baby will help her to realise she was a baby once, too. Taking your older child with you, if you think it's appropriate, to see an ultrasound scan or listen to the baby's heartbeat can help them to understand that it's real, as can allowing them to help you pack a bag for the hospital and choose baby names, provided they are mature enough.

- Make sure that you have secure and reliable arrangements in place for the care of your older child when your baby is being born. When you introduce your child to your baby make sure there are not too many other people there — this is a special moment. One of the most popular tricks is to buy a present for the older child from the new baby.

·   If possible, try to keep your child's world as stable as possible once their little sibling is born — it's best to avoid moving from a cot to a bed and starting potty training when there are disruptions such as a new baby in the house.

·   If your first child is old enough, she may want to be involved in caring for the baby and help to dress and bathe her little brother or sister, but if she doesn't want to, it's important not to force it.

·   A major problem for older children once a sibling arrives is jealousy. Try to allocate some special time every day for you to spend one-to-one with your older child — this will help him to deal with feelings of resentment or being pushed out by the demands of his younger sibling. If you had a bedtime routine, such as a story or songs, try not to break it now. Your partner can mind the baby while you read a story to your older child.

Once the first few difficult and demanding months have passed, most older siblings come to terms with, and start to enjoy, having a younger brother or sister. And before you know it, they will be chasing each other around the house.

Preparing your Pet for your New Arrival

Many pet lovers may be concerned about how their dog or cat will react when they bring home their tiny new baby. You are right to be aware of a number of problems your pet may encounter as it tries to come to terms with changes in the home. Your foremost concern will be for the safety and welfare of your baby, and this means that a dog, for example, may need to have some 'baby preparation' training.

The following tips come from a Dublin dog-training company. For more detailed information on how to train a dog for a baby's arrival, check out the blog: http://petcentralpawsitivepetcare.wordpress.com

·   Your dog should be desensitised to baby equipment, baby noises and baby smells well before baby comes home. CDs with baby sounds should be played at low levels while the dog is eating, regularly carry a doll with you while training your dog to do sits, 'downs' and other essential exercises. Make sure to reward any calm behaviour with high-value rewards.

- It is very important that your dog has a safe, quiet, baby-proof den where he can escape from children, visitors and the general chaos associated with babies. The dog should be trained to go to his den on cue and to enjoy spending time there.

- Children should always be supervised when around a dog by an adult capable of controlling the dog — they should not be left alone or out of eye line, even for a second. Advice regarding baby-and-dog safety must be passed on to relations, grandparents, babysitters and anyone in contact with the dog and baby.

- If you have a cat he will be aware that his territory is changing and that certain rooms in your home are being used more or less than they were. Rather than having to constantly move the cat out of the room where you baby is napping, try to get him used to not being in certain rooms before your baby is born. Choosing one space in the house where you can spend time with your cat away from the noise of the baby will help to keep your cat calm. He may benefit from more toys to keep him amused and a box where he can hide.

- Take dogs and cats to the vet before your baby is born to ensure they don't carry fleas or other parasites and never let a dog or cat lick your baby's face. Washing your hands after stroking your pet will also prevent anything nasty passing to your baby. Never leave your cat alone in a room with your baby.

What is Perineal Massage?

In the last few weeks of pregnancy a woman can massage the area between her vagina and anus (*perineum*) in preparation for childbirth. There is some evidence that massaging stretches the skin so that you are less likely to get a tear or to need an episiotomy during your baby's birth. Some childbirth preparation classes talk about this in more detail.

Basically, you put your thumbs inside your vagina and push towards your anus and out to the sides until you can feel a tingle or stretch. Now hold for a couple of minutes before massaging the area for another couple of minutes. The more you do it, the more supple your skin will become and the more able to cope with the enormous stretching it will need to do during labour.

Alternatively you could try the Epi-no, which can be used from week 37. The Epi-no provides a controlled and gradual perineal stretch by using a balloon which you inflate to stretch your muscles. It also prepares you for the sensation of delivering your baby's head and using muscles to push him out. It can also be used after your baby is born to exercise your pelvic floor muscles.

Available from *www.epin-no.co.uk* for £89.99 + £6 P&P and from some midwives.

What to Put in Your Hospital Bag

As your due date draws near and you anticipate the birth of your baby, it's time to think about packing your hospital bag. Women having a home birth will also need to have similar items, but they will obviously be closer to hand.

It's a good idea to have your bag for hospital ready some weeks before your baby is due, in case you go into labour early. If your bag is sitting packed and ready to go, and you go into labour, you can just grab it and go. And don't forget that friends, family members and your partner will be visiting you in the hospital and can take away dirty clothes for washing and bring clean ones to you, too, as well as anything you may have forgotten to bring.

Below is a hospital bag checklist for both mum and baby.

Mum's Packing List

- TENS machine if you are using one — you will probably have started using it at home ☐

- Toiletries — soap, shower gel, shampoo ☐

- Toothbrush and toothpaste ☐

- Hairdryer (optional) ☐

- Glasses (if you wear contact lenses you may need to take them out during delivery) ☐

- Medications for conditions such as asthma etc. ☐

- Make-up (especially important for when visitors come to visit and you want to look good) ☐

- Lipsalve ☐

- Hairbrush ☐

- Tissues ☐

- 2 bath towels ☐

- 1 hand towel ☐

- 2 face cloths ☐

- 2 short nighties for labour — button-down are good if you plan to breastfeed. Best to buy inexpensive ones as you will probably end up throwing them out. ☐

- Disposable pants or old underwear ☐

- 1 pair warm socks (feet can get cold during labour) ☐

- Stress balls or other gadgets you may be using during labour ☐

- Ipod and earphones ☐

- Your birthing ball — to help the baby's head engage, and to lean on during labour. Obviously this won't fit in the bag! Check that your hospital will allow you to bring one in. ☐

- Water mist spray to keep you cool during labour ☐

- 3 nightgowns or pyjamas for after labour ☐

- Slippers ☐

- Dressing gown ☐

- 2 nursing bras ☐

- An outfit for going home — you will still have a bump, so best not to pack your tightest jeans ☐

- 2 packs maternity pads ☐

- 20–30 breast pads ☐

- Lanolin breastfeeding cream ☐

- Mobile phone and charger ☐

- Camera (with charger) ☐

- Book on baby's first days and breastfeeding ☐

- Something to read — nothing too taxing as you'll be too tired after the birth to concentrate ☐

- Pen and paper for information you may be given ☐

- Health insurance policy number, if relevant ☐

Baby's Packing List

- 3 vests ☐

- 4 sleepsuits or babygros ☐

- 4 bibs ☐

- 1 pair scratch mitts ☐

- 1 hat ☐

- Going-home clothes — vest, sleepsuit, hat and cardigan; warm sleepsuit if it is cold ☐

- 1 cellular blanket ☐

- Sudocrem or another nappy-rash cream ☐

- 1 pack newborn nappies ☐

- Bag of cotton wool pleat ☐

- 2 towels (hooded) ☐

- A small plastic bowl for water for cleaning your baby's bum   ☐

- Soothers — if you are planning to use them   ☐

It's a good idea to ask the hospital whether they supply sheets for babies on the wards — if not, bring your own. All hospitals urge expectant mums to avoid bringing valuables into the building, for obvious reasons. Finally, if it's the middle of the night, then it might be a good idea to bring some food and drinks for your partner. He will need to be able to keep going when the going gets tough! You will need to bring in a car seat before most maternity hospitals will release mum and baby from the hospital. For more on this see page 204.

HOW DAD FEELS AND HOW HE CAN HELP

The third trimester can seem to go very slowly. As your baby grows, this can be an uncomfortable time for your partner with an aching back, heartburn, restlessness, frequent trips to the bathroom and sleepless nights. Your job is to fetch and carry and generally do whatever is asked of you.

You may be concerned about the impending labour and how you will perform when the going gets tough — will you panic and faint, will the midwife ask you to cut the umbilical cord, do you even want to? Even more worrying, will you know when your partner is in labour? Or will you have to deliver the baby yourself?

It may be hard to believe, but this big person you are sharing a bed with will go back to her normal self and you will have a sex life again, although this may take a while. Try to look beyond these past few weeks into the future — if you find you are getting hung up on the birth, talk to other new dads about it.

Adam Brophy, in *The Bad Dad's Survival Guide* says, 'Now is a time to attempt to show some backbone, to offer comfort, to be resilient, to rub swollen feet, offer assurances of continuing beauty and deny the existence of varicose veins… You do this for basic survival.'

Read forward to Chapter 5 in case your partner goes into early labour and you are called upon to step into action sooner than planned.

Chapter 4 ∽

YOUR HEALTH DURING PREGNANCY

When you are pregnant, your body will be working very hard to support your growing baby, and so you will want to look after both of you. This chapter will help you to do that, as well as giving you lots of information on food safety in pregnancy, the benefits of a healthy diet, and some of the common ailments specific to your pregnancy in a handy A-Z guide. Of course, pregnancy is full of myths and mysteries and I've also included some facts about the many old wives' tales that others will tell you!

Many people have concerns about the safety of certain activities during pregnancy, such as sex or exercise. They wonder if it's safe to continue to do the kind of things they used to before they became pregnant. The answer is yes, within reason. There are limitations and you might have to accept that life might not be as it was for a little while. But you will have a beautiful baby to show for it.

SEX DURING PREGNANCY

You may find that your libido changes as your pregnancy progresses: talking to your partner about how you feel and listening to how he feels, will help you both to cope with any problems or 'dry' periods. If you're not having sex, it's important to find other ways to be close and intimate such as cuddles and massage.

If you suffer from morning sickness, most common in the first trimester, it's unlikely that sex will be high up on your list of priorities. But once this time is over, your second trimester could bring a whole new revival of sexual desire with some unexpected advantages, as increased blood flow to your genitals and increased breast sensitivity mean great pleasure in your sex life.

If your partner is concerned about harming the baby, you may need to reassure him that sex during pregnancy is safe unless your doctor advises against it, or for some other reasons (see below).

Towards the end of pregnancy you may feel too cumbersome to really enjoy sex and your bump may get in the way, but changing sexual positions may help take the physical pressure off your body. Many pregnant women find they like to be on top, or enjoy sex in the 'spoons' position. You and your partner may feel reluctant to engage in full sex at this late stage in your pregnancy because you may be concerned about harming your baby, but your little one is cushioned in the uterus and unlikely to be hurt. In fact, sex has been used for centuries to bring on labour (see page 123).

Avoid sex:

- If you've had a number of miscarriages — to be on the safe side.

- If you've suffered bleeding, but check with your doctor or midwife as it may depend.

- If you are having twins or more, in the last trimester, in case it brings on early labour.

- If you or your partner have an STD (sexually transmitted disease) and could pass it on to your baby. Of course, you should seek treatment for any STD.

- If your waters have broken.

- If you've got thrush you may find sex uncomfortable until it has cleared up. Remember, you partner may need treatment, too.

- If your doctor says you should, for any other reason.

REAL STORY

'When it comes to the sex bit I must say it was great for a few weeks but when I could feel my tummy growing, I went off it completely. I felt extremely uncomfortable, unsexy and interrupted with the nausea and needing to pee constantly.'
Natasha

EXERCISE DURING PREGNANCY

Keeping active and exercising can help you carry the average two stone in weight that most women gain during pregnancy. It can boost your energy levels, help you sleep better, reduce constipation and relieve stress and anxiety. Exercise also helps you to get your pre-pregnancy shape back more quickly as you will gain less fat.

The level of exercise you can do will depend on how fit you were before getting pregnant. If you weren't exercising regularly before, but wish to do something now to improve your health while you are pregnant, start very slowly and remember not to overdo it. It's also a good idea to mention your plans to your GP or midwife.

The golden rules are to skip exercise if your energy levels are low and you are suffering from any sickness, and to drink plenty of water to avoid dehydration. Remember, your body will already be working extremely hard to grow your baby.

Enjoying Exercise During Pregnancy

- Gentle and steady exercise is what you should aim for in pregnancy.

- Wear suitable clothing and pay particular attention to good footwear with strong ankle and arch support — pregnant women are carrying a heavy load and need to look after their feet.

- Wear a good sports bra, which will support your expanding breasts.

- Stop often while exercising and drink plenty of water.

Swimming is considered the safest exercise for pregnant women as the water carries your weight, so there is little risk of stress to the joints and you are unlikely to get overheated. Many women enjoy the feeling of weightlessness they get from being in water.

Walking is a safe pregnancy exercise and can be easily fitted into your daily life — try to do some gentle stretches before setting out and wear shoes which support your feet.

Women who were runners before pregnancy may continue to run, with some moderation to their exercise routine, but talk to your doctor first. It is not wise to begin running when you are pregnant if you have never done it before. Wear good shoes, drink plenty of water and make sure you do not overheat.

Cycling in early pregnancy is good because the bicycle carries your weight, but be aware that as the baby grows, there is a greater risk of falling and also putting stress on your back from leaning over.

Yoga and Pilates can be good for pregnant women as they relieve pressure and stress on the body — some instructors run special classes for pregnant women and can adjust stretches to suit your condition. They will encourage you to avoid exercising while lying flat on your back.

Aerobics are suitable for pregnant women, although you will need to be careful about keeping your balance. Classes designed for pregnant women are best. Water aerobics are ideal for pregnant women.

Dancing can be great fun and can be done at home or in a gym class, but you will need to avoid jumping, leaping or spinning round. A class for pregnant women is best.

To be Avoided During Pregnancy:

- Exhausting yourself and getting out of breath while exercising is not good for your body or your baby as you are limiting the supply of oxygen through the placenta. If you can't talk while exercising, slow down, as you are overdoing it.

- Try to keep your heart rate under 140 beats per minute and your body temperature at under 102°F or 39°C as overheating is dangerous for a developing fetus. Do not exercise in very hot weather as this will put extra strain on you and your baby.

- Listen to your body: it will tell you if you are doing too much. If you suffer from dizziness or shortness of breath, stop straight away.

- Any exercise where you could fall, such as horse riding or skiing and anything that involves jolts and quick movements, bouncing, leaping or any risk of abdominal injury should be avoided.

- As your body adjusts to carrying a baby, joints and ligaments stretch, leaving you more prone to injury, so avoid contact sports and running or cycling over uneven ground.

- Towards the end of your pregnancy avoid exercising flat on your back as this can decrease blood flow to your womb, lowering your blood pressure and causing you to feel faint.

- If doing step aerobics lower the step as your pregnancy progresses and be very careful to avoid falling as a growing baby will alter your centre of gravity.

- Stay away from the sauna or steam room, which can make you too hot and may harm your baby.

Stop! If you suffer any of the following:

- Vaginal bleeding
- Shortness of breath
- Palpitations
- Back pain
- Pelvic pain
- Nausea
- Dizziness
- Light-headedness
- Chest pain
- Faintness
- Fluid leaking from your vagina
- Uterine contraction
- Any unusual pain

Pelvic-Floor or Kegel Exercises

Most women will not have heard of their pelvic floor before they become pregnant, but it is common vocabulary among new mums, along with a dawning realisation of what these muscles actually do and how they might be affected by the strains of pregnancy and by pushing your baby into the world. Your pelvic floor is basically all the muscles that run from your pubic bone right through to your lower back. They form a sling shape across your pelvis and are responsible for your being able to control your bladder and bowels, so they're very important indeed. Your pelvic floor can be stretched and weakened by labour and you may find you leak urine after coughing, laughing, dancing or running. This can be extremely embarrassing for a woman but thankfully, there is something you can do to prevent it.

To help strengthen these muscles after birth, you will need to do pelvic floor exercises (or Kegels). You should do them regularly during and after pregnancy and they will strengthen pelvic floor muscles, promote perineal healing and help you to regain weakened-bladder control. They can be done anywhere and no-one will know you are doing them.

The easiest way to find whether you are squeezing the correct muscles (after all, you can't see) is to sit on the toilet and start urinating, then squeeze the muscles to stop urinating, hold them for a few seconds then relax. (You should only do this as a test, though, as holding urine is not recommended.) You should feel a pull if you are using the correct muscles. Try not to tighten other muscles in your legs or stomach while doing your Kegel exercises. Don't hold your breath either as your muscles need oxygen, like any other muscle when exercising.

Once you have found your pelvic floor, hold in the muscles for a count of ten, then release for the same time, before repeating. Try to do ten Kegels every morning, afternoon and evening and in a few weeks you should notice an improvement. You can do these exercises while driving, breastfeeding or lying in bed. The Epi-no, which helps to stretch your perineum, may also help you with Kegels — see page 79.

YOUR DIET IN PREGNANCY

Being pregnant is a special time in any woman's life — from the minute you know you are expecting a tiny life, you need to start thinking like a mum and looking after yourself and your baby in a way you may not have done before. Especially when it comes to what you eat and drink.

Scientists now believe that a woman's diet when she is pregnant can affect whether her baby will have allergies in childhood or develop heart disease in later life, so most mums-to-be will want to ensure they are eating the best foods they can at this time.

Most women find that their appetite changes as their pregnancy progresses and this may depend on whether they suffer sickness or other problems such as constipation. The best rule to remember is to eat when you are hungry and at least every four hours. As long as you are eating healthy unprocessed foods, avoiding anything dangerous and your doctor says your weight gain is normal, you can enjoy your food and not worry about it.

What You and Baby Need

While it's tempting to eat what you want, including gallons of ice-cream, during pregnancy, these days it's known that pregnant women do not need to 'eat for two'. Any excess weight you put on will only have to be lost again after your baby is born. In fact, you don't need to eat any extra calories in the first six months of pregnancy because your body becomes more efficient at using energy when you are pregnant and extracting nutrients from the food you eat. After this, in the third trimester of your pregnancy you will need an extra 200–300 calories per day.

Your pregnancy diet needs to be healthy and balanced with the following types of foods every day:

- Lots of fruit and vegetables

- Plenty of carbohydrates such as bread, rice, pasta, potatoes and breakfast cereals — the wholegrain or 'brown' version of these foods will be a better source of fibre

- Dairy in the form of yogurt, milk and cheese

- Protein such as chicken, meat, fish, eggs, beans and pulses

- Oily fish once or twice a week

- Foods packed with iron such as meat, fish and green vegetables

- Folic acid from green vegetables such as broccoli and fortified breakfast cereals, milk and bread as well as a supplement during pregnancy (see page 2 for more on folic acid)

Pregnant women can get hungry at frequent intervals and to avoid reaching for the biscuit tin, carry some of the following foods with you to snack on:

- Yoghurt

- Fresh fruit, such as bananas or pears

- Dried fruit, such as raisins or apricots

- Unsalted nuts, such as brazil nuts or almonds

If you're working, don't worry, most people are used to seeing pregnant women snack at frequent intervals.

When you get the munchies at home go for a bowl of cereal with milk, toast with mashed banana or hard cheddar cheese or hummous with vegetable sticks. These foods will keep you going for longer than processed cakes and sweets and will pass on valuable nutrients to your baby. If you are suffering from morning sickness, you may find that it is difficult to keep food down, so you will need to snack more often. You may wish to ask your doctor whether you should take a vitamin supplement.

Foods to Avoid
Due to changes in your immune system during pregnancy, you may find that your stomach is more sensitive than normal. To avoid putting you or your baby at risk from the bacteria in what you eat and drink, you will need to be extra vigilant when cooking and serving food. Make sure your kitchen is clean, that you wash your hands after touching raw meat and eggs and that everything you eat is cooked right through.

In addition, keep these foods out of your pregnancy diet as they could harm you or your baby:

- *Undercooked eggs,* due to the risk of salmonella bacteria. This includes soft-boiled, poached etc., which have runny yolks — hard-boiled eggs are fine. Beware of other foods made with raw eggs, such as home-made ice-cream, mayonnaise, mousse or cheesecake. If you order any of these in a restaurant ask the waiter to find out whether they are cooked through or not. Mayonnaise in a jar from the supermarket is fine as it is made with pasteurised eggs.

- *Blue vein and soft cheeses,* due to the risk of listeriosis, an illness which particularly affects pregnant women and newborns. These include Camembert, Brie, Cashel Blue, soft goat's cheeses, Cambozola and Stilton among others. All hard cheeses, such as Cheddar or Gouda as well as processed cheeses, such as Boursin, mascarpone, mozzarella, ricotta and cream cheeses like Philadelphia are fine. Make sure any cheese, milk (including cream, soured cream and crème fraiche) or yogurt (and fromage frais) products you eat are pasteurised.

- *Unpasteurised goats'-milk products,* such as milk or cheese, as they could harbour toxoplasmosis. Toxoplasmosis can also be found in undercooked or raw meat so you shouldn't handle or eat this food.

- *Liver products,* such as paté, due to the risk from the bacteria 'listeria', which can cause listeriosis and because they contain high levels of Vitamin A, which can harm baby's development.

- *Fish,* such as tuna, swordfish, shark and marlin which can prove toxic to an unborn child because they contain mercury. Tuna lovers should limit their consumption to one fresh steak or two cans per week. Smoked salmon is not recommended during pregnancy as it is uncooked.

- *Shellfish,* such as mussels and oysters — or make sure they are thoroughly cooked to kill off any harmful bacteria.

- *Pre-washed bagged salads,* as these can contain bacteria — instead buy whole vegetables and wash them thoroughly before eating.

- *Cured meats,* such as salami which can contain harmful bacteria.

- *Peanuts.* Cut these out while pregnant or breastfeeding if you, your baby's father or other children have a nut allergy. Otherwise they are fine to eat.

- *Refined foods,* such as white bread and sugar as these will fill you up but are low in nutritional value.

- *Junk foods* — these are too high in salt, fat and sugar to be good for you or baby.

- *Caffeine,* which has been associated with an increased risk of miscarriage and low birth weight. Cut down on caffeine by limiting your intake of coffee, tea and cola and switching to decaffeinated brands. Pregnant women are not recommended to consume more than 300 mg of caffeine per day — that is approximately two mugs of instant coffee, four cups of tea or a small amount of cola.

- *Alcohol* — most governments, including the Irish government, recommend that pregnant women avoid alcohol altogether as it is passed to the baby via the placenta. Drinking too much during pregnancy can lead to fetal alcohol syndrome (FAS) with increased risk of low birth weight, miscarriage and malformations.

I'M A VEGETARIAN — DO I NEED TO START EATING MEAT NOW I AM PREGNANT?

If you don't eat meat, you may find that, once you have announced your good news, well-meaning relatives start to voice their concerns about the baby getting enough nutrients. If you eat a varied vegetarian diet with plenty of peas, beans, lentils, seeds and cereals as well as dairy foods and eggs your diet should be fine during pregnancy. Your doctor or midwife may recommend you take an Omega 3 or Vitamin B12 supplement and that you eat more foods fortified with iron. A good way to get more iron from your food is to drink orange juice with meals. Talk to your GP or midwife about your diet and follow the advice of your caregiver — there should be no need for you to suddenly start eating meat while pregnant.

VITAMINS, SUPPLEMENTS AND MEDICINES DURING PREGNANCY

Because what you eat and drink passes to your baby through the placenta, it's important when pregnant to think twice before taking medications, supplements or herbal remedies. Talk to your GP about what is safe and if you take regular medications ask whether you can continue to do so.

All women are recommended to take folic acid during pregnancy (see page 2). If you find out that you are pregnant and haven't been taking folic acid, don't worry, but start straight away. In addition to this your doctor may advise you to consider an iron supplement (usually after the first trimester) as your body needs extra iron during this time due to the extra blood needed to grow a baby — there are a number of pregnancy-safe supplements available. Omega 3 is another supplement that is believed to be beneficial during pregnancy. Women who suffer from indigestion can take remedies and there are a number available which are safe to take during pregnancy. Check with your care provider.

Pregnant women are not advised to take Vitamin A in either a supplement or multivitamin form.

Over-the-counter drugs can often be more powerful than we think and have some worrying side-effects for pregnant women and developing babies. Depending on which trimester you are in when you take them, they can cause breathing problems in the baby, an increased risk of miscarriage and placental abruption (where the placenta separates from the uterus before the baby is born). Codeine, aspirin and ibuprofen as well as cold and flu remedies that contain a potent combination of painkiller, anti-histamines and pseudo-ephedrine must be avoided or only taken under the strict advice of a qualified pharmacist.

Certain prescription medications should be avoided during pregnancy and your doctor will advise you on this: these include drugs for acne, certain antibiotics, anti-convulsants, anti-depressants, anti-cancer drugs, anti-thyroid drugs and thalidomide, which is not commonly available, but which is used in the treatment of certain rare diseases. In addition, some herbal remedies are not recommended for pregnant women because they may cause birth defects or induce uterine contractions. These include: St Johns Wort, ginseng, aloe vera, and some oils. Always ask a qualified herbalist or pharmacist and read labels before buying and using herbal remedies.

If you're considering aromatherapy during pregnancy, make sure you see an aromatherapist specialising in pregnancy as you will need to be sure that the oils rubbed into your skin are safe for you and your baby at this time. Many aromatherapists recommend against having treatment during the first trimester when your baby's organs are developing. Oils that are a definite no-no during pregnancy include basil, cinnamon, clove, parsley, sage, rosemary, myrrh, juniper, bay, thyme and jasmine (there are many more than these but an expert can fill you in). Some oils are safer but only suitable from the fifth month on. The essential thing is to check with an expert here. If you like to burn essential oils at home, check the label to make sure they don't say 'avoid during pregnancy', or ask your pharmacist — these harmless-looking oils can be more powerful than you think.

In the same way that essential oils should be approached with caution during pregnancy owing to their powerful properties, herbal teas should also be viewed with caution. These harmless looking drinks can, in fact, have powerful effects. Some have been used to bring on periods, among other things. Raspberry leaf tea, for example, is often recommended for women who are overdue and want to bring on labour. In general — and you may want to seek advice on this — it's safe to drink peppermint and chamomile tea during pregnancy (although do this in moderation).

ASTHMA IN PREGNANCY

Ireland has the 4th highest prevalence of asthma worldwide with approximately 470,000 people affected (1 in 8 of the population). Pregnancy can be a very worrying time for asthma sufferers and you may be concerned about which medications you can safely take.

The good news is that if asthma is controlled the chance of a normal pregnancy and delivery is the same as that of a woman who doesn't have asthma. You can use your preventer and reliever inhalers safely during pregnancy under medical advice.

Asthma management at this time should never be ignored. Remind your GP that you suffer from asthma and discuss how you will manage the condition when your pregnancy is first diagnosed.

In 2008 the Asthma Society brought out a guide on asthma management for women during pregnancy called *Asthma in Pregnancy*. You can order a copy of the booklet free of charge through the Asthma

Society on 1850 445 464 or download it from *www.asthmasociety.ie*. It is also available from maternity hospitals.

CRAVINGS

A little monster has taken over your body and right now she wants gherkins and ice-cream — together! Your body is doing its job of nourishing a growing baby and cravings are its way of getting the foods that fulfil that role. While in most pregnant women this means sugars found in chocolate and ice-cream or salts from crisps and pickles, for example, bear in mind that your cravings could be revealing a vitamin deficiency. If you're concerned talk to your doctor or midwife.

While it's almost impossible to ignore a craving, if you can, it's a good idea to try to go for a healthier alternative in order to avoid filling up your body with empty calories, which won't nourish you or your baby. If you crave ice-cream, try frozen yogurt; what about popcorn instead of crisps? However, if you're eating a balanced healthy diet, a little of what you fancy is perfectly fine.

Of course we've all heard of pregnant women who want to nibble on coal, but if this applies to you or you are desperate to gorge on coffee grinds you may have a more serious deficiency and should consult your doctor.

Once your baby is born your cravings will miraculously disappear.

REAL STORY

'I lived on ice and ice pops. I was constantly chewing on ice and I couldn't go one day without it. It drove everyone around me crazy with the constant crunching and now my teeth are very sensitive, typical! Another craving was anything chocolate, especially cereals. One thing I couldn't stand was the smell of vegetable soup and mushrooms, and it hurt so much as I really longed for them.'

Natasha

RELAXATION DURING PREGNANCY

Pregnant women may not have enough energy to party or have an energetic social life, but that doesn't mean you can't find ways to relax and enjoy yourself. Here are a few ideas:

- Go for a walk — get outside into the fresh air; it will lift your mood and get your heart pumping.

- Phone a friend — a 20-minute chat on the phone will give you the chance to catch up and will make you laugh. Friendship is good for our mental health.

- Have a DIY pampering session — lock the doors and turn off your mobile then take your time with a manicure or face pack. Soak your feet as they are under a lot of pressure at the moment.

- Have a pregnancy massage to ease aches and pains, but it's best to wait until you are in the second trimester and the pregnancy is well established. Look for a massage therapist who is certified in pregnancy massage.

- Buy some accessories — fun jewellery and colourful bags don't have to be expensive, and you can use them after the baby is born.

- Spend money on your hair — to make you feel better even when you feel you're the size of an elephant.

- Get some flower power — buy yourself a bunch and arrange them in a vase to bring a gorgeous natural scent into your home.

- Declutter your home — pick a wardrobe or kitchen cupboard, take everything out and sort into bags for the bin, the charity shop, E-bay etc., and put back everything you want to keep. This is more therapeutic than it seems and your home will start to feel less crammed with stuff as you work through each room.

- Read a magazine or book — losing yourself in reading is relaxing and an utterly personal experience. In 20 minutes you can read two articles in a magazine or two chapters in a book.

- Have a power nap — 10–20 minutes of sleep can be good for your energy levels, and you'll wake up feeling refreshed but not groggy.

- Get pet therapy — Stroking a cat or dog lowers the heart rate and blood pressure levels, improving your mood, so pin moggy or fido to your knee while you are watching your favourite soap.

- Meditate away stress — sitting still, blocking out other thoughts and controlling your breathing is good for controlling levels of stress. You can do this anywhere — on a train or bus, on the sofa or bed, wherever you have time and space.

- Get some laughter therapy — rent a comedy DVD and chuckle away stress.

- Dance crazy — put on your favourite music, turn it up and dance around the living-room. It doesn't matter how you look because you will feel just great.

- Get knitting — knitting is something you can do in front of the TV, it's relatively easy to pick up once you have learned the essential stitches, not expensive and there are some gorgeous patterns available for babies.

- Do nothing! Sometimes it's good to just sit with a cup of tea and collect your thoughts.

Stop Worrying and Enjoy your Pregnancy

Once your pregnant bump is visible to the outside world you'll be surprised by how many people will approach you with a nugget of advice or wisdom, and not all of it will be welcome. Known as 'old wives' tales', some traditional beliefs, which were widely accepted for centuries, have now been disproved by developments in modern science. Here are some of the most common and bizarre myths that I have discovered and hope will make you smile.

Your cravings and the baby's position can reveal his or her gender.
If you're carrying your baby high, crave chocolate and your face becomes round during pregnancy, you must be having a girl. If you're carrying low, crave sour foods and your face doesn't become round, then you will have a baby boy. The truth is that the way you carry a baby is determined by muscle tone and the position your baby chooses to lie, and the only way to know for certain whether you are having a boy or girl is to have an ultrasound scan after the 20th week of pregnancy, and in some cases, even this proves unreliable. The gender of your baby is determined by whether an X or Y chromosome from the

father fertilises the egg. Another myth is that if your baby's father puts on weight during your pregnancy you will have a girl, and if he doesn't, you will have a boy.

Lifting your arms above your head when pregnant is dangerous.
Old wives' tales say that if you hold your arms above your head, for example when hanging out washing, your baby's umbilical cord will get wrapped around his neck and choke him. The truth is that if your baby's cord becomes wrapped around him or her, this has nothing to do with what you have or haven't done while pregnant, and more to do with how active your baby has been in the uterus. About 20–25% of babies are born with the cord around their neck, or even legs, and some umbilical cords can even end up tied in knots!

Having sex while pregnant could hurt your baby.
Within reason it is perfectly safe to enjoy sex with your partner while you are pregnant because your baby is protected from harm in the uterus. In fact some women enjoy sex more while pregnant thanks to the increase in blood flow to the pelvic floor. See page 83 for more information.

You will lose a tooth during every pregnancy.
This myth is based on the belief that your unborn baby will take away all your calcium so that they can grow bones, and this can lead to tooth loss. However, with calcium supplements readily available and improved diets rich in fortified foods, this is rarely a problem in 21st-century Ireland. Pregnant women are advised to take 1,500 mg of calcium a day from food or supplements. If you are concerned that you are not getting enough calcium, ask your dentist for advice. For more advice on caring for your teeth, see page 114.

You shouldn't take a bath while pregnant.
Baths were believed to expose the baby to bacteria from water travelling up the vagina and into the uterus. But we now know, thanks to science, that water does not enter the vagina during a bath. What you should be careful to avoid is a bath that is too hot (above 38°C or 101°F) as this will cause your body temperature to rise and could be dangerous for your baby. If your waters have broken or you are bleeding, you should definitely avoid having a bath.

Cats are dangerous for pregnant women.
For women who love cats and find their company relaxing it can be upsetting to think that they cannot stroke their cat while they are pregnant — luckily, this myth isn't true. However, there is a real risk from a parasite called toxoplasmosis, which can lead to miscarriage and fetal deformities. It is most commonly found in the stools of cats, which is why pregnant women should never handle cat litter. Let your partner do this, and recommend he wear rubber gloves.

Toxoplasmosis is also more common in outdoor moggies who catch and eat their own food. If a neighbouring cat or stray comes into your garden and may be defecating there, make sure to wear gloves when gardening and wash all fruit and vegetables you have grown. If you are concerned about this talk to your GP or midwife, or talk to your vet about your cat.

Common sense should protect you from contracting toxoplasmosis. If you have to handle cat litter, use tight-fitting rubber gloves and wash hands thoroughly afterwards. If you work on or near a farm, you will have to take extra precautions around livestock. See page 47 for more information.

Microwaves, computer screens and X-rays are harmful to pregnant women.
While it is wise to be wary of over-exposing yourself to these machines, there is no evidence that modern microwaves and computers expose women and their unborn babies to harmful radiation. However, if you need an x-ray your doctor or dentist will be able to advise on its necessity and safety when you explain that you are pregnant.

Spicy foods will bring on childbirth.
This is completely untrue. When you go into labour is much more closely connected to hormonal changes in your body than anything you might eat. Otherwise women who regularly eat spicy foods would have shorter pregnancies!

You shouldn't have your hair dyed when pregnant.
This myth may be connected to the unpleasant chemical smells associated with hair dye, which can seem stronger to pregnant women, who have a more sensitive sense of smell. There is no evidence that hair

dye is harmful to your unborn baby, although some of the chemicals can be absorbed into your bloodstream. However, if you're concerned, tell your hairdresser that you are pregnant and consider having highlights or lowlights where the dye does not reach your scalp. Another option is to change your hair colour to one closer to your natural tone so that it needs less dyeing as the roots grow through. Alternatively, as a precaution, wait until after the first trimester during which your baby's nervous system is forming. Beware that if you dye your hair during pregnancy, it may turn out a different colour, due to pregnancy hormones.

If you get a lot of heartburn, your baby will have a lot of hair.
I'm not sure where this myth comes from, but there is good reason why many women suffer from heartburn when pregnant. As your baby grows and your uterus expands, your stomach is pushed upwards. This makes it easier for acid to move into the lower throat or oesophagus, known as 'reflux', and to cause heartburn. To avoid heartburn sit upright after eating, take safe antacid medicines (ask your GP or pharmacist) and sleep with your head propped up by pillows. (For more on heartburn see page 108.)

WORKING SAFELY DURING YOUR PREGNANCY
Many women have jobs that are perfectly safe during pregnancy when they make a few simple changes. Follow these tips:

- Get someone else to do the lifting and carrying — even bending at the knees to lift something could put a strain on your overburdened back.

- Some pregnant women suffer from swollen ankles, especially if on their feet at work all day — you may need to be moved to a different department. If this is not possible try to put one foot up at a time on a stool or box to relieve pressure, then swap legs. Wearing support tights is also helpful.

- Don't hold the phone between your ear and your shoulder as it could stretch important back muscles you need to carry your baby. If possible, get a hands-free set instead.

- If your company does not have guidelines for pregnant women, suggest to your employer that your workstation is checked out to make sure it is suitable. This is not just to avoid RSI (Repetitive Strain Injury) but to ensure no added stress is put on your body at this time. If this is not possible bring in a small pillow to give your lower back some support and put your feet up on something such as a box or couple of telephone directories under the desk.

- If you are suffering from tiredness it can be hard to take a break at work, but your body is telling you to slow down. Short breaks can be effective if your job involves a lot of thinking or decision-making — even leaving your desk and making a cup of tea can give you a screen break and prevent muscle tension from your sitting in one position. If you can, schedule your time so that you do your most taxing work when you feel at your best.

- Alter your home schedule so that you spend most evenings relaxing at home and have enough energy for work. Gentle exercise such as swimming or a walk may give you more energy and help you sleep.

- If you're suffering from morning sickness, keep a stash of plain crackers or other snack foods in your desk in case you start to feel queasy or faint, and keep up your fluid intake with extra glasses of water throughout the day. Keeping a toothbrush and toothpaste at work will help to keep your mouth feeling fresh.

- Certain jobs are not ideal for pregnant women and your employer should have guidelines or policies regarding pregnant staff. Some airlines do not recommend female staff fly during the first trimester, for example.

- If you find you are hot at work, buy a small desk fan, open the windows for fresh air, and take screen breaks outside the building.

- Invest in some maternity clothes — once the first trimester is over you will start to expand more quickly and squeezing into normal clothes is no longer an option. Put the word out to women you know who have been pregnant to see what clothes you can borrow, buy a few mix-and-match basics, get fitted for a new bra for added support and wear flat shoes.

IS IT SAFE TO FLY WHEN PREGNANT?

This is a difficult one, but what you will find is that different airlines have different policies on this issue, so in many ways the decision is made for you. The best advice I can give is to avoid putting your body and your baby under any unnecessary stress during pregnancy, and that includes flying, unless you have to.

Some airlines do not allow their pregnant female staff to fly during the first trimester due to the tiny risk of exposure to low radiation, however, your exposure from one or two flights is unlikely to be anything close to that experienced by women who fly every day for their job.

Understandably, airlines are not keen on carrying pregnant women in their third trimester. If you are taking a short-haul flight and are between 28–32 weeks' pregnant, you should inform the airline, who may ask for a letter from your GP stating your due date and that you are having a healthy/normal pregnancy. You may not be allowed to travel long haul after week 28 in your pregnancy and after 32 weeks or so airlines may not be keen to take you on any flights.

I would recommend you avoid flying in the last trimester, unless you have to, of course, simply because as you grow, sitting in a confined space becomes more difficult (and getting in and out of the tiny loo is no joke either!). Don't forget that flying can be stressful; you may end up carrying luggage and making connections can lead to dashing about and putting added strain on your body. If you have to fly, the second trimester is best.

If, for whatever reason, you need to take a long-haul flight and your airline gives you permission, try to take a direct flight, drink lots of water, wear flight socks or support tights and walk around often to avoid the risk of Deep Vein Thrombosis (DVT), which is more common in pregnant women. It's also a good idea to carry your medical notes with you, just in case, and to have medical insurance.

Try not to eat the food on these flights but bring your own with you — reheated food can carry risks. Finally, avoid going anywhere that requires you to have vaccinations. A brief chat with your GP, midwife or obstetrician should help you to assess your level of risk — for the vast majority of women flying short-haul presents few problems.

How much weight should I gain during my pregnancy?

Every woman is different and it depends on your weight before you were pregnant. On average pregnant women gain two stone, most of which goes on at a rate of 1 lb per week in your second and third trimesters. If your medical team are happy with your weight gain you shouldn't be too concerned about it. The extra weight is made up of the following:

Baby, placenta, amniotic fluid	13 lb
Extra blood and fluids	4 lb 5 oz
Enlarged uterus, breast tissue	4 lb 5 oz
Extra fat stored for breastfeeding	7 lb
Total, on average	28 lb 10 oz

As your body lays down fat during pregnancy to feed and nurture your newborn baby, the quickest way to lose pregnancy weight postnatally is to breastfeed.

How Dads Feel During Pregnancy

After the high of telling everyone that you and your partner are expecting a baby, the expectant mum spends her time feeling and being pregnant, with all the positive and negative symptoms of this unique condition, but by and large you carry on your life as before. But there's one big difference — you may not be suffering from morning sickness, but you will have concerns about how you and your partner will cope with pregnancy, childbirth and parenting.

Having some knowledge about pregnancy and what happens to a woman's body and to her mind will help you to cope very well during this time. You may have seen your sisters or friends being pregnant and talked to them about it, but if you haven't been up close and personal to a pregnancy, it can seem strange and hard to grasp.

You have to adjust to your partner's mood swings caused by hormonal changes in her body, her cravings for crazy foods at crazy times and physical changes as she progresses through the pregnancy. You are expected to live with a woman who at times seems like a stranger and to be understanding and supportive when you may have no idea what is going on.

The best thing you can do is to read up on pregnancy so you have some understanding of what your partner is experiencing, and many men want to find out as much as possible about pregnancy so that they can play as full a part as possible in their partner's journey.

YOUR HEALTH DURING PREGNANCY. AN A-Z GUIDE

This section will act as a reference point for you, so that you can look up any pregnancy health issues you may have (hopefully you won't get many!). There is no guarantee that you will suffer from any of them and there's nothing wrong with you if you don't.

For every woman that 'glides' through pregnancy without sickness, stretch marks or piles, there are several who are counting down the weeks until their baby is born because they are in pain, discomfort or cannot sleep. The good news is that any ailments are likely to disappear as soon as you feel the joy of holding your baby in your arms.

When I was expecting my little girl everyone told me how lucky I was not to suffer from morning sickness and stretchmarks, but mother nature had a few other little gems in store for me. First, my teeth were sore — the dentist couldn't see anything, but I certainly wasn't imagining it; then leg cramps would attack while I was fast asleep in the dead of night and my other half had to pound and massage my leg to bring the circulation back; next it was constipation — lovely; and finally I ended up spending a night in hospital two weeks before my daughter was born with agonising pains in my ribs — stretching out and lying flat seemed to ease this.

Luckily most pregnancy conditions are minor and easy to cope with and the vast majority miraculously disappear once your baby is born. The following list covers the most common pregnancy health issues and how to alleviate them.

Back Pain

Back pain in pregnancy is usually caused by hormones that relax the ligaments in your body, specifically those in your pelvic area and the muscles in your abdomen, to make space for your baby — which can affect your ability to stand up straight. Lower-back pain also comes from carrying so much weight in one specific place and from increased pressure on the spine.

To avoid your back pain getting worse as your baby grows:

- Walk with your shoulders back and abdominal muscles pulled in to lengthen your spine.

- Always bend at the knee and not the waist when picking things up.

- Avoid stretching to reach things.

- Sleep on a firm mattress.

- Try not to stand for long periods — and if you need to, rest one foot on a box or stool for a few minutes and then swap to the other foot.

- Consider buying a special belt or other products which help back support during pregnancy.

- Try not to stoop to balance yourself — bad posture when pregnant will not help to alleviate back pain.

- Wear sensible shoes — completely flat shoes will not give your arches support, but higher than 1–2 inches may unbalance you. Towards the end of pregnancy you may not be able to see your feet! Wear slip-ons as bending down to tie up laces or do buckles will be difficult.

- Apply a hot water bottle to the sore area for some relief, or relax in a warm bath.

- When getting up from a lying-down position, roll over onto your side and push up with your arms to avoid straining your back.

- In the later stages of pregnancy sleep on your left side — this gives the best blood flow to your baby and will allow you to rest your back.

- Sleep with a maternity body pillow, available from maternity shops and a number of websites.

- Try swimming or aqua aerobics to help strengthen your back and tummy muscles during pregnancy.

- Yoga or Pilates pregnancy classes can help to strengthen muscles to give your back more support as well as help you to relax.

- If you're in severe pain and your GP cannot suggest anything truly effective, you could consider seeing a qualified osteopath. He or she will help you to walk and to carry the weight properly. If you use an alternative practitioner, check that they are fully qualified to work with pregnant women.

Blocked Nose

Most common in the last trimester, a continually stuffy nose is caused by increased progesterone in your body. Some women swear by wearing those nasal strips you often see rugby players wear, but not in public!

Breast Changes

Your partner may enjoy your expanding boobs during pregnancy, then be disappointed to find they are sometimes out of bounds. Larger and heavier breasts with more prominent veins and darker nipples are caused by pregnancy hormones, but the downside is that they are sometimes tender and sensitive to touch. There's not a lot you can do about this and as the pregnancy progresses this is likely to ease. Some women (and their men) are disappointed to find their expanded chest goes back to its normal size post-pregnancy.

Breathlessness

Your respiratory system increases the depth and frequency of breaths when you are pregnant, so you may feel like you are breathless. Combine this with your growing baby pushing up against your diaphragm and squeezing your lungs and you can see why many pregnant women need a breather every now and again. If you have severe breathlessness, you should see a GP.

Carpal Tunnel Syndrome

Tingly fingers and numbness can be a problem for a small number of women in pregnancy, and some might even find it difficult to type or write. Carpal tunnel syndrome is caused when the carpal tunnel in the wrist, through which the nerves to your fingers run, becomes swollen. If you think you have this problem, talk to your GP. Ask your local pharmacy whether they sell carpal tunnel wrist guards, sleep with your hands higher than your heart to decrease swelling, and avoid low carrying such as when shopping.

Constipation

Pregnancy hormones relax the body's ability to push food through the intestines, leading to constipation, which can be painful and uncomfortable. It's important to try not to strain on the toilet in order to avoid developing piles. Also, drink an extra glass of water morning and night, eat more fruit and vegetables (dried fruit is also good and raw veggies), start the day with a high-fibre breakfast cereal and a glass of prune juice. Eat plenty of fibre, including brans, wholegrains and pulses and probiotic-rich foods such as yogurt which will keep your digestive tract healthy. Moving around and being active will also help.

Dizziness and Light-headedness

This is caused by pressure from your expanding uterus on your blood vessels. You may feel dizzy when getting up or sitting down as blood shifts away from your brain as you move. Instead of jumping up, get up gradually, and make sure to eat and drink often to avoid low blood-sugar levels.

Drier Eyes

You may find that the balance of fluids in your eyes during pregnancy changes, leading them to be drier than usual. If this is the case, try to blink more often, to drink lots of water and get enough sleep. You can buy a bottle of 'tears' from your pharmacy — made from the same pure saline solution that your eyes naturally produce. This may help to relieve itchiness.

You may need to switch contact lenses or change to glasses while pregnant.

If you suffer from allergies or hay fever, talk to your GP, because anti-histamines are not recommended in pregnancy.

Fluid Retention

Some pregnant women suffer from swollen (oedema) ankles, especially if they are on their feet at work all day. The solution is to soak your feet in cold water as soon as you get home then put them up above your hips. In later pregnancy this is not advisable, as it's not a good idea to lie on your back, so lie on your side instead. Swelling hands are not unusual in pregnancy and some women end up going to the jeweller to have their rings cut off, so if you think yours are becoming tight, take them off now. Drinking more water will also help with fluid retention. Women carrying twins are more likely to develop oedema and sometimes carpal tunnel syndrome. If you're concerned your swelling is severe, see your doctor, as it could be an indication of pre-eclampsia (see page 73).

Frequency of Urination

In other words, needing to visit the toilet more often than usual. This is most common in the early weeks of pregnancy due to hormonal changes and in the latter stages when your baby's bigger size compresses your bladder. Drink your normal amount of water plus an extra large glass every day, but avoid drinking too much just before bed. Try to find out the location of public toilets near where you shop or walk so that you are never 'caught short'. If coughing or sneezing leads to some leakage, wear a panty liner so that you don't have to worry about it. Pelvic-floor (Kegel) exercises during pregnancy and once your baby is born should alleviate this problem.

Headaches

Common in the first three months of pregnancy, headaches are caused by the massive increase in blood volume in your body (40% over the pregnancy). The solution is to get enough rest, to avoid noisy places, to make sure rooms are properly ventilated and to make lighting subtle. Ask your GP what kinds of pain relief are suitable for pregnancy.

Heartburn and Indigestion

During pregnancy, the muscle at the bottom of the oesophagus relaxes and allows stomach acid up from your stomach. These acids and digestive juices cause a burning sensation. Heartburn can be very uncomfortable and your GP should be able to recommend a safe over-the-counter remedy. Other tips for coping with heartburn and indigestion are:

- Eat smaller meals more often and avoid getting bloated on big meals.

- Try drinking a cup of peppermint tea after eating.

- Try not to lie down for at least an hour after eating to prevent stomach acid moving up.

- Avoid foods that you know trigger heartburn, such as spicy meals, fatty food, caffeine, alcohol and citrus fruits and drinks.

- Try not to eat two to three hours before going to bed.

- Try drinking warm milk an hour before bed.

- Sleep on a higher pillow at night.

- Try chewing gum during the day as it produces more saliva, which neutralises the acid in the stomach.

- Avoid wearing clothes that are tight round your stomach.

Itchy Skin

An itchy abdomen is normal during pregnancy when your skin is stretching such a lot to accommodate your growing baby. These tips may help:

- Massage calamine lotion into your skin.

- Take a cool bath.

- You may find that soothing creams help.

- Wear loose clothing made from breathable fabrics, such as cotton, to avoid rubbing or irritation.

- Be wary of extremely itchy skin accompanied by a rash because it could be a sign of slowing liver function or jaundice known as obstetric cholestasis (see page 59), which can be dangerous for you and your baby if undiagnosed. If you're concerned, see your doctor or midwife as soon as you can.

Leg Cramps

You're in a blissful sleep when – oww! — your leg is killing you and you have to jump up and down on it. Leg cramps are common in pregnancy, especially in the second and third trimesters. If it strikes in the same leg each time, lie with a hot water bottle over the affected leg. Cramps could be caused by your baby lying in such a way that the blood supply to your legs is decreased, and by not taking enough calcium in your diet, so try upping your intake of yoghurt, milk, cheese and sardines. Sit in the bath before bed and give your calves a gentle massage, then rotate them to stretch and relax your muscles.

Leaky Boobs

In the later stages of pregnancy it's not unusual for women to produce colostrum or pre-milk from their breasts, the milk that newborns benefit from before full milk supply comes through. This can leak during sexual stimulation, but it's nothing to worry about. Wear washable or disposable breast pads, available from pharmacies.

Moodiness

It's normal to be emotional during pregnancy and friends and family will not take it personally if you suddenly burst into tears for no apparent reason — at least they shouldn't anyway. Some mums have told me that their memory falls apart when they are pregnant, they lose their self-confidence and become very reliant on their partner for reassurance and support. Dads-to-be say their partners lose their sense of humour, panic over things they considered unimportant before and pick fights — but it's not our fault! On a more serious note, though, if your sad feelings persist and you are finding it difficult to cope, seek help from your GP. See the information on antenatal depression on page 45.

Morning Sickness or Pregnancy Sickness

A whopping 60–80% of pregnant women suffer from morning sickness, making it the most common pregnancy health problem. Many women will feel nauseous in the first trimester of pregnancy, while others are unlucky enough to get it right through their pregnancy. Try the following to help with the symptoms:

- Eat something bland such as dry toast or a cracker first thing in the morning to head off sickness.

- Ginger is found by some women to be good for sickness — munch on a ginger biscuit or drink ginger-root tea (in moderation) from health food shops. Always check the safety of herbal teas.

- Eat little and often and don't miss meals. Your body still needs food.

- Eat fewer fatty foods, as they tend to make nausea worse.

- Eat slow-release carbohydrates such as porridge, rather than quick-release ones such as white bread.

- Bananas prevent nausea and make a good snack.

- Foods rich in iron such as beef, eggs and leafy green vegetables can help to ease nausea.

- Make sure to replace fluids lost in being sick.

- Try wearing a travel acupressure wristband which some women find useful (available from pharmacies).

- Take a ten-minute walk which can help to decrease nausea.

- Carry antibacterial wipes in your bag, just in case.

For most women morning sickness eases off at around 13 weeks when their baby is starting to put on weight and has developed most of his or her vital organs. Pregnancy sickness is more common in multiple pregnancies and in women under 30, as well as women experiencing their first pregnancy. It is not usually dangerous for the baby, although it's never good to lose weight when pregnant.

If none of the tips above help, and you are losing weight and cannot keep liquids or food down, don't ignore it, see your doctor. You may be suffering from *hyperemesis gravidarum* (a severe form of pregnancy sickness) which affects around 1% of pregnant women. You may need to be put on an intravenous drip to replace fluids or on drugs to control nausea in hospital.

Pelvic Pain and SPD

Pains around the pelvic area are common in early pregnancy and especially a first pregnancy because the uterus is stretching for the first time with the help of a hormone called relaxin. Often referred to as 'growing pains', aches low down on either side of the abdomen are caused by your pregnant body stretching and thickening muscles and ligaments in order to support your growing belly. These aches and pains often kick in around the fourth month of pregnancy when you are beginning to show. Gentle walking or swimming may relieve it or have a 30-minute rest with your feet up.

Some women develop *Symphysis Pubis Dysfunction* (SPD), a severe pelvic joint pain where the bones in your pelvis have moved due to the pregnancy and are grinding together. SPD can affect women from week 12 of their pregnancy and is more severe in some women than others. This condition can be excruciatingly painful, with pains on the inside of your thighs and lower back and your pelvic bones clicking together when you move. The pain of SPD is made worse by walking, going up and down stairs and is often worse at night. Tips for easing the pain include sitting down to get dressed, getting down on one knee to lift anything instead of bending over, and when getting out of a car, swinging your bottom right around towards the door and putting both feet down together — it's important to avoid stretching your legs apart, which will be painful.

Your doctor may recommend mild painkillers, wearing a special belt, visiting a physiotherapist, moving little and often and in some cases, bed rest.

In most cases symptoms of SPD will stop after your baby is born.

Perspiration

Pregnant women feel warmer than other people, as their resting metabolic rate goes up during pregnancy. Dress in layers so you can take them off one by one, drink lots of water to replace lost fluid, and sleep in a cool room.

Piles or Haemorrhoids

Developing piles or haemorrhoids is quite common in pregnancy with 20–50% of women affected. Symptoms include pain and bleeding in the anal region as veins around your anus stick out and become itchy. Piles are caused by straining on the toilet due to constipation, so the first thing to do is to prevent constipation by following the tips on page 107 on diet. Other ways to avoid developing piles are to sleep on your side, to lie down several times a day, to soothe the area with hot and cold pads, to take a warm salty bath and to wash regularly. There are some good haemorrhoid creams available over the counter — ask your pharmacist which are suitable for pregnancy. If it's really sore, buy a child's blow-up swimming ring and sit on that — it might also be useful after your baby is born and you are sore in the perineal area.

Restless Legs (RLS)

Restless Legs Syndrome usually occurs to a small percentage of mums-to-be in the last trimester of pregnancy. This can feel really weird — like a creeping or burning sensation inside your legs that is not exactly painful, but can only be relieved by moving your legs about. This can be really difficult to live with because relaxing by lying down to read, or putting your feet up to watch TV, for example, will just make it worse, so you need to move about often. It's also not great if you're trying to get some much-needed sleep.

Treatments include checking out that you are getting enough iron and folate by visiting your GP, stretching your legs, having a massage and avoiding caffeine.

Sciatica

Your baby can become so big towards the end of pregnancy that he lies on various organs and muscles in his mum's poor body, leading to all sorts of uncomfortable aches and pains. Sciatica is a pain that starts in the lower back, stretches over your bottom and down one leg — understandably, moving around and finding a comfortable sitting and sleeping position can be difficult.

Sciatica sufferers have told me that sitting cross-legged can be good because your abdomen is resting on your calves instead of pulling against your lower back. Sitting on a high stool with one leg extended downwards is also comfortable for some mums-to-be and sleeping on your left side with a pillow between your legs can help you get some quality shut-eye.

Skin Changes

Some women find that something funny happens to their skin during pregnancy — the skin around their nipples (areolas) grows darker and moles and freckles darken too. This is known as hyperpigmentation. Others develop *linea nigra*, a dark line from their belly button down to their pubis from the fourth or fifth month, thought to be due to an increase in the body's production of melanin during pregnancy and which is harmless.

Small itchy red spots can also be common during pregnancy and are most common on the hands and trunk. Your complexion may also be affected by pregnancy hormones and you feel like a teenager again. If you have spotty skin, go for oil-free skin products and make-up, drink lots of water and make sure you get enough fruit and vegetables in your diet. 'Pregnancy mask', known as 'chloasma' is a darkening of the skin on the face where brown spots appear, most commonly on the forehead and cheeks. These fade a few months after baby is born but are very sensitive to sun exposure. Always wear sun creams with a high sun-protection factor, stay in the shade and wear a hat as your skin may be more sensitive to the affects of sun at this time.

Sensitivity to Smell

One slightly surprising result of pregnancy is a heightened sense of smell. Suddenly smells such as wine, cigarette smoke, certain foods and perfume can make you feel sick. This is down to your pregnancy hormones affecting your senses. There's really not much you can do about this, except to avoid frying food, for example, as well as cigarette smoke and request that your partner abstain from aftershave!

Sore Ribs

Your growing baby is making space for him- or herself in your body and in the process your internal organs will be pushed out of the way — this can result in your upper abdomen becoming quite sore and, if a nerve gets caught under your rib cage, it can be agony. The good news is that when your baby's head engages for delivery the pain is likely to ease as he or she won't be able to reach so far up. In the meantime, gentle movement may dislodge your baby to a more comfortable position.

Sore Teeth

Your gums become swollen and inflamed during pregnancy and tend to bleed easily, so it's important to look after your teeth and get regular dental check-ups.

Some pregnant women suffer unexplained soreness or have a strange metallic taste in their mouth and this can often be put down to increased levels of progesterone and oestrogen in the blood making gums softer, to snacking more often which puts more strain on your teeth and to morning sickness which can expose your teeth to stomach acid, which attacks enamel.

If your teeth are sore or bleeding take another look at your care routine, floss every day and use a soft brush. By all means have your teeth examined, but because of the painkillers needed for dental surgery, it's wise to wait until after your baby is born. Your dentist will be able to advise you about the safety of dental x-rays and taking antibiotics during pregnancy.

Stretch Marks

A common side-effect of pregnancy, when the sheer size of your bump literally stretches the skin beyond its natural elasticity and leaves you with pink or brown lines running along your abdomen and sometimes on other parts of your body too, including your thighs, hips, bottom, upper arms and breasts. Your likelihood of developing stretch marks in pregnancy is down to your skin type — if your mum got them, it's likely you will, too. Slathering on Vitamin E cream before stretch marks really set in can help to keep skin supple but will not prevent them: but rest assured the marks will generally disappear into silvery lines some time after your baby is born.

Vaginal Discharge

Some women find that they have greater vaginal discharge when they are pregnant and this is perfectly normal. However, if your vagina is sore or itchy, or if the discharge smells strange or unpleasant or changes to a yellowy or greeny colour, you could have an infection so it's wise to see your doctor.

If this symptom affects you, wear pant liners, don't use perfumed toiletries when bathing or showering, watch what fabric detergent you use, avoid wearing tights for long periods of time and never sit in a wet swimming costume as all of these will encourage an infection or yeast imbalance (see Thrush, page 74) to flourish.

Varicose Veins

Some women develop varicose veins during pregnancy. These often run in the family, but only really appear during pregnancy due to increased pressure from the uterus on the pelvic veins, expanded blood volume and pregnancy hormones. The result is bluish veins on the back of your legs that are prominent and can be sore. Follow these tips to ease soreness:

- Put your legs up above your hips when relaxing.

- Sleep with a pillow under your feet.

- Wear support tights.

- Eat more Vitamin C to keep your veins elastic.

- Walk 20 minutes per day.

- Don't wear heels.

- Flex your ankles when standing or sitting for any period of time.

- Don't sit for long periods with your legs crossed.

- Your varicose veins will probably go away after your baby is born.

You should see your GP, midwife or obstetrician if:

- Vomiting is persistent, you become dehydrated, you are losing weight or cannot eat a normal amount of food in the day.

- Aches and pains become severe, especially in the pubic bone region in late pregnancy.

- You have severe abdominal pain or vaginal bleeding, as it might signify a threatened miscarriage or early labour.

- You have a severe headache, blurry vision, dizziness or vomiting. If it is not relieved by usual painkillers it could be due to pre-eclampsia (see page 73).

All of the conditions above are related to the changes your body is experiencing during pregnancy. Some will affect you in all three trimesters of your pregnancy, while others will come and go, depending on the trimester. The very good news is that once your baby is born and your body starts to recover and get back to normal, they will be gone.

Chapter 5 ∾

LABOUR AND GIVING BIRTH

Here it is — the day you've been waiting for, when you will meet your little baby for the first time. It's also a day that many women will face with dread as they recall the horror stories others have 'considerately' shared with them and the images of screaming women in labour that commonly appear on our TV screens. These interpretations of childbirth generally do more harm than good as they make it harder for women to relax into labour and let their bodies do the job they were designed for.

Women having babies in Ireland today are well educated and informed. We like to feel in control of our working and home lives, and yet giving birth puts totally different demands on us. We have to overcome our natural instincts, to flee pain and discomfort, and instead try to see it as a good thing because it is our body doing what it is designed to do and working hard to bring our baby closer to being born — this is understandably easier said than done for most of us.

And that's not the only thing we can't control about childbirth — the magical Expected Due Date (EDD) that you've had in your diary for seven or eight months is just that, 'expected'. Only a small percentage of babies are born on the day we expect them to be and some can hang onto mama for days or even as much as a couple of weeks. If this happens to you, it can be tempting to ask the obstetrician to 'do something' because you are fed up with being pregnant and the baby must be ready to come out *now*, but patience really is the better option.

Waiting until your baby is ready to be born on his own and your body has started the birthing process, even though it seems like the whole world is phoning you daily asking for news, is generally a better option than being induced in a hospital setting. There are, of course, good reasons why women are induced, which we'll look at later.

The good news is that if you've been attending antenatal classes, have spent some time talking to your birth partner about how you want him or her to support you during the birth, thought about what you'd like to happen during labour, written a birth plan and trust your midwife or doctor, you will feel more confident about the whole birth experience and it is less likely to be intimidating or scary.

Keeping an open mind is also important — some women find that their preferred method of pain relief, an epidural, is not necessary after all, while others are taken by surprise by the intensity of their contractions. Every birth is different and no-one will judge you if you need more or less pain relief than the next woman.

Writing a Birth Plan

A birth plan is an informal guide written by you to the kind of birth you want. It doesn't have to be an extensive document: a few notes or bullet points written on a piece of paper will be enough. What's important is that you have thought through the whole experience in your mind and focused on what may happen during childbirth.

The reason some hospitals welcome birth plans is that they express what the woman wants before she becomes overwhelmed with pain and unable to explain her wishes (during contractions anyway!). You can put your plan in your hospital bag and the midwife will discuss the pros and cons of your wishes, then add the plan to your charts so that other hospital staff can consult it. Some hospitals have standard forms you can fill in if you wish: ask at antenatal appointments. You can also download birth plans from the internet.

Depending on whether you are having your baby in hospital, in a Midwifery-Led Unit or at home, make sure to ask what facilities are available to you during labour at your antenatal visits, as this information will help you to write your plan. Will there be a birthing pool you can labour in? Should you bring a birthing ball with you? Can you play your own music? Will your midwife bring gas and air (the Entonox mask) to a home birth? How soon should you go to the hospital or call the midwife?

While writing down your wishes can help you to focus on what you do and don't want, it's important to retain some flexibility. Doctors and midwives will always put the health and safety of you and your baby first, even while trying to respect your wishes. And bear in mind that it doesn't make you a failure if your birth doesn't work out as planned.

Questions you might want to consider for your birth plan:

- Do you want to labour in water? (There are pools for labouring, not birth, in the midwifery-led units in Our Lady of Lourdes, Drogheda and Cavan General Hospital.)

- How long do you wish to stay at home once your contractions begin?

- Do you want ARM (Artificial Rupture of Membranes) in hospital? See page 144.

- Do you want to be able to walk about during labour?

- Do you want to set the scene with music or candles?

- Do you want to film your child's birth?

- Who do you want to be your birth partner?

- What position do you want to give birth in?

If you want pain relief, would you be happy to have:

- Transcutaneous Electrical Nerve Stimulation (TENS) — where a low-level pulsed electrical current is used to control pain?

- Pethidine — an injection in the hip, usually in the first stage of labour?

- The Entonox mask (50% oxygen and 50% nitrous oxide, also known as 'gas and air')?

- An epidural, an injection in the spinal area which dramatically cuts down on pain?

- Forceps, ventouse or a caesarean section, if necessary?

- How do you feel about an episiotomy, where the vagina is cut to allow easier delivery? Would you prefer a tear?

- Would you prefer alternative pain relief such as acupuncture, meditation or hypnosis, if it is permitted?

- Would you prefer for the baby to be cleaned before he or she is handed to you?

- How do you want the placenta to be delivered — naturally, or with an injection to speed it up which is more common?

- Do you want the midwife to place the baby on your chest straight after birth?

- Do you want to breastfeed the baby immediately after birth? (It can help to establish breastfeeding.)

- If the baby's father is present, does he want to cut the cord?

- Are you happy for your baby to be given a Vitamin K injection after birth?

REAL STORY

'The birth plan was so useful when I went into the hospital (I had attached it to my file) as the midwives had read it and knew exactly how I wanted things to go — as naturally as possible once the baby was safe and well. My midwife reminded me about it during labour too.'
Helen

WHEN YOU'RE OVERDUE

You've been waiting nine months for this day — your due date. Everything is ready, and yet in many cases, especially for first-time mums, the day passes with no action and mum starts to get a bit fed up with lumbering around, feeling huge. She just wants to get on with it.

While it can be tempting to use modern medicine to hurry things along, most babies will be born within 14 days of your EDD, and if you get to this point with no action, your doctor will most likely recommend induction. Often women are told that if they don't go into labour over the weekend they will be booked in for an induction on Monday, so you get some warning, and baby often makes an appearance just before the deadline. The reason why doctors are not keen to leave your baby in his watery home past 42 weeks is because of a risk that the placenta may start to fail.

You may be excited and nervous at the same time, but waiting for something that may or may not happen today can make time literally drag. If you don't feel up to much, then lying around catching up on DVD box sets can be a way to kill time, but if you have energy why not get out and about — a 20-minute walk every day can lift your spirits and combat boredom, even if you only return with magazines and chocolate! Stocking up your bathroom and freezer with your favourites is also a good way to use your time — you will scarcely have time to shower in the first frantic few weeks of your baby's life. Many women report a spring-cleaning obsession around this time, however big they are, as the nesting instinct kicks in.

If you want to move onto the next exciting stage, there are some more natural things you can do to help things along, although I'd advise you to talk to your midwife or doctor first.

- Some women have found the following helpful: Raspberry leaf tea, available from health food stores, is thought to help the muscles in your uterus to prepare for labour, which is why women less than 32 weeks' pregnant are advised not to drink it. If you don't like the taste of the tea, you can opt for tablets instead. I tried this tea but can't say it made much difference. Caulophyllum is thought to be good for helping to start labour when you are overdue, although I would advise you to consult a qualified homeopath before taking it. Acupuncture can help women who suffer from back problems during pregnancy and a qualified acupuncturist may be able to help bring on your labour if you are overdue.

- Nipple stimulation may feel a bit strange when you feel about as attractive as a hippo, but the thinking is that you do what a newborn would do when breastfeeding, so you rub and roll the whole of the areola or dark part of your nipples for 20 minutes or so, which releases a hormone that helps to bring on labour.

- Gentle walking is good for a number of reasons, and it's not unusual to see women who are 'ready to pop' pacing the streets with partner in tow. The walking motion keeps everything mobile and gravity will help your baby's head to engage if it hasn't already, but I wouldn't advise a strenuous hike and don't forget to take your mobile.

- Spicy food is thought to bring on childbirth, although no research has been undertaken to prove this. Anecdotally, many women insist it has helped, but this may be an old wives' tale. I suppose there's no harm if you like to eat curry.

- Sex can do the trick — prostaglandins in semen help to ripen the cervix for birth and orgasm releases oxytocin in a woman's body. But many couples find this option unrealistic as neither feels like it when there's quite literally three in the bed.

- Sweep of membranes — strictly speaking this is a medical intervention and you may not want it. Your doctor or midwife stretches open the cervix, then runs her finger in a 'sweep' across the amniotic sac. This process may lead to hormones being produced that bring on labour.

We've heard of women trying one or more of these methods to bring on labour, with varying degrees of success. Whatever you do, we'd advise you talk to your midwife first and remember that your baby will come out sooner or later, whatever you choose to do.

How You Know You are in Labour

Recognising the point at which you go into labour is not an exact science, and it is different with every pregnancy. Just as some women dash off to the hospital at the first twinge and end up being sent home again, some mums-to-be hardly notice that they are having contractions until they are partially dilated and the baby is well on his or her way.

During your final checks with the hospital your doctor or midwife will be looking to see if the baby's head is engaged and what position the baby is lying in. Those having home births will have their bumps palpated (felt by hand) by their midwife. Many women will notice that the baby has 'moved down' into their pelvis, which can be a welcome relief as they can breathe more easily and may enjoy a surge of energy.

Often referred to as 'nesting', this energy spurt can mean that you are able to throw yourself into making final preparations for the arrival of your baby. While some mums-to-be find they lose 1–2 lb in weight in the final couple of weeks, others don't.

In early labour your cervix will start to soften in preparation for your baby's journey through the birth canal — this process can take days or happen overnight and you probably won't be aware of it.

Antenatal classes tell pregnant women to look out for three clear signs that labour may have started — contractions, a 'show' and ruptured membranes (your waters breaking). When all three happen together, your contractions are regular and strong and your cervix is 3 cm dilated, you are considered to be in established labour.

However, in real life, you may get contractions with a show and your waters won't break, broken waters and no contractions — or any combination of these.

Contractions

A contraction is not like any ordinary abdominal pain across the general area of your tummy, but more like a squeeze under your bump and around your lower back. When you experience a contraction it gets tighter for a number of seconds and your stomach seems to tense, before being released. If the pain wakes you up from sleep, makes you breathe deeply and hold onto something for support — it's a contraction.

Some women get Braxton Hicks, or fake, contractions. They feel like contractions but eventually fade away instead of getting closer together and longer in duration. These can start from as early as 30 weeks, tend to last less than a minute and are not very painful. Braxton Hicks may be annoying but they are a sign that your body is getting ready for the real thing.

If you're having contractions, start timing them in order to work out your next step. Using your mobile, a digital watch or one with a second hand, write down the time gap between the start of one and the start of the next, and write down how long the contraction lasted. It's hard to say how long they should last or how far apart they should be at each stage as every labour is different, but in general you may start off with a contraction every 15 minutes that lasts several seconds and as your labour progresses, they will last longer — maybe 30–60 seconds. If they are far apart and you can cope with the pain, taking a bath can help as the water supports your bump. You may be in very early labour, but if it's your first pregnancy this stage can take many hours, so anything you can do at home such as sitting on your birthing ball while watching TV or setting up your TENS machine may help.

In general, if the contractions are coming closer together and last 40 seconds or longer, it's time to think about calling your midwife/doctor or the hospital, or planning your journey to hospital. If you decide to phone ahead, you will be asked how long you have been having contractions for (say, x hours), how often they are occurring (every x minutes) and how long they are (x seconds, for example). You will also be asked if you have had a show (see below).

Because first babies take longer to appear, first-time mums can wait at home for longer. If you live close to the hospital you can generally stay at home until you have to use your breathing techniques and grab hold of something when you get a contraction. By the end of labour contractions will be much closer together, with little breathing space between them.

A 'Show'

In pregnancy a mucous plug seals off the uterus, protecting your baby from harm. Before or during labour, the plug is dislodged when the cervix begins to stretch and appears as a bloodstained discharge or 'a show'. It may look like a pink or brownish jelly and come out in small pieces. Some women have a show two or three weeks before going into labour, so this is not something to panic about. You may wish to inform your midwife or hospital, and if you are already having strong and regular contractions and get a show, this may be a sign that you should consider going to hospital.

If you are losing bright red blood, go to the hospital as quickly as possible as this could be an indication of a rare problem where a part of the placenta comes away from the wall of the uterus.

Ruptured Membranes — Waters Breaking

We've all seen films where there's a huge gush of fluid from between the legs of a heavily pregnant woman in the middle of a dramatic scene, but this isn't always how waters break. As the baby makes his way down and out of the uterus, his head presses down on the 'bag' he has been living in for the last nine months and the amniotic sac of fluid quite literally pops. In many cases there is only a trickle of clear fluid with a yellow tinge.

If the fluid is green or brown, your baby may have opened his bowels, passing meconium. Depending on the grade of meconium, your midwife or doctor will be able to tell whether your baby could be in distress or not so, if your waters break, it's advisable to contact your medical team more quickly than with the other signs of labour. In most cases babies are absolutely fine, but it's wise to be over-cautious and your doctor or midwife may want to take blood samples from the baby's head and monitor his heartbeat.

If your baby's head is not engaged there is a very small risk the cord may be pulled down with a gush of fluid (cord prolapse), and you should go into hospital to be monitored, even if you go home again once you know things are fine. If your baby is breech, go to the hospital straight away in case the cord is brought down with the gush of water, which could limit the flow of oxygen he is receiving. It's particularly important to ring your doctor or midwife if your waters break more than three weeks before your due date.

Some hospitals recommend you come in anyway if your waters break, as a labour of more than 24 hours could put the baby at risk of infection. You may go in, the midwife will make a note of when your waters broke and monitor the baby's heartbeat before sending you home to get some rest with instructions to return in 12 hours.

If you're concerned about your waters breaking at an inconvenient time (when you're not sitting on the toilet) wear a sanitary towel, sit on a towel in the car and put a mattress protector, towel and bin liner under the sheet on your bed.

If it's your first baby, you may get contractions and a show well before your waters break.

What to do when you are in early labour:

- Don't panic! You could have mild contractions for 48 hours before labour becomes truly established.

- Call your partner if he is not there — he will need to be on standby and may want to be with you during the early stages of labour.

- Stay at home, unless your waters break or you have been told to come to hospital at the first signs of labour. Many first-time mums realise later that they went into hospital too early, and would have preferred to spend the early part of their labour in the comfort of their own home. The longer you can safely leave it and the more established labour is before you reach the hospital, the better your birth is likely to progress.

- If you have hired or bought a TENS machine, now is the time to use it. You will need help fitting it and you will need to be patient as the electrical current takes some time to get to the desired level. TENS is designed to help you cope with pain but it will not take away the pain, so don't expect a miracle.

- Try to get some sleep or rest if it is night-time, or keep upright and moving around if you feel up to it. Keeping upright will allow gravity to help your labour along.

- If your waters haven't broken you may find it helps to sit in a deep warm bath, or you could sit on a low stool under the shower.

- It's important to feel the baby move at this stage — if you cannot feel any movement, phone your doctor or midwife.

- Try to eat and drink something — you will need your energy.

- If you think you are suffering from diarrhoea, don't worry, this is quite normal and often the body's way of emptying your bowels before labour becomes truly established. If this is severe, seek advice.

- Time your contractions so that you know how your early labour is progressing.

- Have your hospital bag ready to go.

- Start thinking about your breathing and anything you have learned in antenatal classes. Try not to hold your breath during a contraction as this will deprive your muscles of oxygen and make your labour progress more slowly. Breathe in through your nose and out through your mouth.

- Try out different positions to see how they help you cope with the pain of contractions — walking around, getting on your hands and knees, bouncing or sitting on your birthing ball, straddling a chair or leaning over furniture work well for many women at this stage.

- Ring your midwife if you feel your labour is changing or you are concerned. You may be asked to go to the hospital to be monitored.

- If your contractions have reached the length and frequency that indicate you are in established labour, then it may be time to go to hospital. Having to hold onto furniture and use your breathing techniques is a good sign that your contractions are the real thing.

- Look forward to the arrival of your new baby.

POSITIONS OF BABY FOR BIRTH

Your baby can be lying in any number of positions in the uterus, but the most common is the anterior, head-down position and your midwife or doctor may talk about the head being 'engaged' and in a good position for birth. Posterior refers to when the baby's spine is facing yours, which means that he has to move around to the anterior position during labour. Breech babies can present in a number of ways and twins can also lie in a variety of positions. Here are some diagrams of how your baby or babies might be lying:

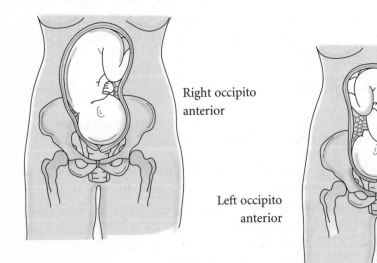

Right occipito
anterior

Left occipito
anterior

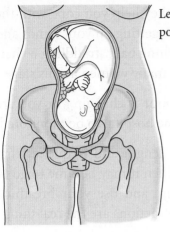

Left occipito
posterior

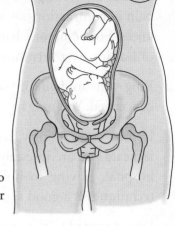

Right occipito
posterior

Frank breech

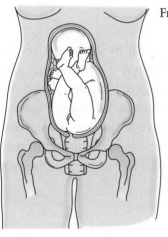

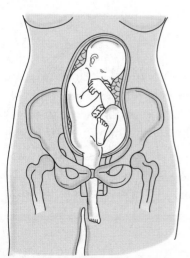

Full or flexed breech

Footling breech

Twins can be:

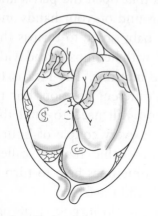

Both twins head down

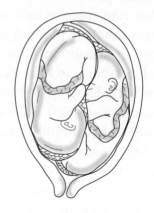

One twin head down and one breech

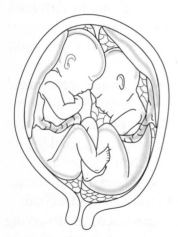

Both twins breech

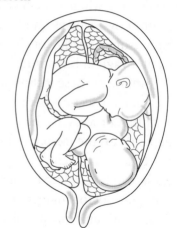

One twin transverse

WHAT IF MY BABY IS BREECH?

Breech babies (their bottoms are down instead of their head) are usually spotted on ultrasound scans and when your midwife palpates (feels) your tummy. It's also not unusual for a pregnant woman to get a feeling that something is strange and the baby is banging her in the ribs. If your midwife or doctor suspects your baby is breech in the last six weeks of pregnancy you may be given another ultrasound to confirm this. Then you have a number of options before deciding what kind of birth you may have.

A breech baby under 37 weeks may decide to turn on his own. If he doesn't, you can try exercises and positions that open the pelvis and allow him space to turn, such as crawling around on your hands and knees. Another position that can give your baby space to turn is the knee-chest position. Mum kneels on her bed, with her hips spread wide and her head and shoulders resting on the mattress. The idea is to gently nudge the baby into moving into a different position, but to make it work you will need persistence: you will need to hold the position for around 15 minutes and repeat it every couple of hours. Other women have told me that a homeopathic remedy called Pulsatilla from a qualified homeopath can sometimes help to turn a breech baby, and some even say that hypnosis did the trick.

If your doctor is trained in it and willing to do it, ECV (External Cephalic Version) can work. Normally done in the last two weeks of pregnancy when your baby is hopefully big enough not to turn back again, ECV involves an obstetrician and midwife manually turning the baby from outside your tummy. It's not comfortable, but if you really want a vaginal birth it might be an option.

If none of these techniques work, then your doctor may recommend a caesarean section because breech babies can be damaged during the birthing process if they are lying in a difficult position. This also depends on the hospital's breech delivery policy. Generally speaking it's better for your baby to experience some of the labour process before a caesarean takes place because this will help to expel fluid from his lungs, but your doctor may prefer to schedule an elective caesarean section.

If you can find an obstetrician who is experienced at delivering breech babies and your baby is lying in a good position, you may be able to attempt a vaginal birth. However, if things don't go well, you may end up with an emergency caesarean section. Your doctor will always put your health and the health of your baby first.

Posterior Birth

Also known as 'back labour', a posterior birth can be a challenge for any woman. Instead of your baby's head facing your back and his back facing your tummy, he is facing the opposite way around — his face is looking out of your bump and his back is aligned with yours. This means that he has to turn a full 180 degrees in order to get into the best position for birth.

If an ultrasound or palpation by your midwife during pregnancy reveals that your baby is facing posterior, you may try to turn him around before birth. This can be done by adopting the scrubbing-floors position, i.e. on all fours to widen the pelvis and give baby space to turn; by sleeping on your side, sitting on a birth ball and kneeling upright when you can. Avoid anything that closes up the space available in the pelvis, such as crossing your legs.

If your baby is still posterior when you reach your due date, you are likely to be overdue — this is because posterior babies are unable to engage into the pelvis until labour is well established. If your doctor recommends induction and you want to try for a natural birth, you will need to discuss this.

You will know that labour has started when you experience almost constant back pain, and being on your back will be unbearable. Some babies will turn around in early labour while others can take many hours to turn, which can be very uncomfortable for you with all the pain in your back.

Leaning over a birthing ball, straddling the toilet or a chair and getting on your hands and knees are all positions that may help back labour and your partner can give invaluable lower-back massages. Your labour may be long but in most cases babies turn around into the ideal birth position.

Home Birth

Just under one per cent of all births in Ireland happen at home, and for some women this is the preferred option. Many women believe that you are not allowed to have a home birth for your first baby, but this is not true. First births are often the slowest and give you enough time to transfer to hospital should your midwife be concerned about anything. If your pregnancy is considered low risk, then you may be suitable for home birth, although a limited service is available.

Being in a familiar setting can help you to relax and you can have all of your antenatal appointments and checks with your midwife at home, too. If you're interested in a home birth, contact your local hospital early on to see if they operate a home-birth service and contact the Home Birth Association of Ireland as soon as your pregnancy is confirmed (see page 24).

If it is not possible for you to have a home birth through a hospital service, you may hire a Self-Employed Community Midwife instead and an HSE grant will contribute to the cost of her services. Medical insurance may also cover some costs. There are very few private midwives operating in Ireland and if you want one you will need to contact them as soon as you know you are pregnant.

During antenatal appointments you can discuss pain relief options with your midwife, but these are generally limited to drug-free exercises which you can learn in antenatal classes, a birthing pool and the Entonox mask, which is carried by midwives. However, women who have home births report less need for pain relief as they labour at their own pace. Those women that labour in a birthing pool say the water supports their abdomen and back and allows their skin to stretch and let baby out, so they may suffer fewer tears.

The two Midwifery-Led Units currently operating in Ireland, in Cavan General Hospital and Our Lady of Lourdes in Drogheda have pools, although currently women are only allowed to labour in them and have to give birth outside the pool. For a home birth you can rent or buy a birthing pool as well as a pump to inflate it and tap connector for around £100 from *www.madeinwater.com*. Ask your midwife if he or she is trained in water birth, if you want to have your baby under water.

Before you go into labour practise inflating your birthing pool (a job for your partner) and filling it. The water will need to be at body temperature (37°C), but these pools are designed to reflect heat back into the water and keep it warm.

Once you are in water, use whatever position you are comfortable with in the pool, there will be space for your partner to get in with you should you wish. For more information, check out *www.waterbirth.org*.

WHO WILL HELP ME GIVE BIRTH?

Giving birth can be an empowering experience or a profoundly scary one, especially for first-time mums, who have no idea what to expect, how much pain they will experience or for how long. That's why it's important to have a supportive and understanding birth partner who will be with you throughout the process. In most cases a woman will prefer this to be her partner and the father of her child, but when he is not the ideal choice then she may choose her mother, sister or a friend.

The birth partner's job is to offer support and to interpret the birthing mother's desires and feelings to the midwives. Some women hire the services of a doula to help them during the birthing process (see page 27).

Your care provider throughout the whole experience, who is trained in assisting normal births, is the midwife and there may be one or two involved depending on your birth and where you have your baby. If a midwife is concerned about anything during the birth, she may request the backup of an obstetrician, who specialises in births that need assistance such as with forceps or ventouse deliveries. If you have a caesarean section this is an operation that will require a medical team (see page 146). Your partner should be allowed to be with you during a c-section.

THE THREE STAGES OF LABOUR

Thinking of labour as being composed of three stages can sometimes be confusing when you've never been through it before. There *are* three distinct stages, but they are of vastly different lengths of time; most of the action happens during the first two stages, at the end of which you will be holding your bundle of joy. Broadly speaking, the first stage of labour is the longest and can last anything up to 24 hours (some are even longer than this) — it can seem like forever and you may use every method of pain relief available before you reach the end, or it may not be as bad as you feared. The second stage, in contrast, is relatively short and can last from around 30 minutes to two hours — at the end of which your beautiful baby comes into the world. And the third stage often passes relatively unnoticed.

First Stage

During the first stage of labour regular contractions of the uterus lead to dilation (or opening) of the cervix (neck of womb), rotation of the baby and his descent down into the pelvis. This long stage of labour lasts until your cervix is dilated to 10 cm. As the first stage progresses contractions come closer together and last for longer.

The early part of the first stage of labour is called the *latent* stage and it lasts until you are 3–4 cm dilated, at which point you are considered to be in *active* labour. Sometimes getting to 3 cm can take 12 hours followed by only 2 hours to reach 10 cm: every woman is different and there are no hard-and-fast rules.

Your pain-relief options during the latent stage are the TENS

1

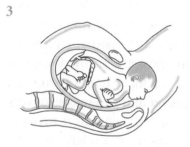

The cervix is now dilated to 10 cm and the woman can start pushing her baby out into the world.

2

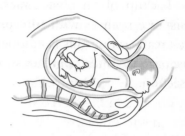

The top of the baby's head is 'crowning' and can be seen.

3

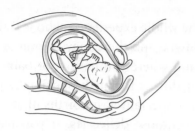

The baby's head has fully emerged from the birth canal. He is facing his mum's back.

4

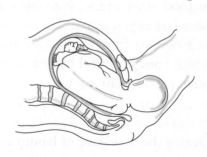

The baby's body has turned so that his head is facing upwards.

5

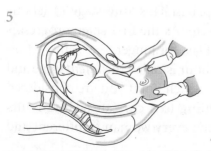

The midwife gently helps the baby's shoulders and body out into the world. The baby is born.

machine and Pethidine. During the active stage and up to around 8 cm many women find an epidural takes away the pain and allows them to rest, especially if they are worn out with the effort taken to get this far. If you're waiting for an epidural and in pain, gas and air (Entonox mask) may help, and this method of pain relief can also be used from 8 cm onwards.

New thinking around childbirth shows that stress levels in the first stage of labour can actually slow down the natural birthing process. This is why it's often best to stay at home in a relaxing environment without too much stimulation until you have reached the active stage, and also why your midwife will most likely advise you not to come into the hospital until your contractions are longer and closer together than you might otherwise be comfortable with. Don't worry, you are unlikely to have the baby there and then — most births (and especially firsts) take longer than you might think.

Also, it can be extremely frustrating to arrive at hospital only to be told you are not in labour when you know you have been getting contractions for hours. Most midwives will be reluctant to admit you to the labour ward until you have reached 3–4 cm and are considered to be in active labour. At this point you will be put in a room, a midwife will look after you, monitor your progress and keep an eye on how the baby is doing.

Second Stage

The second stage of labour involves the birth of your baby and is usually extremely physical and demanding. As your baby moves through the birth canal towards your vagina you will feel the need to push, but if you do this before you have reached 10-cm dilation there may not be enough space for your baby to come out, which could hurt both of you. The last few minutes before you are ready to push can be very difficult for some women but it's important to focus on what your birth partner and midwife or doctor are saying. The aim is to end up with a controlled birth with both you and baby undamaged by the experience.

There is a technique to pushing that is not always easy to get the hang of, but essentially you will need to push into your bottom during a contraction while keeping your face relaxed (a tall order, I know!). Your midwife and birth partner will coach you through this to make the most of each exhausting push. Most women push for about 45 minutes to 2 hours, but this varies, and you don't really notice the time passing.

As the baby's head crowns, or appears through your vagina, your midwife may ask you to pant — this is to avoid you pushing too hard and ending up with a tear, although it's fairly common for women to end up with a small tear as the perineum is stretched so tight. You may experience a stinging sensation now.

Your baby will be born head down, facing towards your back, then he will slowly rotate to look outwards. The midwife will manoeuvre his head, followed by his shoulders, then the rest of his body out into the world. Your baby is born! The umbilical cord is clamped and cut, or you may ask for it to stop pulsing naturally first, so that baby can receive all the blood in the cord, which it does after about five minutes. At this stage you can hold your lovely baby. Babies are often placed on their mums' tummies for warmth and will automatically try to latch on to your breast, or if you prefer, he can be cleaned up and put in a blanket first. This is a very special time for mum and dad.

Third Stage

The third stage of labour, when the placenta is delivered through the vagina, completes the birthing process and takes 15–30 minutes. You may get contractions again for this, but they won't feel anything near as strong as what you have been through. You probably won't notice what's going on because you will be totally focused on your new baby. Some hospitals give women a drug called syntometrine at this stage — this can make the third stage shorter and lead to less blood loss, but depending on how the labour went, some women can feel nauseous and dizzy as a result.

After your placenta has been delivered you may need to be stitched up due to a tear or episiotomy. This won't hurt as you will be given a local anaesthetic.

ACTIVE BIRTH

Active birth has become more popular in Ireland in recent years, where women prefer to be upright and moving around during the birthing process rather than being continually monitored while they lie on their back on a bed. Gravity is considered a great help during labour as is opening the pelvis by sitting on a birthing ball, straddling a chair or getting down on hands and knees, and many women find these positions more comfortable during contractions. Some hospitals, such as the Coombe Women and Infants University Hospital, are now using birthing balls in the labour room as they recognise their usefulness, and others, such as the Midwifery-Led Units in Our Lady of Lourdes in Drogheda and Cavan General Hospital, allow a woman to labour in a birthing pool. There are pools in Cork University Maternity Hospital and the Rotunda Hospital, but at the time of writing these were not opened for use.

These days women are more likely to try different positions to help them cope with contractions. During the first stage of labour squatting can be good, kneeling while leaning over a birthing ball or bean bag, or standing while leaning over the back of the sofa can all help your cervix to dilate and baby to move down the birth canal. Antenatal classes can be useful for mums-to-be where they can learn about and practise different positions. Birth partners can find out how best to assist women during contractions such as by lower-back massage.

If you are on your back in bed for the pushing and delivery stage of labour, ask the midwife to prop up the back support so that you are in a more upright position and not pushing your baby against gravity. Some women like to squat while pushing, others will kneel up against the back of the bed and others prefer to give birth while lying on their side.

Active birth is all about you taking control of your birthing experience, expressing your desires clearly to your partner and midwife and being willing to try something new — it doesn't mean you can't use pain relief or change your plans.

LABOUR WITHOUT PAIN RELIEF

If your approach to labour is that you will take whatever drugs are on offer, thanks very much, that's absolutely fine. After all, modern pain-relief drugs were designed to make the whole labouring experience less painful, so why not use them?

However, what other women who've recently been through childbirth will also tell you is that, especially during early labour, using alternative methods of coping with the contractions made a big difference. This allowed them to stay at home for longer, which can only be a good thing, as long as your midwife says it is safe.

Many of the following techniques are covered in antenatal classes and others you will need to arrange yourself:

- Breathing — something we do all the time of course, but breathing properly through a contraction is crucial to maintaining a sense of control and letting the pain bring you closer to your baby being born. The aim is not to tense up but to relax as much as possible — a good way to do this is to open your eyes and focus on something in the room as a distraction. Breathing in through your nose and out through your mouth can also help.

- Relaxation — telling yourself that the pain will only last for a few seconds instead of dreading the next contraction can help you to relax. Consciously relaxing different parts of your body such as your face and hands can also help — you probably don't even realise that your whole body is tensed and 'fighting' the contractions.

- Meditation — not for everyone, but if you have practised before labour this technique could help to distract you from the pain. You will be consciously aware of everything that is happening, but can almost 'remove' yourself from it.

- Massage — one for your partner, massage during labour can be a great help, although he should wait until your contraction is over. Every woman is different: you may need a rub on a sore part of your labouring body and it's important to tell your partner what is helping and what is just irritating.

- Moving around — in Active Birth (see above) keeping mobile can take pressure off your back and distract you from the pain, which is why it's not unusual to see women pacing the corridors in maternity hospitals, partner in tow.

- Water — there's a good reason why women in early labour instinctively head for the bath. The water supports their bump and takes the pressure off during contractions, and women end up with less perineal tears and damage. Birthing pools are becoming more popular in Ireland, although are not widely available yet in hospitals.

- Your voice — It seems groaning, chanting or singing can actually help you cope with pain. Shouting positive things like 'yes!' after a contraction can also send a powerful message to the brain that you are in control.

- Other ideas — some women swear by stress balls, which give them something to do with their hands, wearing an eye mask in hospital to block out the sight of strange people and medical equipment and the power of being plugged into relaxing music in their ipod. At the end of the day, if it works for you, use it.

PAIN RELIEF

If you do decide to avail of pain relief, there are a number of options:

Transcutaneous Electrical Nerve Stimulation — TENS machine

This is a battery-powered electronic device that transmits electrical pulses through disposable self-adhesive electrode pads that are taped onto your back. Designed to be used at home as soon as labour starts, you need to rent your obstetric TENS machine from a pharmacy about six weeks in advance. You collect it one week before your due date and can keep it for around three weeks, in case your baby is overdue.

You will need your birth partner to attach the pads to your back and connect the wires up to the machine. Then you set the pulses to the level that eases the pain for you. There's also a boost button that you can press when you get a contraction.

The good news about TENS that it does not involve drugs and that you can use it easily at home. However, you will need to have realistic expectations — it will help you cope better with contractions but won't necessarily take away the pain.

It can take up to an hour for the electrical pulse to reach the required level, so put it on early. When it is working, you will feel a tingling sensation on your skin.

Some mums told me that they thought their TENS wasn't working, until they pulled it off and got the full force of their contractions!

Make sure to follow all safety instructions.

You can also rent a TENS machine from *www.medicare.ie* 01 201 4900.

Pethidine

This injection in your hip is a synthetic version of morphine. Used during the first stage of labour, it takes the edge off pain and allows you to relax through contractions. It takes 20 minutes to work and lasts for up to 4 hours.

Some mums say it makes them feel sick, while others enjoy the respite it gives them from pain, allowing them to get some rest during a long labour.

If you request and are given Pethidine, it's likely your midwife doesn't think your baby will be born in the next two or three hours, so rest while you can. The reason midwives are reluctant to give you Pethidine after 6-cm dilation is because it can affect your baby's breathing if it has not worn off before he is born. If your labour speeds up and baby comes quicker than expected he can be given a reversal drug to offset the effect of Pethidine. Pethidine is available in hospitals.

'Gas and Air' — the Entonox Mask

A 50/50 mix of oxygen and nitrous oxide, the Entonox mask (sometimes a tube which you suck on) is available in hospital and carried by midwives attending a home birth. Getting the full benefits of using the mask is all about timing. You hold the mask over your mouth and nose and take deep breaths in when you need to, but be warned — it takes 20 seconds of breathing in to get the benefits of the gas-and-air mixture, so you will need to start sucking before your contraction reaches its peak.

'Gas and air' is ideal for use towards the end of the first stage of labour when you reach about 8 cm. Some women find that it makes them thirsty or drowsy — the feeling of being 'out of it' can also make you swear and call your birth partner names!

Epidural

Some women have told me that the epidural is the Holy Grail of childbirth and others have said that they proposed marriage to the anaesthetist! An epidural is the only method of pain relief that will completely take away all your pain. Your monitor will show that you are having contractions, but you won't be able to feel them.

An epidural involves the injection of anaesthetic between two vertebrae in the lower part of your spine and must be carried out by an anaesthetist. It is put into your back between contractions, usually at about 5 cm dilation, and you will need to lie completely still while it is being done. Then a tiny tube is attached to the epidural site, taped to your back and up over your shoulder so that your midwife, and sometimes you, can control how much anaesthetic is being given.

You will need to be catheterised so that your bladder can drain itself of urine, as you will not be able to feel that you need to urinate, and will be given an intravenous drip in case medicines need to be administered and for fluid intake.

If you think you might need an epidural at some point during your labour, tell the midwife as soon as you arrive at the hospital because the anaesthetist may be busy with other labouring women or assisting a caesarean section.

There are some disadvantages to having an epidural. Your labour is less likely to be active as you will be hooked up to various monitors and needles, and an epidural can make it harder for you to push because you can't feel your body's natural movements, so you may be more likely to have a ventouse or forceps birth. Sometimes waiting for the epidural to wear off before pushing can help a woman to push and avoid more interventions at birth, but this will depend on how your birth is progressing.

Another side-effect of the epidural is a rare problem where the needle cuts a membrane around the spinal cord. You will not feel anything while your epidural is working, but after the birth may suffer from a bad headache. This is repaired by your anaesthetist doing a 'blood patch', injecting blood from your arm into the site to 'patch' the hole or tear.

Epidurals are available in all Irish maternity hospitals.

Monitoring your Baby

Once you have been admitted to hospital your midwife may want to monitor your baby's heartbeat with a cardiotocograph, or CTG. This can be done in a number of ways, although the most common is by strapping two elastic belts with pads on to your bump — the midwife will move them around until she has found your baby's heartbeat, then you will need to sit still for a period of 20 minutes or more while the results are printed out on paper.

While some women are happy to be monitored continuously if their midwife suggests it, others prefer to be upright and moving around. If this applies to you, ask your midwife whether you can be unhooked from the monitor after the time is up. There are alternative methods of listening to your baby's heartbeat which can be used, including a hand-held fetal Doppler, or monitor, and Pinard stethoscope, that can be used intermittently, leaving you free to move around the rest of the time.

In general, being active and upright during labour will help things to progress more quickly. Continuous monitoring by cardiotocograph has been linked with an increased risk of caesarean section and instrumental vaginal birth. Also, if you are lying down your baby has to travel 'uphill' to move down the birth canal which can slow your labour down. If you are having a low-risk pregnancy and do not want to be continuously monitored, discuss it with your doctor or midwife at an antenatal appointment. Women with high-risk pregnancies are more likely to be continuously monitored.

You may be waiting for your baby to arrive for several hours and your midwife will keep an eye on you with regular checks of the monitor print-out or with a Doppler device or Pinard stethoscope as well as giving you an internal examination every couple of hours to see how far you have dilated. If you start to feel strange or are unduly worried about anything and the midwife is not there, ask your partner to find her and make sure that everything is all right.

INDUCTION

If you have reached 42 weeks and there is no sign of baby, your doctor is likely to want to induce your labour. This is because there may be concerns that the placenta is no longer working properly. Other reasons for induction include concern that your baby is not growing well, that he may be in distress, or that you have pre-eclampsia, diabetes or obstetric cholestasis. Unexplained bleeding can also lead some doctors to want to move things along.

If your waters break and labour doesn't start spontaneously within 24 hours, you are likely to be induced in order to avoid the risk of infection to your baby, although in most first births it is more likely that your contractions will be well established before your waters break. Sometimes women are booked in for induction but before they reach the date, they go into labour naturally. Others are admitted to the hospital on a specific date and may be kept in while various methods of induction are used.

There are various medical methods used to start labour before the body begins the process by itself:

- Prostin is a synthetic version of prostaglandin, a natural hormone that gets the cervix ready for labour. It is applied to the neck of the womb by a midwife or doctor using a pessary gel. It doesn't guarantee success, so if the first application doesn't work, you may be given another a number of hours later. Because induction can sometimes lead to stronger contractions, you are likely to be kept in hospital when prostin is administered.

- Artificial rupture of membranes (ARM), also known as breaking your waters, is sometimes done by a midwife if you are having contractions, although different hospitals have different policies. If you do not want your waters broken, you can ask for them to break spontaneously. The midwife uses an instrument that looks like a plastic knitting needle to nick the bag of fluid your baby is lying in. If the baby's head is not engaged there is a small risk of the cord coming down before his head which could restrict oxygen, so you will need to be continuously monitored. After your waters have been broken your body will produce more prostaglandin which will speed up labour.

- A syntocinon drip is sometimes used to stimulate contractions, and if you have already started contracting, it is likely to make them stronger and more frequent.

While there are sometimes good reasons for induction, some women say they were uncomfortable with their experience because the drugs made their contractions much more powerful and they lost their sense of being able to use relaxation and breathing techniques to stay in control. Their labour quickly moved onto the active stage and they felt unprepared and were more likely to have an epidural, even if it wasn't in their birth plan.

INTERVENTIONS DURING BIRTH

In theory, childbirth should be a natural experience that does not require medical interventions, but the reality can sometimes be different. While the majority of women will push their baby out into the world with no problems, others may experience a tear or require medical help such as forceps, ventouse or a caesarean section.

Tear

In one of my antenatal classes I remember the instructor holding up a tissue and pulling it from both sides — she said, 'This is how thin your perineal skin will become during childbirth'. Then she ripped it apart! Every woman in that room turned pale and prayed it wouldn't happen to us. And yet tears are relatively common in vaginal births.

While some women never tear, others will end up with a tear for every birth. During the pushing stage your midwife will be telling you when to push hard and may say 'stop pushing, pant' — this is usually to allow the perineum to stretch a bit more before your baby's head emerges. Listening to your midwife at this crucial time will help avoid a tear, and many women say that doing pelvic floor exercises (Kegels) and perineal massage (see page 78) during pregnancy may help to keep the skin supple and more able to stretch.

Don't worry if you tear, though — it's certainly not unusual for a woman to need some stitching after birth. You won't feel the stitches going in as a local anaesthetic is used, they will dissolve after a couple of weeks and you will be pretty sore in that area for a while anyway. In certain cases, your stitches might become infected and it's important that you have them checked if you think this might be the case. Your doctor will be able to prescribe something for the infection. An inflated airline neck cushion or rubber ring is also a useful place on which to rest a sore bottom.

Episiotomy

If your doctor thinks that your perineum may tear badly during your baby's birth and could leave you with urinary problems in the future, he or she may suggest an episiotomy to give your baby more space to be born. This involves cutting the perineum from the vaginal opening, and if you haven't had an epidural, you will be given a local anaesthetic so that it doesn't hurt.

If you want to avoid having an episiotomy, talk to your doctor or midwife before the birth and put it in your birth plan. Ask them to help you avoid tearing or needing to be cut with controlled pushing, and follow the tips above for avoiding a tear.

If you have a tear or episiotomy try to bathe twice a day to keep the wound scrupulously clean and don't be afraid to ask the hospital for painkillers — you've been through enough and will not be in a fit state to look after a demanding newborn if you are in pain.

Forceps

The squeamish amongst you may not like to think too much about a forceps delivery as it involves an obstetrician fitting a pair of scoops around your baby's head in order to ease him out through the birth canal. The decision may be taken by you and your doctor if you have been pushing for a while but your baby has moved into a position where he is stuck. In many cases this also means giving you an episiotomy in order to give the baby enough space to come out. Your baby is likely to have marks on either side of his head, but these will disappear with time.

Ventouse

A ventouse is a soft rubber vacuum cap that is placed over your baby's head. Then gentle suction is applied and the obstetrician manoeuvres your baby through the birth canal while you push. You may not need an episiotomy with a ventouse birth, but every birth is different. Your baby's head may have a cone-like appearance for a short time, but this will return to normal.

Caesarean Section

ESRI Perinatal Statistics show that the rate of caesarean sections in Ireland increased from 19.69% in 1999 to 25% in 2007 and most childbirth experts believe this is too high. The World Health Organisation (WHO) say caesarean sections should make up no more than 15% of all births.

Natural childbirth experts believe that currently there is too much medical intervention in what should be a normal experience and that induction and giving women drugs in a hospital setting during labour increases the chance of having a caesarean birth.

However, there are a number of medical reasons why your doctor may recommend an emergency caesarean, including your baby's head being stuck in the wrong position and concerns that he might be distressed.

Once the decision has been made to have a caesarean, the medical team will move fast and your baby can be born within minutes. You will have to sign a consent form and if you have not had an epidural, will need to be given a local anaesthetic in the area around your spinal cord. This will numb your abdomen during the operation but you will be awake and able to see your baby as soon as he is born. In rare cases a general anaesthetic is used.

You will be connected to a drip, and a catheter will be inserted. Water will be sprayed on your abdomen to make sure that you cannot feel any pain. Most c-sections now involve a bikini-line cut, a horizontal incision in your abdomen, and you may sense some tugging. Unless you ask to watch what is happening, a screen will be put up so that you cannot see.

Your medical team will number several people who will all be wearing sterile gowns and masks. These may include an obstetrician, surgical assistant, anaesthetist and nurse, a scrub nurse, midwife and paediatrician. Your partner will also be there, dressed in scrubs, and can hold your hand and give you support during the whole process.

It takes around 15 minutes to deliver a c-section baby who will be shown to you over the screen and then checked over by the paediatrician. Caesarean babies are less likely to have expelled all the fluid from their lungs and sometimes need some time in an incubator in order to give them oxygen and keep them warm.

Your baby will be given to your birth partner to hold and they will meet you in the recovery room once your incision has been sewn up.

Elective Caesareans

Some people refer to women who opt for elective caesareans, where you are scheduled in some time in advance for a caesarean section, as being 'too posh to push'. However, women may choose an elective caesarean for a number of reasons, including avoiding damage to their pelvic floor related to a previous tear, a fear of the pain of childbirth, having had a previous traumatic birth experience, or if they are suffering from a phobia. There are also medical reasons for elective caesarean sections.

Your doctor is more likely to recommend an elective c-section if your baby is lying in a transverse or breech position, if you are having twins where one is breech or transverse, if you are carrying triplets, or if you have placenta praevia, pre-eclampsia or other medical conditions.

There are disadvantages to any caesarean — it is major surgery that will leave your movements slow and painful for some days. After the operation you will be attached to various drips, drains and catheters but most of these will be taken out after about 24 hours. Your caregiver will be keen for you to be mobile soon after the operation as this will aid recovery. You could end up feeling weak and nauseous, your stitches will be sensitive and walking will be slow and painful.

One thing that women who have sections worry about is being able to breastfeed their baby, and it is undoubtedly more challenging due to your wound. If you want to breastfeed ask your doctor to allow your baby into the recovery room and for help with feeding him while lying on your side, so that he is not near your stitches. It is possible to breastfeed after a c-section, but you will need to be determined. Ask for all the help you need from the neonatal nurses or midwives at the hospital, making sure that they bring the baby to you to be fed. Invest in a good supportive cushion and get moving as soon as it is safe to do so.

After a c-section, you will most likely stay in hospital for longer than mums who have had vaginal births, maybe five days, to recover. You will not be able to drive for about six weeks and your general recovery period will be longer. You will need lots of help at home, especially if you have an older child.

About Vaginal Birth after Caesarean (VBAC)

Many women worry that if they have one caesarean section they will never be able to experience a vaginal birth, but this is not necessarily the case. There is a small risk of uterine rupture in subsequent births depending on why you had a c-section before, and the kind of incision made, and you will need to take the advice of your doctor, but it is possible for more than 50% of women to have a natural birth afterwards. It is currently unlikely that you will be able to have a VBAC home birth, however, due to changes in the Memorandum of Understanding between midwives and the HSE (see page 25 for more information). However your baby is born, the decision should be made on safety grounds first.

SEEKING INFORMED CONSENT

Your informed consent, or agreement, is required for a range of screening tests such as amniocentesis and chorionic villus sampling (CVS) as these carry a small risk of miscarriage. And your consent is also required, whether verbally or as a signature on a form, for a number of procedures during labour, including vaginal examinations, a sweep of membranes, breaking your waters artificially, continuous fetal monitoring using a CTG (cardiotocograph), inserting drips, performing an induction of labour, performing an episiotomy, using forceps and obviously, performing a caesarean section.

Informed consent means that you are informed in detail about the pros and cons of every procedure, given a full set of options and a choice of whether you want something or not before you are asked to consent to a procedure. Of course, if the procedure is an emergency, there may be less time for discussion and your doctor will have to make a call based on medical need.

If you are concerned about practices in your nearest hospital ask to speak to the Director of Midwifery and use your birth plan to explain clearly what you are happy and unhappy to have during childbirth.

WHAT ARE APGAR TESTS?

As soon as your baby is born he will be checked by a doctor in order to assess his health — and given an 'Apgar' score. This takes only a few minutes and in the vast majority of cases, babies are given the all-clear. The Apgar test was devised in 1952 by Dr Virginia Apgar, an American anaesthesiologist, to determine whether newborn babies needed medical attention by checking their Appearance, Pulse, Grimace, Activity and Respiration. The test is done as soon as a baby is born and then repeated five minutes later. Each quality is marked out of two and a score of seven or more out of ten is considered good. If Apgar levels are considered low, a doctor may decide your baby needs some medical attention, such as oxygen or some time in an incubator.

WHAT WILL MY BABY LOOK LIKE?

While your baby will be the most beautiful creature you have ever set your eyes on, he may not in fact look his best. Immediately after birth some babies can look blue but this soon turns to a healthy pink once he has taken a few good breaths.

He may look a big squashed due to the pressure of travelling down the birth canal, and the bones in his head are not yet fused, which is nature's clever way of making it possible for him to be born. He is likely to be covered in blood — this will be yours, not his — and sometimes a gooey white substance called vernix.

Forceps babies may have marks either side of their head and ventouse babies' heads can be slightly pointed. All of this will disappear in a few days.

Your midwife may use suction to remove fluid from your baby's lungs, so he may not cry straight away — but in seconds should be howling!

Boy babies are born with what look like huge testicles and girls often have enlarged labia — this is perfectly normal. New babies also commonly have small white spots on their faces.

WHAT HAPPENS AFTER THE BIRTH?

Your baby will still be attached to you by the umbilical cord, and if you wish, you can ask for it to stop pulsing so that he gets all the blood from you that he should, or your midwife will clamp and cut it.

He will be put under a warming lamp while a doctor does the Apgar test. While this is happening, your placenta may be delivered and you may have stitches.

You may ask to hold your baby before he is cleaned up and checked or afterwards. He will be placed on your tummy for warmth and you may feed him.

First-time mums generally stay in hospital for one to three days, but some hospitals offer an Early Transfer Home Scheme (ETHS) where you return home 6–24 hours after your baby is born as long as you both are healthy and a midwife visits you at home for a certain number of days. (For more on this see Chapter 2, Practical Considerations.)

If your baby is born at home, the midwife can help you to have a shower, or to dress the baby, and the two of you can rest in your own bed. She will then visit you both a certain number of times to check on your progress.

STEM CELL COLLECTION

Some health insurers in Ireland make a contribution towards the cost of 'cord blood stem cell preservation'. Medicare Health & Living offer this service in Mount Carmel private hospital in Dublin. For more information check out *www.medicare.ie*.

Stem-cell transplants have been used in treatments for childhood leukaemia and inherited blood disorders. After your baby is born the umbilical cord is clamped, a needle is inserted into the cord and the blood is collected. The blood is sent to a laboratory where stem cells are collected and frozen in liquid nitrogen for future use.

The Belfast Cord Blood Bank was set up in 1993 and initially used to store cord blood collections from siblings of children with leukaemia in Northern Ireland. There is no public cord blood bank in Ireland.

Since the introduction of new regulations in 2008 a licence is needed to extract and store cord stem cells.

STILLBIRTH

When a baby dies after 24 weeks of pregnancy, either in the womb or during labour, this is called stillbirth. It's difficult to imagine anything more traumatic for the parents. Although stillbirth does not affect a large number of pregnancies in Ireland due to various medical checks, such as ultrasound scans during pregnancy, the Irish Stillbirth and Neonatal Death Society, ISANDS, says that each year in Ireland 'approximately 500 babies die around the time of birth. As a result a large number of parents, brothers and sisters, grandparents and friends are bereaved'.

Trying to understand why their baby has died can be very difficult for parents as doctors often cannot put it down to any single cause.

In general, a pregnant woman should contact her doctor to check that everything is well, if in her second or third trimester:

- She hasn't felt her baby move in a 12-hour period and he doesn't react to a prod or to sugary food or drink.

- She has an uncontrollable itch which might indicate obstetric cholestasis (see page 60).

- She experiences sudden weight gain and swelling, headaches, dizziness and stomach pain, as this might indicate pre-eclampsia (see page 73).

Not surprisingly, it is very difficult to deal with a stillbirth and parents will need to mourn and grieve for their baby. In some cases counselling and the support of other parents who have experienced a similar loss may help.

ISANDS produce and distribute a booklet called *A Little Lifetime* to all maternity hospitals and units in the country. This booklet has helpful and important information to support parents at the time they are told the sad news that their baby has died or is expected to die shortly after birth.

For more information on the help and support available through ISANDS check out *www.isands.ie* or phone 01 872 6996.

Dad – Labour and How You can Help

Childbirth has changed a lot for men in the past 50 years or so. Women now expect you to be there for every stage of the whole messy process. But you will get the chance to meet your new baby the moment he opens his beautiful eyes to the world.

How You may Feel

Not long to go now and you will see your baby for the first time. While it's perfectly normal for the pregnant woman to feel nervous about going through labour, do you ever get the feeling that your anxieties are not being recognised? It's true that it won't be you screaming out in pain as your baby comes into the world (unless she breaks a finger through squeezing it so hard!) but that doesn't mean you will necessarily fly through the whole experience. After all, childbirth is one of the most dramatic events in life and it tests the mental and physical strengths of both women and men.

As the due date approaches you may find yourself worrying — after all, you have no idea when your partner's labour will start. Will you be at home or at work? Will you miss the birth? And you have no idea how things will go either. What will be expected of you? Will you be up to it? You may worry about seeing your partner in pain and not being able to do anything about it. Your instinct will be to protect her, but your job will be to encourage and support her.

How to Get Ready

'Be Prepared' may be the Scout's motto, but when it comes to labour and childbirth it is good advice. In the same way that books such as this one advise pregnant women to attend antenatal classes and write a birth plan, it's important for you to prepare, too. Try to go to antenatal classes and attend midwife and doctor visits with your partner when you can. Ask questions and take an interest. Reading birth stories such as the ones included in this book in the next chapter, can also help you to get an idea of how labour can go — no two labours are the same and no-one can predict what will happen. Also, watching documentary films and TV programmes that depict real births can be informative, if difficult to watch. Avoid films and soap operas with birth scenes in them as these tend to be overdramatic and may just make you both anxious.

Talking to your partner is also important during the last few weeks in order to allow both of you to express your concerns and hopes. Telling your partner that you are excited rather than terrified (even if that is far from the truth!) will help her to focus on the positive. This experience will change you both as people and approaching it as a team will make you stronger. If you know any other couples who have recently had babies, talk to the new dads — they will be more than willing to tell you about their experience and may even give you some good tips.

If you're a squeamish person who feels nauseous at the sight of blood, I hope you have explained this to your partner already. She may be happy for you to step out of the room occasionally during labour in order to take a breather, however, please don't underestimate how important your presence will be to her when the going gets tough.

Your partner may also suggest hiring a doula, a woman experienced in supporting a woman through labour and birth. A doula will usually be an additional support rather than a replacement for you.

How You can Help

Before labour begins there are a few preparations you can make to ensure a stress-free journey to hospital. Pain will affect your partner's ability to think straight, so try not to rely on her to remember everything.

- In the majority of cases a woman will experience contractions for a few hours before she feels ready or her midwife says she should go into hospital. If you are not at home this should give you time to get there.

- She should have packed a hospital bag of essential things for herself and the baby and you may need to put some things in it at the last minute. Placing a list on top of the open bag of what to include will help you to remember.

- Start timing her contractions using a watch with a second hand or a stopwatch — the midwife will ask for the length of time between the start of one and the start of the next, and also how long they last for. Write this down as you may forget.

- When your partner is showing signs of being in labour, one of you will need to phone the midwife or hospital. You will be asked how many weeks' pregnant she is, for details about her contractions and whether she has had a show or her waters have broken.

- Once you have decided to go into hospital, put your partner in the back seat of the car supported by pillows. Under no circumstances should she try to drive herself to hospital. If you haven't arrived home before she needs to go, have a family member or neighbour on call to drive her in and you can meet her at the hospital.

- Make sure there is enough petrol in the car and you have change for parking at the hospital.

- Put some food and drink for yourself in a bag — labour can be a long process and often takes place through the night when there are no shops or cafés open.

- If you are planning a home birth you can inflate and fill the birthing pool if you are using one, and make any other preparations.

How You can Help During Labour

In basic terms, your job during labour is to be solid and supportive through a long and sometimes stressful process, so get ready. You may not feel that you are making much of a contribution to the whole process, but your partner needs you more than you realise.

Once you have arrived at hospital your partner will be examined by a midwife to determine how dilated she is. Hospitals have different policies for admissions, but in general once she is in active labour (3–4 cm) she will be admitted to the labour ward. She will be given a bed but can move around.

The midwife may ask if your partner has elected to have her waters broken or if she has a preference for pain relief. This is your chance to produce the birth plan and convey your partner's desires to the midwife, although if she is between contractions she will be able to explain what she would prefer herself. Depending on how the labour progresses she may ask you to help her walk around, to massage her lower back, help her balance on a birthing ball, or do breathing and relaxation exercises together. The best rule to follow at this point is to do what you are asked — you are the support team and she is the main event.

She will probably shout and scream and may call you awful names, and throughout all this you need to keep saying she's doing really well and the baby will be born soon. Try to accept that you cannot make the pain go away, and focus on what your partner and the midwife need you to do.

If you are having a home birth and your partner wants you to get into the bath with her, don't hesitate.

If your partner needs intervention such as forceps, ventouse or a caesarean section she may feel scared, so keep holding her hand and talking to her — say the baby will be out soon and the pain will be over. You will need to listen carefully to the midwife at this time — your baby will soon be born and your partner may need encouragement in pushing and breathing.

Don't worry if you feel scared — this is perfectly normal. In the same way that your partner needs to keep focused on the baby, you do, too — and when you see your son or daughter for the first time prepare to be bowled over. You will certainly be relieved but don't be surprised if you cry — childbirth is a very special experience that you will never forget.

In the words of two-time dad Adam Brophy in *The Bad Dad's Survival Guide*, 'The only person in the room who has had no preparation for this Somme-like scene, and without a physical distraction, is you. And you are expected to remain supportive, encouraging and meditative throughout. All the while you are rushed from pillar to post by nurse, midwife and matron as they take it in turns to either disappear as Mum appears about to die, or line up to insert various lengths of arm into the part of your partner that until now you thought only you got to play with...' According to Brophy, meeting your baby for the first time 'hits like a brick to the heart. It puts every heart-wrenching teenage crush and subsequent rejection in the shade.'

Congratulations — you are a dad.

Chapter 6 ∾

BIRTH STORIES FROM
WOMEN IN IRELAND

'I know that a lot of women say gas and air can make you feel sick, but I found it was great. After about 6 hours of sitting in the bath with contractions quite far apart, I got a show so we went to the hospital. I was 5 cm dilated! I was having contractions in the car on the way and had to lean on a wall when we arrived. They put me in a wheelchair to go to up the labour ward. They broke my waters and said there was some meconium but nothing to really worry about and it was probably a bit too late for an epidural, but I could try gas and air.

'The midwife was very encouraging and said I was doing brilliantly. I didn't mind the gas and air, but it's important to take several breaths before your next contraction — so my husband was watching the monitor and would tell me a contraction was coming and to get back on the mask. The one time I didn't do it, I got the full force of the contraction, which was really powerful. After that I used it when he said, which really helped. It was like he was coaching a football team! It got me through the next two hours and then the midwives said it was time to push. I was afraid of the pain of coming off the gas but it was fine.

'The midwife said not to worry if your baby doesn't cry straight away because we want to make sure there is no meconium in the airways, but within seconds they had cleared it and she was crying. It was a great moment. I had two stitches and my husband marvelled at our daughter while I was sewed up and the placenta was delivered, which didn't hurt a bit. Then she was put on my chest and latched on straight away.'

Lucy, Dublin

'I was a nine-months'-pregnant single-mum-to-be, living alone in a remote part of Ireland. I'd been having lower-back pain all day, taken paracetamol, had a hot bath and paced my tiny sitting room for most of the day, but I was sure I wasn't in labour. Watching ER that night one of the doctors was giving birth and suddenly it hit me — I might be in labour. I rang my mum and told her I wasn't feeling great. I never mentioned the possibility of labour, so she told me to drive over to her so I wasn't on my own. That was five-and-a-half miles of driving at about ten miles an hour and stopping in the middle of the road every time I got a spasm of pain down my leg. Luckily, country roads are quiet on March evenings!

'Mum realised I was in labour straight away but couldn't convince me. She made me ring the labour ward and talk to a midwife who told me to get to the hospital ASAP.

'It was a nightmare journey, with bumpy roads and mum driving like a F1 driver. She reckoned if she got stopped by the gardaí she was going to ask for a police escort. As we got to the nearest town she wanted to bring me to the hospital there, but I was having none of it, they don't have a maternity unit.

'We got to the hospital in a record one hour and I was examined straight away — 4 cm dilated so up to the labour ward immediately. I was examined again and had already gone to 10 cm! Out the window went all my good intentions in the birth plan. I was pleading with my mum to make them give me an epidural, but the baby was coming too soon and there wasn't time.

'So instead I was hanging off the bed sucking for my life on the gas and air, which didn't seem to be doing much except making me feel light-headed and dizzy — a bit like being drunk. I didn't feel like it helped the pain much, but maybe it would have been worse without it.

'My gorgeous son was born about an hour or less after we arrived at the hospital. I fed him myself straight away, but the gas and air had left me feeling very sick and I couldn't face food until breakfast a few hours later.'

Jillian, Co. Clare

'I had my first baby in January 2005 and after nine hours of pain I decided to have an epidural. It worked fairly well, although it had to be topped up five times in the eight hours until my gorgeous son was born. Unfortunately I was one of the minority and suffered with a post-epidural headache. It took a while for me to figure out I even had a headache as I also had a postpartum haemorrhage which required repair and blood transfusions. The headache was terrible. When I sat or stood up my head felt like it was exploding. I really wanted to breastfeed my baby so I tried my best to sit up and struggle through the pain.

'After a day or so, I was brought to theatre where the anaesthetist did a 'blood patch', injected some of my own blood back into the epidural space to try and plug the hole and cure the headache. I was told that nine times out of 10 this worked. It was a painful procedure and I had to lie still and flat on my back for 12 hours afterwards. I have these vivid memories of one of the midwives holding my son over me as I tried to feed him lying down. But the next day the headache returned along with the day-three baby blues!

'The day after that I was brought back to theatre where another anaesthetist did another "blood patch". This time they knocked me out with a sleeping tablet afterwards and took my son to the nursery for the night. Thankfully, this did the trick and the headache stayed away. I was so happy to leave the hospital with my little boy and I was able to continue breastfeeding him. The experience totally turned me off epidurals, but not having babies. My son is now at school and he has a sister and a baby brother! Needless to say, I did not have an epidural again. My daughter's birth was much easier and quicker. I stayed at home as long as I could and she was born 40 minutes after I got to the delivery room. The birth of my third baby was quite long to start with but from 5 cm to him being born took about half an hour!'

Antoinette, Athlone

'When I went into labour with my second baby I had contractions every 30 minutes for more than 24 hours — I wondered if he would ever come out. Eventually we went into the labour suite — I was so exhausted I had an epidural. This time it was a better experience because we were able to let the epidural wear off so that I could feel to push. A doctor came in at the last minute and ordered the midwife to prep a room for a caesarean. The midwife was convinced the baby would arrive soon and thought a section was unnecessary, and I really didn't want one after going through so much. A few minutes later our baby boy was born.'

Name withheld

'I had backache all evening on Sunday. We went to the cinema, and on returning home I went to bed as normal but found it hard to sleep. Around midnight, after tossing and turning, I noticed regular little pains coming and going. I felt like a child on Christmas Eve with the excitement. The pains got stronger as an hour turned into two hours. At around 2.30 a.m. I decided to get up and have something light to eat. As the pain got worse I felt the best way to deal with it was to bend or crouch down on my hunkers.

'Everything I had read suggested you go into the hospital when the contractions are 10 minutes apart and lasting 60 seconds. Mine were 5 minutes apart and lasting 30 seconds. Fear of the unknown and terrified of having the baby there and then on the bedroom floor, us novices decided to head into the hospital.

'I still remember a huge pothole in the Phoenix Park over which we drove during one major contraction. On arriving at the hospital I was given a physical and was told that I wasn't even in labour yet, not a fraction of dilation. I was moved to the pre-labour ward. My cubicle had a fit ball (which did prove helpful) and a funny-shaped labour chair along with the bed. It was suggested that I walk the corridors, which I did. A radiator or windowsill was my crutch each time I had to cling onto something when the contractions hit me. My partner was great at pushing my lower back and trying to make funny comments to make me laugh.

'At least I knew I was in the safest place. I could, in a way, relax. If anything happened now, at least I was in the hospital, I was close to the holy grail — the epidural. My biggest fear all along was that I would be too late for that very special needle.

'At around 1 p.m. my pain was really really bad. I couldn't talk, keep my eyes open, eat, sit, anything. John called a midwife to check on me and right enough, at long last I was 1 cm dilated. Time to go to the labour ward.

'The first thing I asked for was the epidural. By this stage some of the contractions were so bad I was getting sick. My waters had to be broken which scared me, as the implement used looked like a large knitting needle. It wasn't sore at all though and rather than a huge explosion of water, as I had expected, there was just a constant trickle which went on for a long period of time. Wires and machines were set up and before long an angel dressed in a three-piece suit and with a quite serious face entered the room. OK, not quite an angel but the pain-relief he gave made him worthy of the name. I was a bit apprehensive of getting the actual epidural itself. It is, after all, a very large needle entering the area around your spine and is not without its risks. It wasn't as bad as I had imagined.

'It was so strange looking at the machine which records the strength of contractions. The strength was clearly getting more intense and yet all I could feel was a bit of a tensing in my abdomen. By mid-afternoon, whether due to the epidural or the tiredness or having gone through 16 hours of labouring, I felt strangely comfortable, almost like I was a bit tipsy! Things were moving very slowly so my consultant administered oxytocin.

'At 8.30 p.m. it was decided that I was ready to push. This was for me the scariest part. The bottom of the bed was removed and it was all hands on deck and one person took one leg, someone else took another and all sorts of encouraging ways of getting me to push were orated. I tried and tried but nothing was happening and as the baby's heart rate once again fell, I heard two dreaded words: "episiotomy" and "forceps". I dreaded the pain of the episiotomy but actually it wasn't noticeable. What was noticeable was the size of the forceps — they reminded me of the tools you use when barbecuing. The thought of where they were going to go was not pleasant, however, as things were getting more serious I didn't exactly have the time or wish to dwell on that. The last few minutes passed like a blur and at 8.50 p.m., my lovely softly spoken consultant lifted up a little, red, wrinkled baby boy.

'The afterbirth and the stitches had to be done then, but now the excitement of having my little bundle completely smothered out any pain that might have been there.'

Sinead, Dublin

'From when I found out I was pregnant all my priorities changed, and anything else seemed to be of little importance. I didn't suffer from morning sickness, but I was extremely tired from weeks 9 to 13. I had a urinary infection, which can be quite common, and when I was five months' pregnant I had an upper-respiratory-tract infection because my immune system was low.

'When I was 20 weeks' pregnant my waters started leaking. I went to the hospital and had an internal examination and an amniotic fluid test. Luckily enough, the membranes were still intact, the cervix was very thick with no sign of dilating, the amniotic fluid test result was negative and the baby's heartbeat was steady.

'When I was 26 weeks pregnant I was let go from my job, which was a bit of a shock but a blessing in disguise as I was very stressed at work. At 37-and-a-half weeks I had water leaking again, several "tightenings" and a jelly-like discharge. I was hoping the baby would be OK, but getting excited thinking, "Maybe this is it", but it wasn't! At five days' overdue, I finally went in to have my baby.

'Labour started at 4.30 a.m. with a dull pain in my back and I woke wondering if it was labour or not; 15 minutes later I had another and I knew for sure. All of my labour was back labour, even though the baby's head was engaged facing to the rear. My waters broke at 7.30 a.m. and the contractions were three minutes apart.

'We got to the hospital at 8 a.m., but I was only 2 cm dilated. By 12 p.m., I was 4 cm and I took two Panadol. From 2 p.m. I used the TENS machine, having tried the birthing ball and the gas and air, which I didn't like at all, as it tasted funny and dried up my mouth. At 4 p.m. I was 8 cm and had another two Panadol. At 5.30 p.m. I was 9 cm dilated and wheeled into the delivery room.

'In the delivery room, I couldn't start to push as I was only 9 cm but I could feel the baby's head grinding in my pelvis and I needed to get her out! After 50 minutes of pushing they asked if I wanted them to break the waters? 15 minutes later at 7 p.m. my baby was delivered using the vacuum. I had a second-degree tear as I didn't want an episiotomy.

'It was the most incredible experience of my life, her cry was the most beautiful song to me and when I held her to my chest, I was so utterly proud and pleased. Half an hour later, her head moved down my breast and she latched on herself. I love being a mother. I feel truly

blessed to have such a wonderful daughter, and so proud that I'm her mammy!'
Nuala, Co. Meath

❧

'Three weeks before my first-born was due, I developed high blood pressure so I was admitted to hospital. It never came back to being normal and when, after a few scans, my baby appeared not to be gaining weight, they decided to induce me at 37 weeks.

'The contractions came fast and strong and I was vomiting, but it didn't work so they tried a second dose. Again the contractions came strong — the pain was horrendous. They tried a few times to break my waters but it didn't work so I was sent back to the labour ward. They gave me Pethidine which did actually help with the pains and told my husband he should go home as nothing was happening. The next morning he came back and after 12 hours of more pain, a doctor came in and assessed me. She told me I wasn't going to be able to deliver the baby, so an emergency section was ordered.

'Everything went so fast, there were a lot of nurses buzzing about me, an anaesthetist was putting lines in my arm, someone else was putting a catheter in, lots of questions were being asked — it was very scary. Our baby girl (7 lb 5 oz) arrived about ten minutes later. She had breathing difficulties, so was rushed to special care. The doctor advised us that this sometimes happens after a c-section, because not as much fluid is expelled from the baby's lungs in comparison to vaginal births. Our beautiful baby girl was put on a ventilator and lived for just 18 days.

'I wanted a baby very badly and braved getting pregnant again. They took very good care of me, the pregnancy went well and I knew I would have an elective caesarean from the start. At 38 weeks I had the operation, a totally different experience, very laid-back and easy-going. The anaesthetist actually sang to me on the way to the theatre, which did actually calm my nerves.

'Another lovely baby girl was delivered and found to be perfectly healthy. She and my husband were put in a little room connected to theatre, and it seemed like it was taking a lifetime to get me stitched so I could be with them and snuggle my baby. In less than half hour I was reunited with Dada and baby — a very happy moment and the relief could not be explained.

'Since then I've had three more elective sections. The hardest part is in hospital those first few days afterwards when you can't move too much, and getting out of bed to get baby to feed him or her is really hard. Usually the next day I'm able to get up and walk about a bit, maybe as far as the bathroom. When the nurses see you are mobile again they remove the catheter and any drips. You are allowed to shower, and told to take the dressing off as it gets wet in the shower. After my first section I had stitches that had to be removed, but with the others they were dissolvable. I would recommend an elective c-section but only if there was a medical need. The recovery time is longer and the stay in hospital is also longer.

'I know how in the press the term "too posh to push" is used a lot. I'm sure there are a lot of celebrities who opt to have an elective section, but in the long-run it really isn't the easiest choice. You don't have to go through labour, but you are being cut open and it's not a choice I would make if I had it. It's not the women that should be getting the stick, it's really the doctors who perform these sections for no medical reasons.

'I would say it is harder to care for baby after a c-section as you can be quite sore, and bending and moving around can be sore for a time afterwards. You are not permitted to drive for six weeks also, which is hard, not being able to get out of the house.'
Kate (name has been changed)

'I was nine days overdue and lying in hospital after four unsuccessful attempts at bringing on labour with prostin gel. I was having contractions but nothing was happening. I couldn't sleep or make my way to the bathroom unaided and was in tears with the pain. Then I was offered a Pethidine injection — within ten minutes I was fast asleep with no pain and the relief was immense! I would recommend this to anyone, it's amazing!

'I had always imagined having my baby without a c-section, but in the end it was necessary and I was more scared than I thought I could ever be. The team of doctors and nurses were great and really tried their best to keep the atmosphere calm, even though I had taken hold of the arm of one of the nurses and couldn't let go. After ten minutes it was

all over and I was holding my beautiful baby boy. I couldn't believe how fast it was. I also found the recovery from my section easier than I had expected; the scar didn't hurt as much as I thought it would.'
Joanne, Dublin

'Three years ago my partner and I decided to start trying for a baby — I have chronic Crohn's disease [an inflammation of the intestines] so we had to plan carefully because of my medication and keeping my condition under control. It took a year to get pregnant but unfortunately I miscarried after a couple of weeks. After two months, I fell pregnant again. I sailed through my pregnancy but had morning sickness throughout.

'At 32 weeks I had a scan that showed there was very little fluid around the baby, so I was admitted and the baby was monitored for a week. I was discharged but had to go in for scans every couple of days. At one of these check-ups they decided I would have to come in the following day for a c-section. I was very excited, not nervous at all, but my partner was in pieces.

'I was wheeled down to theatre at 11 a.m. and they asked my partner to wait outside and gown up. Inside there were two midwives, an anaesthetist and two surgeons. I was first given an anaesthetic in my back — it was just a sore pinch, nothing major. All I felt was my legs getting heavy and then the team carefully laid me down and put a screen up over my stomach so I wouldn't be able to see. At 11.50 a.m. our baby boy was born. The staff couldn't have been more helpful.

'I couldn't get out of the bed for 24 hours. The first night the nurses took the baby just to let me get a rest. I had dissolvable stitches, so they just fell off themselves. The incision was tender, but nothing major, just stiff, if anything. I had been told horror stories before going in, but was pleasantly surprised that after 24 hours I was weak but able to walk around and look after the baby. I was kept in for five days and was given pain relief daily. Before I was sent home, they took a blood test and it showed I needed iron tablets for two weeks, which was fine.'
Leanne, Cork

'My first baby was by emergency caesarean as he was in the breech position. I was so overwhelmed by his birth as it was my first baby that I didn't really care how he came into the world, I was just so glad that he arrived safe and sound. Soon afterwards, I noticed the other new mums in the ward coming and going as they had had natural deliveries and were able to walk around soon afterwards. As I was breastfeeding as well, I found it quite difficult to move around. I felt that it took me a long time to recover from the caesarean. I have since had another little boy who was born by a natural delivery. I really pushed for the natural delivery as my memories of the aftermath of the first baby were painful. To compare both I found the natural delivery much quicker to recover from. I was up and about soon after and overall felt much better about myself. I know that it was completely necessary medically to have the operation but if I had a choice I would definitely choose the natural way.'
Alison, Dublin

'My first son was 14 days' overdue and was induced after having my waters broken. I was put on a drip and had gas and air until 4 cm then got the epidural out of fear of the unknown, despite being adamant going in that I was not going to get it. When I was fully dilated it became apparent that my baby was in distress and the team arrived with amazing speed — the obstetrician performed an episiotomy and used the ventouse to deliver the baby in about five minutes.

'My second son was ten days' overdue and I had what the midwife described as a "precipitous" (fast) birth. Luckily I was already in hospital after having high blood pressure for a few days. The pains started at 10.15 a.m. I called a midwife. She checked me and I was not dilated, so she said there was no hurry to the labour ward. At about 11.20 a.m. the pains were nearly on top of each other and she brought me to the labour ward. The obstetrician checked me, I was 5 cm, so he broke my waters. I remember getting the gas and air at 11.45 a.m. At 12.15, the midwife was taking down my details and ringing my husband when she asked me my telephone number — I couldn't answer because I was having the baby. She rushed over and three pushes later baby was out. My husband arrived just in time to cut the cord.'
Liz, Co. Meath

'I had a "show" during the day on Saturday — gooey stuff in my knickers! Then that night as I got up from my chair at about 2 a.m., I thought I had wet myself — and then realised my waters had broken! I rang the hospital and they said I should come in.

'The midwives poked and prodded a bit and checked the baby's heartbeat and told me I'd have to stay in as labour would start soon enough as my waters were nearly all gone. It suddenly hit me that I would be leaving, minus bump and with baby. I was put into a room with another woman who had a newborn. I told my partner he should head home for some sleep and I'd text him once things kicked off. Anyway, he hadn't been gone long when, at about 5 a.m. contractions started. I hobbled down to the midwife saying I thought it was starting. She examined me, my partner arrived back, and two more midwives examined me in between contractions. It all seemed to be happening so quickly and was so intense. I just did all the deep breathing, leaned over the bed, and my partner put pressure on the small of my back. They seemed to be poking down below in between every contraction. I was so out of it. Anyway, next thing I knew the midwives said I better get down to the labour room as I seemed to be nearly fully dilated already. They wheeled me down the hall in a wheelchair, I had a massive urge to push and they told me to wait.

'I got to the labour room and sampled the gas and air — wow, loved it! Then I started pushing and our son was born at 8.17 a.m. I only had a small tear.

'I am pregnant now with baby number two and am planning a home birth this time. The care I'm receiving from my midwife is superb.'
Denise, Cork

'On my second birth I was two weeks' overdue when contractions started. We arrived at the hospital at 2 a.m. I was 3 cm dilated and my midwife asked did I want any drugs? I said yes to an epidural which was ordered straight away. I thought I was going to be in this pain for hours. I was moved to another room for what seemed like ages, then my

midwife came back and checked where I was — 4 cm. She asked would she break my waters as it could give me some relief, I said, yes would try it. After my waters were broken, the midwife was washing her hands when I got the shock of my life — the baby was on its way and I could not stop it! The midwife came over to look and she could see the head. Two pushes later my baby was born. The epidural man arrived just as the baby was delivered.'
Clodagh, Co. Mayo

'We realised our baby was posterior position [back-to-back] from the midwife palpating during the pregnancy. I tried to turn the baby by scrubbing the floor on my hands and knees which allows more space for the baby to turn around. We had planned a home birth but were registered with the hospital so we could have tests and the option of transfer if needed.

'I was expecting to go overdue by ten days because both my mum and sister had done so, and my midwife was measuring me every week and said the baby was still growing so I knew everything was fine. At 14 days' overdue I went to the hospital for them to check the placenta was still functioning properly, to have fetal-heart-tracing done and an ultrasound to check there was still enough fluid around the baby. I had been having minor Braxton Hicks.

'On day 15 a different obstetrician gave me a dire warning about the risks of going post dates, and I had to explain why I didn't want an induction but wanted a natural birth. On day 16 which was a Friday I had another fetal-heart-tracing, a sweep and was booked in for an induction on the following Monday. That night at 11 p.m., I took Pulsatilla, a homeopathic remedy that I had been given in a birthing kit from a homeopath during my pregnancy. Soon after I got a show, felt a pop in my lower back and texted my midwife. By 12.30 my contractions were stronger and regular and I was sitting on a birthing ball leaning over onto furniture and on my hands and knees. My husband was kneading my back with his thumbs (which were sore for days afterwards) and getting the pool ready.

'At 2.30 a.m. I got into the birthing pool which was brilliant and by 6.30 a.m. I was fully dilated. My midwife suggested different positions but wasn't pushy at all. She said that as things weren't progressing I should get out of the pool which I did at 8.30 a.m. I was exhausted but the baby wasn't distressed. She said she thought we would have to go to the hospital. So I waddled to the car in my slippers and dressing gown and lay across the back seat. I had my hospital file with me so we could go straight in. As I was walking up the ramp in the hospital I had a massive contraction and had to get on my knees. I was put in a wheelchair and taken straight to the delivery suite. The midwife there coached me through pushing. They wanted to put in a catheter and prepare for forceps and episiotomy but I said no. Twenty minutes later an obstetrician came and wanted to do the same but I asked could I have no episiotomy and ventouse instead. In two pushes my daughter's head was delivered and another one for her body. Because it was an assisted birth they had to cut the cord and check the baby out, but I would have preferred it if the cord had not been cut until it had stopped pulsing. They gave me Syntometrine to deliver the placenta which was still fine. The baby latched on straight away. I had a third-degree tear and was given a spinal block to have it stitched up. I stayed overnight and came home the next day.'

Aifric, Dublin

❧

'I had my first baby in hospital. My boyfriend and I got stuck in traffic on the way and it took ages to get there. I was five days' overdue. Everything was going really well but I was finding it tough and starting to lose concentration so I had Pethidine. It was enough to help me over the hump and give me time to refocus my mind. I sat on a birthing ball in the shower and my baby was born after pushing for 30 minutes kneeling on the floor. I didn't have a tear or episiotomy. All together the labour lasted seven hours so it was quite quick for a first birth.

'With my second baby we decided that for practical reasons, such as not having a car and not wanting to leave our older child with a babysitter, we'd have a home birth. I was five days' overdue again. The midwife advised me not to bother with a birthing pool as my first labour had been fast and there wouldn't be time to use it. I woke up at 2 a.m. with contractions close together. We moved to the sitting room and called the midwife. The community midwife had rented us a TENS machine and my boyfriend put it on me, but he didn't realise he had turned it up to the max and practically electrocuted me! Once we had worked out how to use it properly, I turned it up with each contraction but when they were on top of each other I had it on boost all the time.

'I found that the pushing stage was easier at home because I wasn't under pressure to push for harder or longer as I was in the hospital. Again I didn't have a tear or episiotomy.

'What gave me peace of mind was the safety net of knowing that there would be an ambulance on call should we need to get to the hospital, and a doctor could come out to us in case of emergency with a police escort so they'd be with us in 5–6 minutes.

'At 4 a.m. our baby was born. It was so quick I probably would have given birth in the car on the way to hospital. Our older child woke at 7 a.m. and came down to see her new sister. The nicest part was not having to leave home.'

Aoife, Dublin

'My first birth was traumatic because after the epidural in hospital, I couldn't push, my blood pressure was high and my baby's shoulders got stuck. I had an episiotomy and the doctor used forceps, but I was in agony as the local injection didn't really work. In fairness to all concerned he was a big 10 lb 8 oz. But I was very shocked by the experience and in an incredible amount of pain. I was very bitter about it for a long time. It wasn't until the birth of my second son that I was able to put those ghosts to rest.

'When I became pregnant five years later I knew there was no way that I wanted to go anywhere near a hospital to give birth. I contacted the Home Birth Association, who sent me a list of independent domiciliary midwives in my area and I contacted Mary. We hit it off straight away and I booked her for my birth. All of my check-ups were at home, which was great. Mary held a group session three weeks in a row at her house for five couples, where we watched a home-birth video and she gave us a "class" on natural childbirth, explaining everything and answering questions. I was very confident about giving birth at home.

'At 1 a.m. my waters broke spontaneously, I called Mary and she arrived within the hour. Not a lot was happening as I had no contractions yet. Mary advised that I go back to bed to get some sleep and she went to rest in the spare room. After an hour and a half the contractions became quite strong. Mary suggested we go out for a walk around the estate (at 4 a.m.!) and we walked for nearly two hours, it was fantastic because for each contraction I was looking at something different and chatting away. Mary suggested we head back when my breathing changed and I was working harder on each one. I got into the bath for a rest and I stayed in it for about an hour.

'When I got out of the bath, I started to panic a bit and basically chanted, "No, No, No" and refused to push, so in effect my body birthed my son itself because I wasn't helping by pushing. He was born at 7.40 a.m. I have wonderful pictures of us kneeling on the bathroom floor, me starkers with my new baby covered in goo in my arms. I got back into the bath again with the baby for while, to have a wash down then I went into my bed to lie down and wait for the placenta to deliver. Mary didn't cut the cord until after the placenta was delivered. She then examined it completely and showed us all the different blood vessels and tubes in the cord which had sustained our son for nine months. She weighed the baby and he was a healthy 9 lb 6 oz. I didn't have any stitches, or tear or anything like that, he was born so gently that my body had time to stretch to cope with it. Being in my own home, in my own bed, having a shower in my own bathroom was brilliant. Mary came every day for a week to check on both of us.

'When I became pregnant again I booked Mary immediately for another home birth. I went over by a week again, contractions started at about 10 p.m., I called Mary by midnight when I knew it was the real deal. This time I stayed downstairs just pottering about doing washing, tidying up etc, anything to keep myself occupied. Mary came down to me at about 2.30 a.m., when she heard me starting to work harder at the contractions. I basically just walked around the house, up and down the stairs lots of times putting washing away, even when the contractions got really hard. I found it helped to distract myself. At about 4.25 a.m. Mary examined me and said I had a bit of a way to go yet, but I felt it was close. She told my husband to run me a bath, but as I was trying to get up off the couch after the exam I rolled over onto my knees on the floor and didn't manage to get up, baby was coming! This was the best position to be in, I was leaning onto the couch, husband was sitting beside me and Mary behind me. The baby was born in one long push at 4.50 a.m., after just 20 minutes' pushing. He was 10 lb 4 oz and gorgeous. He was born with a Unilateral Incomplete Cleft lip but thankfully his palate was unaffected. He had surgery when he was three months' old to correct his lip and he is gorgeous.

'When I became pregnant with my fourth son we had moved out of the city and I looked into the home-birth option but there was no midwife at the time covering my area. I booked with a private consultant this time and my son was born by emergency c-section as he was transverse and I went into labour a few days early. On my fifth pregnancy I decided to opt for an elective section. Everything went well except for the spinal anaesthetic. It took 40 minutes to get it in and about 15 needles. The anaesthetist apologised and told me that I had the option of a general anaesthetic, but I didn't want that at all, I told him to keep trying and he got it eventually. My daughter was born safe and well.'

Claire, formerly Dublin

‿‿

'For my first pregnancy, I attended a consultant obstetrician privately as I wanted to get to know the person who would attend my birth. One week after the due date I had a cervical sweep, which I found painful. By 11 p.m. that night I decided I needed to go to hospital. I had already put on the TENS machine. On arrival, the midwife broke my waters.

'I walked the corridors and although I was having contractions, examinations showed very slow progress. I was put on a syntocinon drip and the pain became unbearable. Progress to dilation was slow and I asked for an epidural. Then, there were IV drips, continuous monitoring, many internal examinations and fetal-blood sampling. All this time I was immobile on the bed. Dilation did not pass 4 cm. I was told that my obstetrician would be in by 8 a.m. and would probably perform a caesarean. At that stage, I felt relief as I could hear babies being born elsewhere and I thought I would never birth my own baby.

'I was brought to theatre. I felt tremendous tugging and some discomfort but I did not want a full anaesthetic. It was a huge joy and relief to hear my baby cry. I stayed in hospital for ten days. Breastfeeding was very difficult. She found it hard to latch on and was very unsettled. Sheer determination, total support from my partner and a belief that breastmilk was the very best food for her ensured that eventually we did succeed with breastfeeding.

'When I became pregnant the second time, I learned about upright positions and movement for labour, breathing techniques and relaxation to cope with pain. I also learned that it's the birthing mother that makes the decision about what happens in labour, following recommendations from midwives and doctors. It was an eye-opener and it helped me realise what had happened during my first birth and how unprepared I was.

'I attended the consultant obstetrician antenatally again as I knew I had an increased risk of a repeat caesarean and he had a good reputation as a surgeon. I felt I had him on standby. I was determined to do everything possible to have a natural birth. I was determined to avoid the epidural as it was likely it would slow the labour so much that another caesarean would be necessary.

'On my arrival at hospital around 11 a.m. on the due date, I was 8 cm dilated. Labour started at home during the early morning. I had been practising breathing, focusing and movement to cope with the contractions. I remained standing in the labour room holding my husband. I was asked to get on the bed for examinations, then immediately took a standing position again. It took all my concentration to keep from panicking and being swallowed up in the intensity of the contractions.

'Then I felt the waters going and the contractions changing. This did not feel like pain. I still needed to focus but the physical feelings now were of ecstasy and power. The midwife began to insist I get on the bed. I eventually agreed to kneel on the bed facing the head of the bed. Sitting or semi-reclined would have been agony. Although my body was involuntarily pushing, I did not forcibly push at all during contractions but just let my body do the work and did not stop it. After about an hour, when I was very happy to remain as I was as the physical feelings were unexpectedly wonderful (I would describe them as orgasmic!), the midwife returned to the room saying, "We need to get the baby out", so I decided to push a little more forcefully. The pain of the head crowning encouraged me to push further and at that point, the baby emerged.

She was passed to me and nuzzled in immediately.

'I had a natural delivery of the placenta (without drugs) and had given birth without any tears or grazes. Breastfeeding was easy and my baby was calm and relaxed. I was elated.

'Less than two years later, I was pregnant again and I planned a home birth with an independent midwife [Home birth after caesarean is currently more restricted now in Ireland — see page 25].

'By 5 p.m. I was having regular contractions and so I rang the midwife. She suggested I take a bath and ring her back. In the bath, I was feeling uncomfortable and within minutes I felt strong pushing urges. I called my husband and asked him to call the midwife — the baby was coming. The head emerged while he was on the phone to the midwife. The midwife said I should get out of the bath which, at that stage was impossible. Instead, we decided to drain the bath as I held the baby's head, still on all fours. I talked my husband through the process of how he would hold the baby as he was being born. My third child was born, caught by his father, and passed to me to hold. The midwife arrived running up the stairs and I recall saying that it's a boy and he's breathing.

'The midwife re-filled the bath. My eldest daughter came to see her brother. After about 40 minutes, I cut the cord and delivered the placenta. I got dressed and into bed having given birth without any tears or grazes. My little boy fed and slept beautifully.'
Name withheld

'I had a check-up with my consultant the day before my EDD and had a sweep — it was a little bit more uncomfortable than I had anticipated and I had slight bleeding afterwards. At 11.15 p.m. that night I was lying down in the spare bedroom when I felt my waters break! I hopped out of the bed just in time and walked like a geisha to the bathroom, trying to keep the carpet from getting soaked. I pulled down my PJ bottoms and there was a big gush — the waters were clear and warm and kind of slimy! I cleaned myself up — put on my pads and started shaking. It was really starting — oh my God!

'I went upstairs and woke my husband. I phoned the hospital and spoke to a very nice midwife who said that as my waters had broken I'd better come in to be checked over. So we waited until about 1.30 a.m. until going in. This is where the fun began — I was examined by a midwife who said, "This is your first baby is it?"

'"Yes," I replied.

'"Well, are you sure your waters broke?"

'I said. "There was a gush and a fine big puddle in the middle of my bathroom floor!"

'"Well," she said, "It doesn't seem as if they are broken." I was really irritated at this point knowing full well my waters had broken and I was starting to feel strong period-like cramps. I was then informed that sometimes your "hind waters" can break and re-seal and you don't go into labour at all! I was disgusted — how annoying!

'So I went back out to the waiting room where the pains became more frequent and lasted about 30 seconds. I was then examined by a doctor, who said I wasn't in labour but they'd keep me in overnight. So I went up to the ward and got into bed at about 3.30 a.m. and sent my husband home. Then followed the longest night of my life — I had cramps one after the other at two-minute intervals but was told I wasn't in labour. I felt like such an idiot! Had I imagined my waters breaking? Was I imagining the pain? I put on my TENS machine which irritated the hell out of me and promptly tore it off again! I didn't understand that the nurses meant you had to be 3 cm dilated to be considered to be in labour and I had sent my husband home with my birthing ball — the only thing I wanted at that time.

'The consultant came in to check on me at 8.30 a.m. and said that I was in "early labour" — music to my ears! He told me to take whatever pain medication I needed and to consider the epidural as these aren't the dark ages!

'So I finally got down to the labour ward at about 9.30 a.m., where an irritated midwife told me I wasn't in labour! At this point I was ready to punch someone because I was in agony. She told me I was only 2 cm dilated so I told her I'd quite happily go back up to the ward. I was thinking, "I really don't want to be in the same room as you, you ould cow!" (Labour pain and lack of sleep weren't making me very reasonable!)

'She examined me five minutes later and said I was 3–4 cm now and in established labour. At this point she advised me to try gas and air which I didn't want, as I had memories of going to the dentist and being knocked out with gas, which always smelled weird and made my head spin! But I tried it and it actually helped — I think I felt it gave me some control over what was happening to my body. An hour after that I opted for Pethidine — which was just lovely! And by lunchtime I was ready for the epidural! The midwife didn't take too kindly to that, she actually seemed quite disappointed in me and I felt awful for asking but my baby was in a posterior position and the contractions were all across my lower back and tummy and I was worn out!

'She suggested we break the waters to speed things up but advised me that the contractions would be more painful. I asked her what was best for the baby and she said to break the waters before the epidural was administered so that's what we did.

'The anaesthetist arrived at around 1 p.m. He was lovely and put me at ease straight away. I was terrified of getting the epidural, having seen the size of the needle! But all I felt was the tiniest pinch when the local anaesthetic was administered.

'When the epidural began to work I was in heaven and told the anaesthetist I loved him and had married the wrong man! He laughed — I think he gets that a lot.

'Finally at 5 p.m. I was fully dilated and then had to wait an hour due to the epidural, before I could push. So at 6 p.m. I started to push — I was terrified at this point but the midwife (who at this point was my best friend as we had gotten over our initial unease!) wisely pointed out, "The baby has to come out, love!" So I pushed and pushed and pushed and pushed — with my husband encouraging me and looking totally freaked out at the same time. After an hour and a half the consultant examined me and told me the baby was in a posterior position and wasn't going to come out. At this point the baby was in distress so they decided a section was the only way to go. The sense of disappointment in myself was overwhelming — but I just wanted my baby out safely.

'So down to theatre I went and the baby was delivered at 8 p.m. He didn't cry at first, which was a bit of a worry, but after a few minutes he started wailing so I was delighted! I was so relieved I didn't feel the time passing until I was back in recovery with the baby in my arms.

'I'm pregnant again and may be having an elective caesarean this time. I will be braver and not allow anyone to speak to me like I'm a toddler and I won't be afraid to ask questions or make my wishes clear.

The staff were wonderful but we have to accept that giving birth is not something we have any control over.'
Aoife, Cork

~∾~

'Five years ago we welcomed our first son into the world using hypnosis. It was a long (22 hours) but gentle labour, most of which I spent at home. So discovering I had complete placenta praevia [where the placenta covers the mouth of the uterus] on my second pregnancy, and had no choice but to have a c-section, was very disappointing for me.

'Pregnant for a third time (now with no complications) I first found an amazing Irish doula who found a very VBAC [Vaginal Birth After Caesarean]-friendly consultant. Our discussion of the birth plan went well and he seemed totally on board with all my "no-intervention" requests.

'Saturday afternoon (two days after my due date) my waters began to leak and I got excited that I was finally going to meet our third boy! I texted my doula who assured me that labour probably wouldn't get started until I had put our other boys to bed! She was so right... by 8 p.m. the house was quiet. I took out my CD, sat on my ball, dimmed the lights and began to relax. By 10 p.m. I knew I was in active labour and felt ready for her company. I laboured at home, peacefully until 2 a.m., when a particularly strong surge told me it was time to head to the hospital.

'My heart sank when, after a midwife checked me, I was "only" 3 cm. But once I was in the delivery room upstairs, my doula helped me focus quickly and I soon forgot the tone of the midwife downstairs. I shut out everything around me and focused on her voice and two hours later (seemed like 20 minutes) I was 9 cm! My surges were very strong at the end and never closer than 6 minutes apart but I found that visualising the baby's journey down really helped. At 6.40 a.m. I gave birth to a beautiful, healthy 8 lb little boy.

'So although this labour and birth was very different to my first, hypnobirthing was again a vital tool in bringing my baby naturally and peacefully into the world.'
Name withheld, Dublin

~∾~

'I was carrying twins and my waters broke at 38 weeks and 2 days. I thought it couldn't be worse than my first delivery as my first child was over 10 lb and required a lot of intervention to get him out, eventually arriving grudgingly via forceps. So at least we knew the twins would be smaller and I had visions of them just popping out.

'By the time I arrived at the hospital, the contractions hadn't really started so after putting a trace on the babies to make sure they were fine, I was offered something to eat and a cup of tea.

'About midnight the contractions started, I tried sleeping but was too excited so set out pacing the corridors instead. I had read somewhere that in case there are complications and you have to have a section on the second twin (very rare actually) you're better off having an epidural so that was ordered. By the time that was working properly I think I was about 7 cm dilated. The epidural was great in that it took the edge off the contractions but I still knew when they were coming so knew when to push.

'At 7.30 a.m., after a little pushing, the midwives delivered our first daughter. The consultant had been called but in the end it all happened very quickly so by the time he arrived, the head was out. In fairness she was so far down in the final weeks she could have walked out. My husband told me afterwards she had to be suctioned but I don't remember any of that — I was focusing on getting number two out at that stage.

'And number two was also head down but wasn't co-operating too well on the pushing front. After about 20 minutes my consultant said: "If she isn't out in the next five minutes, we'll have to do something". That was enough of a threat — nobody was coming near me with forceps again so on the next push she was out. It was 7.50 a.m.

'Despite my night's activities, I was actually feeling quite fine, relieved it was over, delighted with my beautiful little girls and looking forward to starting breastfeeding, which both of them managed within an hour of birth.'
Siobhán, Dublin

Chapter 7 ∾

| THE FIRST FEW DAYS

Congratulations — you have a beautiful baby! Right now, you will feel as though you have used up every ounce of strength in your body getting to this point. But hang on — here's a little person who needs your complete focus 24 hours a day, just when you feel exhausted and need to lie in bed for a week. For first-time mums this can be something of a shock, and even mums on their third or fourth child feel unprepared for this special but exhausting time. Even though you may have been reading about how to look after your precious baby, you didn't necessarily think you'd be doing it on no sleep!

How you will Feel after the Birth

It's hard work pushing a baby out of your body and very rare for any woman to do it without breaking into a sweat. In fact, from talking to new mums I'd say that it's quite normal to feel like you've been in a boxing ring, or as one mum told me, 'I looked like I'd been in a car crash with no make-up, bloodshot eyes, huge freckles and my husband insisted on taking pictures!'

The good news is that the human body is excellent at healing itself and most after-effects of giving birth have passed in a week or two, with a slightly longer recovery time if you needed stitches or a caesarean section. The even better news is that you will have a brand new baby to show for it.

Going through labour could be compared to running a marathon when you are not trained for it. You have been relatively inactive during pregnancy and then are expected to do something that's extremely hard work, and all while you are in pain — a tall order for any woman. A long labour — and most first babies take a while to arrive — can be especially tiring. If your midwife advises you not to eat, you can end up with depleted energy resources. Pain can also drain your energy as can blood-loss, which can make you feel low.

Apart from achiness all over your body and a huge sense of exhaustion, new mums can sometimes be surprised by the after-effects of giving birth. Some women end up with bloodshot eyes caused by using their face during pushing; these will disappear after a few days. A sore chest caused by straining the chest muscles during pushing is also not unusual; having a hot bath or shower should help while your muscles recover. If you had backache while pregnant you might be disappointed to find it's still there, but this is not caused by carrying a heavy baby out front, but by abdominal muscles which are too weak to support your back; these recover with time.

Another after-effect of giving birth is bleeding, as your uterus shrinks after birth and your body discharges the lining of the womb. This is called *lochia* and you will need to wear maternity pads (like large sanitary towels) which have the added advantage of giving you something soft to sit on as this delicate area may be understandably sore if you had a vaginal delivery. A few days after your baby is born your bleeding should become darker in colour and then stop two or three weeks later. If the bleeding remains bright red for longer than two weeks, tell your midwife or doctor.

It's also quite normal for new mums to be quite sweaty for the first week or so as the body gets rid of pregnancy fluids. Passing water can be difficult and even painful straight after the birth because sometimes the bladder can be bruised or numbed during delivery. If this is the case, you may not feel the need to go, but it's important to pass water in the first few hours in order to avoid developing a urinary-tract infection. If the midwife is concerned, she may insert a catheter to empty your bladder. In the coming days you will find you visit the toilet often as your body empties itself of pregnancy fluids through your urine.

Some women may find that they are leaking urine, called 'stress incontinence' — this is caused by strain on this area during labour. Doing pelvic floor or Kegel exercises to tighten muscles will help this function return to normal over time (see page 88). Even though you may not feel your pelvic floor muscles in the days after your baby's birth, it's still important to exercise them. It may be more comfortable to start your Kegels in the bath or lying on your side in bed, and try to hold them for a few seconds longer each day, so that you can ultimately hold them for ten seconds each time. All this will help your muscles to heal more quickly.

Some women find their first bowel movement after giving birth fills them with dread. Many worry that their stitches may break, but this is not the case; however, straining can give you piles, so it's important to avoid constipation. Do this by eating wholegrains and plenty of fruit and vegetables, drink water and walk around as much as you can to keep things moving.

After your baby is born your body will be using up energy as it starts contracting the uterus. This can lead to cramp-like afterpains that last for more than a week and are stronger when breastfeeding. However, your uterus will soon shrink to its pre-pregnancy size and the pains will disappear.

If you had a tear or an episiotomy and had to get stitches, you will need to look after these carefully. Don't be afraid to ask for painkillers in the hospital and they will give you a prescription for when you leave — don't worry, they won't prescribe anything that will harm your baby if you are breastfeeding. Stitches used in maternity hospitals, and done by your midwife at a home birth, dissolve by themselves, so there is no need to have them removed, and they should heal in a few weeks, although the area may still be sore for a while after that. Avoid wearing tight jeans and go for loose clothing if you can. Gentle pelvic-floor exercises can help with stitches.

Women who have had a caesarean section have a longer recovery period because it is abdominal surgery and the operation results in a greater loss of blood. They have to wait for the spinal anaesthetic to wear off, they may feel nauseous, the catheter has to be removed and they will suffer from afterpains. Doctors recommend getting up 8–24 hours after surgery and wearing elastic stockings to prevent Deep Vein Thrombosis (a clot in the lower leg) due to reduced mobility. The first few days can be difficult and your wound will be sore, but nurses will show you how to hold your baby if you are breastfeeding. Lying down on your side to feed your baby will take the strain off your stitches. You cannot drive for six weeks, but within a couple of months everything should be back to normal.

About three days after giving birth, your milk supply will come in and it can be quite a shock — suddenly your breasts are three times their normal size, sore, swollen, hard and painful and some women even get a slight fever or temperature. This is called *engorgement*. The good news is that this stage only lasts a day or so until your body learns to make the right amount of milk for your baby. Feeding your baby plentifully during this time will help, as will wearing a properly fitted nursing bra.

After a few days of feeding, you may have sore nipples. There may even be some bleeding and cracking. This is part of the toughening-up process, as they adapt to feeding a baby. Putting cool cabbage leaves or cold packs in your bra and using a lanolin ointment can help. Within a few days this stage should pass. Make sure, if you are breastfeeding, that the baby is taking the whole nipple including the areola (around the nipple) into his or her mouth when feeding, to avoid nipple soreness.

It's quite normal, two to three days after the birth, to feel weepy as your hormones adjust to no longer being pregnant. On top of the exhaustion that follows labour, you may be trying to establish breastfeeding, getting little sleep and be scared of the responsibility of caring for a newborn 24 hours a day — feeling down at this time is perfectly normal and termed the 'baby blues'. Your partner can help by taking the baby when he can, to allow you to rest, and visitors will happily come back another time if you are finding it hard to cope. It usually eases after a few days and shouldn't be confused with postnatal depression (PND) which tends to set in weeks or months down the line, is much more serious and may require treatment. (See page 224.)

On top of the physical aftermath of giving birth, you will need to look after your baby. Being together is good for both baby and you as bonding is a natural part of your new relationship. Being together at all times is called 'rooming in' and is now the norm in most maternity hospitals in Ireland. You can take this opportunity to learn how to care for your baby, to feed and change him, when hospital staff are available to help, making you more confident going home.

Many new mums are so overwhelmed by the birthing experience that they fear they may not bond with their baby, and sometimes this can take a little time. But don't worry, before long you would do anything for your baby.

A few hours after your precious baby is born you will both be transferred to a postnatal ward where you can have a shower and put on some comfy clothes. I remember the sheer bliss of tucking into tea and toast and just staring at my new daughter lying fast asleep in her little trolley — you won't be able to take the smile off your face, and rightly so. Allow yourself some time to let it all sink in, give yourself a pat on the back and make the first phone calls with the good news.

Don't be surprised if your baby sleeps a lot the first day as he is also tired from being born, and this is your opportunity for a doze while your partner breaks the news. In fact, this is an excellent piece of advice, but one that many new mums neglect to follow, especially when they get home. After all, there is so much to do! But now is not the time to be superwoman; your rest and recovery is important to both you and your baby, so let your partner and any other helpful friends or family members worry about everything else, and get your head down.

One subject that is commonly discussed by mums is the food in hospital. While this will vary enormously depending on the circumstances of your hospital stay, it's fair to say that the food is edible and nutritious, so try to eat, as you need your strength. At least you are not having to try to find time to buy the food and cook it yourself. Also, whether you are going public, semi-private or private, there will be opportunities to talk to other women who are in the same boat as you.

Some women prefer to go home as soon as they are allowed after giving birth, others would move into the hospital permanently if they could. Just the thought of everything that awaits them at home can keep them glued to their hospital bed until they are prised off it. Whether you stay in hospital or not, it is important to rest as much as you can, to eat well and to take it easy.

Lastly, I hate to say this, but you will not magically be able to fit into your pre-pregnancy jeans by the time you are leaving the hospital. You will still have quite a bump for a while, so don't beat yourself up about it. It can take quite a while for a woman's body to return to normal after having a baby, and the best way to help this process is to look after yourself with a healthy diet and some gentle exercise.

If you decide to avail of an Early Transfer Home Scheme (ETHS) and you and baby are assessed as healthy, you can go home as early as six hours after the birth. Women whose babies are born during the night can go home in the morning. With the ETHS, after you have gone home you will receive daily midwife visits to ensure that you and your baby are doing well and be given advice on feeding, the Guthrie/heel-prick test and your baby will be weighed — the midwife will usually make up to five visits.

When to Get Help

Don't worry about taking painkillers for the first couple of weeks after giving birth — there is no need to suffer in silence if you are sore and in pain. But if you suffer from any of the following, tell your doctor:

- excessive bright red bleeding

- pain in the lower abdomen a few days after delivery

- a temperature after the first 24 hours

- dizziness

- vomiting

- sharp chest pain

YOUR BABY AFTER BIRTH

After your baby's birth he will be examined by a midwife or doctor to check his Apgar score (see page 149), and he will be measured and weighed. He will also be fitted with ID bands, usually on his wrist and ankle. You may wish to try feeding your baby before or after this check is done. At this point your breasts will be producing colostrum, also known as first milk, a thick, yellowy substance designed to keep your baby healthy until your milk comes in. It is easy to digest and high in protein, carbohydrates and antibodies.

In most Irish hospitals newborns are given Vitamin K to prevent haemorrhagic disease of the newborn (HDN). This is where bleeding can occur in various parts of the body because babies are born with low levels of Vitamin K, which is needed to clot blood. You may wish to discuss this with your doctor or midwife during an antenatal visit. If you wish a home-birth baby to have a Vitamin K injection, discuss it with your midwife.

About day four or five after the birth you will be asked to bring your baby back into the hospital, if you have gone home, to have the Guthrie/heel-prick test. If you have taken an early transfer home, or have had a Domino delivery, the midwife may do the test when she visits. If you are not sure where the test will be done, check with your midwife. The test involves pricking your baby's heel and putting blood on a card, which is then sent to the lab to screen for phenylketonuria (PKU), a rare inherited metabolic condition that can be caught early and treated. None of the parents at the clinic I attended understood what the test was looking for — we were all too freaked out by the idea of blood being taken out of our new babies — but essentially PKU is a condition where a baby does not have an amino acid needed for normal development and a substance builds up in the blood which can lead to serious health problems. And if it's any consolation, my five-day-old daughter didn't even wake up when she had her heel-prick test!

Understanding your Baby

Let me tell you a secret — at this early stage, babies are a law unto themselves. You will find that your one tiny newborn has the ability to turn two grown adults into blithering wrecks in a matter of days. However, you won't mind all this disruption one little bit, and even when your baby sleeps, you won't be able to because you will be staring at him to make sure he is breathing.

I remember avidly reading books which outlined routines that would guarantee new parents some sleep after a few weeks, and within days had thrown them out the window. Now is not the time to worry about routines, normality or even hanging out the washing. This is a special time for you and your baby and as tiring as it is, you will never get it back again, so don't worry about trying to poke your baby awake during the day so that you can get some sleep at night — the time for that will come later, when he is big enough. While it's true that new babies have no concept of day or night, they also sleep — a lot — and if you can catch a few zzz when they do, you'll be doing well.

If your baby is crying, at this stage it can be hard to work out why. There's a checklist of things you can go through to work out what he might be upset about. Once you have found out which one it is, a period of silent bliss will ensue. And just to confuse parents, all babies are different — so she could be crying because she's hungry, has wind, has a wet or dirty nappy, is tired, too hot or cold or is in pain. Later, when your baby is a few months old, you can add boredom and teething to this list, but by then you will know each other better and it will be simpler to work out. At the moment, try to understand that you won't always be able to provide a miracle cure. However, you might find that popping him in a sling whilst you hoover will soothe him, or even dancing around with him, rocking him gently can help. Many parents find that fresh air or a trip in the car lulls their baby to sleep.

Your baby's first poo may come as something of a shock. It is actually meconium — a tar-like substance that has been sitting in his gut for some time. It will be a dark green colour, but that's normal. After your milk supply is established this will change to a runny yellowish colour that can shoot out like lava out of a volcano, so try not to be too close when this happens (I won't forget when it happened to me in the middle of the night!). Bottlefed babies will produce firm brown poo.

If you are in hospital don't be afraid to ask for help with feeding and changing as this is a new experience for you and there is lots of expertise on hand. Midwives will be busy, but will check on how you and baby are doing every so often.

In the first few days you will seem to spend all day and night feeding and changing your baby — she won't be able to take big feeds yet and will often fall asleep with the effort of feeding. It's not uncommon to breastfeed newborns 10 or 12 times a day and change as many nappies too. After the weeks and months go by, this will settle down to fewer feeds, fewer changes and more fun, so you definitely have something to look forward to.

Disposable nappies are popular and easy to use, especially when your baby is getting through loads every day, but in recent years there has been a renaissance in the use of the traditional cloth nappy. For more on both sides of the debate, see page 208. When your baby is brand new, you will need to be careful of his clamped umbilical cord, so fold the nappy down at the front to avoid rubbing against it. It will drop off in a week or two. Always wash your hands after changing a baby's nappy, and more frequent hand washing from all visitors wouldn't be a bad thing either.

When communicating with your new baby, try to get as close as possible as he won't be able to see further than about 30 cm. He will, however, recognise your voice and will feel calmed by it.

Babies born by c-section may still have some fluid on their lungs — this can be sore for them and they may scream for attention or have coughing fits. This can be hard for mum, who may not be able to move quickly due to stitches. If your baby looks like he is struggling to breathe or you are concerned about him, always call a midwife.

Some babies can be very windy when they are small, and you seem to spend hours patting his back. You can be amazed by the amount of gas that escapes from his rear end too, often accompanied by projectile poo.

Most new babies are happy to hang out in babygros and other all-in-ones and we'd advise you to have lots of these in supply as he will likely get through three or four sets of clothes every day. The most practical are those that button up the front as you can get them on and off quickly while your baby lies safely on his back. Many babies hate being exposed and will scream until you get their new nappy and clothes back on. Your washing machine will become your new best friend.

New babies are not very efficient at regulating their body temperature and you may be surprised to find she has cold hands or feet. This is why we see tiny babies wrapped up in several layers including socks, mitts and a hat. The ideal room temperature for a baby to be in is 16–20°C.

Some new babies develop a yellow look to their skin from around two to five days old. This is called jaundice and is caused by their liver not being able to break down red blood cells. It is relatively common and usually nothing to worry about. To help his liver to start working properly, you will need to increase the amount of fluids he is taking, by more frequent feeding. Most babies will recover on their own after a few days, and the yellow tinge will disappear. But if you are concerned that it is not going or if he is not urinating very much or feeding well, tell your midwife or GP. You and your baby are still under the care of the hospital until your baby is six weeks old, or of your midwife if you had a home birth.

This is your baby, you will get to know and love each other with time and patience, and even though you may doubt it now — try to put some trust in your instincts about what is best for your baby and yourself. You will be given plenty of advice, some helpful and some unwelcome, but at the end of the day, you are now a parent and can make your own decisions.

Bathing your Baby

Bathing your baby for the first time can be a nerve-wracking experience — a new baby is slippery and so small that you fear you will drop her. Ask at the hospital or the midwife when she visits whether they will teach you how to do it and wash her hair — there's a definite technique. Some mums say their baby got so upset by being given a bath, that they simply ran a bath for themselves and brought the baby in too. The skin-to-skin contact and smell of mum helped the baby to relax. Also, you don't have to bathe a newborn every day — they don't really get too dirty and their skin is too delicate to be exposed to water too often. Avoid putting products into the bath water for the same reason, just plain clean water will do fine.

Some tips on bathing your baby:

- Your baby's bath water should be around 36°C. You can buy thermometers that float in the water and also check by dipping your elbow into the water.

- Lay out a towel, vest, nappy and babygro.

- Hold your baby firmly as she might be slippery. You can buy a large sponge in baby equipment shops that fits in the bath to prevent slipping. Make sure her head and neck are supported as you wash her with plain water.

- Clean your baby's eyes by dipping one ball of cotton wool into cool boiled water. Wipe over the eyes once only, from inside to outside, discard and use another ball for the other eye.

FEEDING YOUR BABY

One of the first things you will be asked in hospital is how you are feeding your baby, and it's a good idea to give it some thought before she is born. Keeping an open mind and taking each day at a time are both important.

Breastfeeding

The World Health Organisation (WHO) recommends that women breastfeed exclusively for six months, with continued breastfeeding up to two years of age. However, breastfeeding rates in Ireland remain among the lowest in Europe.

There are good reasons by WHO promotes breastfeeding — studies have shown that feeding babies this way provides the best nutrition and allows antibodies to pass from mum to baby, helping to lower the occurrence of ear infections, diarrhoea and respiratory infections as well as protecting some babies against allergies, asthma, diabetes, sudden infant death syndrome (SIDS) and obesity.

Breastfeeding is also good for mum as it helps lower her risk of pre-menopausal breast cancer and may help decrease the risk of uterine and ovarian cancer as well as helping to contract her uterus and get back into shape quickly after the birth.

Women who breastfeed need to eat 500 extra calories per day and your baby will enjoy the taste of the different foods you eat through your milk. Breastmilk is made of lactose, protein and fat, which is the ideal food for a baby's digestive system.

Some women who think they don't like the idea of breastfeeding try it and feel that it is the perfect food for their baby. The milk is available at any time and always at the right temperature. They continue it until their baby is weaned onto solids and can drink cows' milk at 12 months, or until they need to return to work. But not all women find breastfeeding easy and natural — it needs practice and support.

The next chapter of this book covers breastfeeding techniques in detail, however, I would advise all women willing to try it to attend a support group. Maternity hospitals and local health centres run support groups which are good for getting you started in the early days and weeks. Other groups are run by Cuidiú (The Irish Childbirth Trust), which has a list of trained breastfeeding counsellors who will answer any queries you might have and La Leche League, a mother-to-mother voluntary group whose services also include telephone counselling and home visits. For more information on breastfeeding technique, see pages 217–20.

Bottlefeeding

While breastfeeding is the best way to feed your newborn baby due to his immature digestive system, and the majority of women are able to do it with some support for at least the first few weeks of their baby's life, having a traumatic birth with a lot of medical intervention can make it more difficult to establish and some women move onto bottlefeeding.

Commercial formulas have improved enormously since their invention in the mid-1800s and are getting closer to replicating the ingredients in breast milk. However, some of breast milk's more complex ingredients have not yet been identified and cannot be manufactured.

Infant formulas are now made from cows', sheep and goats' milk although the vast majority of babies will be fed with a cows' milk formula. For the small number of babies who are intolerant to dairy products, soya milk might be more suitable. Always consult your GP or paediatrician before making a change to your young baby's diet.

If you want to bottlefeed, the hospital may supply you with some pre-made formula in small bottles — you may even be able to buy some to take home with you to save you from having to sterilise and prepare bottles of formula for the first few days. However, this can prove expensive over time and most parents will buy a steriliser and at least six 4 oz and six 8 oz bottles, as well as tins of formula. You may also need a bottle brush, plastic jug, plastic knife, sterilising solution or tablets and obviously, a kettle.

It's important to be scrupulous about cleaning bottles, measuring out formula and making sure it's at the right temperature in order to prevent your baby developing any intestinal problems. The subject of bottlefeeding is covered in detail in the next chapter.

Mums have told me that with bottlefeeding they know how much their baby is taking, but they are concerned that the baby is not getting enough milk from breastfeeding. I can reassure you that it's extremely rare for a woman not to be able to adequately feed her baby through breastfeeding: as long as she is eating enough her body will adjust to her baby's needs and supply just the right amount of milk. Any woman who has pumped out milk from a breast will be amazed by how much milk is in there.

DUMMY DEBATE

Dummies, soothers, dodies, comforters — there are lots of different names for these little rubber nipples attached to a plastic ring. Small babies love to suck and when nothing else will settle them, are comforted by sucking on their fingers, their clothes or a soother. People tend to have strong opinions about soothers — they love them or loathe them. If you want to try using one, take it to the hospital. Breastfeeding consultants will tell you that a breastfed baby won't need to suck as much because she gets more done on the breast, but I know babies fed by bottle and breast who have become addicted to their soother. Some parents try to wean their baby off the soother when they are continually woken in the night in order to put it back in, and others wait until their child is older and can be reasoned with. At the end of the day, it's a personal decision, but for at least the first year all soothers will have to be run through the steriliser.

BABIES WHO COME EARLY

If your baby is premature or unwell when born you will need extra help to get you through this difficult time. Your baby may be in a Special Care Unit or Neonatal Intensive Care Unit (NICU) for some days or weeks. It may be very difficult to leave the hospital when your tiny baby is still there and you may wish to pump breastmilk which can be given to him. Skin-to-skin contact with a premature baby is extremely beneficial. You may not feel relaxed about your baby until he has reached a healthy weight and is strong enough to go home.

The Coombe Women and Infants University Hospital is currently the only maternity hospital running a parent-support group, although some other hospitals in the country are working to set them up. On one Saturday per month parents of babies who have been in the intensive care unit can meet up with midwives, a social worker and physiotherapist in the Coombe to talk about any issues relating to their baby.

You can also get some good advice from Tiny Life, a support group based in Belfast who run a helpline. Phone: 048 9081 5050; *www.tinylife.org.uk*.

REAL STORIES

'One thing I didn't expect after the birth was how much it would sting when going to the toilet! Ouch! It definitely helps to have a sports bottle of warm water beside the toilet and squirt it down below as you're peeing! Witch hazel was great too. And what you just can't prepare yourself for is the lack of sleep!! Everyone says it and it really is true — you need to sleep when the baby sleeps!'
Denise

'On the arrival of my beautiful baby boy we saw that he was born with a cleft lip and tongue tie, which was a bit of a shock, but the staff at the hospital were brilliant. I was breastfeeding and needed a lot of extra support to get that established and if it was not for the continued support of a lovely lactation specialist in my local maternity unit, I would never have done it.'
Liz

'The first two days were the worst. I wasn't sure if the baby liked me, or even if I liked him. I felt like I was holding him wrong, feeding him wrong, changing him wrong — everything you could possibly do wrong I thought I was doing it. Once we got home we settled into a routine and spent some great time together. Now we are doing great, although there are still times I think I'm not doing things right but I'm sure that's just first-time nerves.'
Joanne

'When my son was born I had a light tear which didn't need stitches and I breastfed straight away. My milk came in two days later and I'm not going to lie, it was uncomfortable, but once my baby started feeding properly we were laughing and I was very proud of myself for sticking with it. I felt very tired and a bit like a sack down below, as if my insides where falling out and found it very hard to move around and get up from a sitting position. My tear stung like hell when going to the loo so my doctor recommended Epsom Salts in a bath which was great. It was a very emotional few weeks with tiredness, baby blues and just a total shock to the system being a mammy for the first time.'
Martina

'I had an episiotomy with the first baby and a second-degree tear with my second. The recovery from the episiotomy was not too bad because they used a continuous stitch that was dissolvable, so I just had lots of warm baths to ease the tightening of the stitches. I had no problems after about three weeks and it was just sensitive for about the first 12 weeks. I found it a lot harder to recover from the tear — because of the nature of the tear it had thinned the skin so the stitches did not take. It was very sore for the first 12 weeks and sensitive for at least another 12 weeks after that.'
Liz

'After my emergency caesarean, I found breastfeeding difficult and painful to start with, but I managed to do it OK with help from the midwives. I don't think there was a time when I thought I would give up. I remember on day one Sophie slept for about five hours solid and I was worried I ought to wake her up for more, but I think she had had such a big feed she couldn't keep awake. The other good thing was I wasn't pressurised in going home before I felt ready to go; I wasn't sure how I would cope at home when I could hardly walk. I also had good painkillers so I don't particularly remember being in much pain.'
Bridget

How Dad Feels and How He can Help

You and your partner have just been through the most amazing experience ever. When you are old and grey you will remember seeing your baby's face for the first time and how you felt at that proud moment.

Once you have accompanied your partner and baby down to the ward and made the all-important phone calls to family and friends to break the good news, you might think you deserve to go home and have a few hours' sleep. Hold it there, Mister! Your job is not done, and you'd better get used to being tired because it will be a constant in your life for several months yet.

Your first job is to provide a protective shield around your partner and baby so that they don't become too overwhelmed with well-meaning visitors, just when they are both about to drift off into much-needed sleep. Find out about visiting times, ask your partner who she would like to see and when and convey the news. Don't worry about offending people — there will be plenty of opportunities for them to visit later. They will need to respect hospital quiet times which are designed to allow patients to sleep and eat, but you may be given a visiting card so that you can spend more time with your partner and new bundle of joy.

One thing I remember from my ward in hospital were the number of flowers — and the number of new babies sneezing their little heads off, so you might want to encourage visitors to go easy on these. All visitors must wash their hands before entering the ward and those with colds might be better off staying away from mum and baby until they have recovered.

While your partner is in the hospital, you can have one or two nights' undisturbed sleep at home, so think yourself lucky. She will be feeding your baby and getting him to sleep, just before being woken up by someone else's hungry baby.

There's plenty you can do at home to help, though. Take home any washing and do it, fill the fridge with healthy food. If relatives or friends offer to help, ask for healthy cooked meals you can put in the freezer, set up the crib in your bedroom, keep the house clean and do any of the last-minute shopping that you might have considered bad luck before baby actually made an appearance. For example, my husband had to go out and buy some newborn babygros as our daughter was swamped in 0–3 months.

Also, don't forget to feed mum. She may wish you to bring in extra food to supplement what is supplied in the hospital and now is not the time to argue.

Many new mums have also told us that a little present from the new dad can really cheer them up when they are exhausted and sore. It doesn't have to be expensive, but is recognition that she has given you your precious baby.

An important job for dad to do is to practise putting the baby car seat into the car. The hospital won't let you out the door unless your baby is safely nestled into a seat. You will need to buy a new one to ensure it is safe and make sure it says UN ECE *Regulation 44-03 with an E mark* on the label.

Wetting the baby's head can cause tension between new parents. Your mates will ask if you're going to do it, and my advice is, if your partner is in hospital, do it then. Once she and the baby are home, she won't be able to cope with you and your mates drinking and singing into the wee small hours. And she can't deal with your absence either.

Parents who had their baby at home will not have to contend with hospital visits and visiting times, but Dad will still need to keep a lid on the number of visitors. If your partner is up, dressed and making tea, people will assume she is coping fine, but when they have gone on their merry way she will be up twice or more in the night feeding the baby. If, by contrast, she greets guests in her dressing gown, they may not stay as long, which can only be a good thing. While it's wonderful to share your great news in the early days, all of you need time to yourselves to adjust to such a major change.

If relatives arrive and make critical comments about your partner and how she is feeding, holding or calming the baby, be ready to jump in and defend her. The last thing she needs is to be made to feel inadequate when she is just getting the hang of this most life-changing event. She needs your support and will be eternally grateful for it.

Try to think of ways you can help with the baby instead of waiting for your partner to ask you to hold him so that she can go to the loo or have a shower. Don't just *offer* to change nappies and get up in the night — do it, and don't complain. This is a back-breaking time that you will all survive, but not without a lot of give and take.

Encourage your partner to sleep when the baby does and you can hang out the washing, shop for food and cook meals — a new mum is up at all hours so she needs plenty of energy from healthy food.

Finally, talk to each other. Recognise that this is a stressful time and that you will come through it stronger and still laughing, but only if you keep communicating. You will forget all about the hard times when your baby is sitting up and laughing with you.

Chapter 8 ～

| THE FIRST SIX WEEKS

RETURNING HOME

It's time to go home, whether you've been in hospital for only a short time, or a few days. I remember walking out the hospital door three days after I'd entered it, blinking in the sunlight as I fully realised the enormous new responsibility in my arms. We struggled to fit our little girl safely into the back of the car and debated for five long minutes whether our tiny baby was safe to make a ten-minute journey.

Parenting is scary, especially for first-timers. Those who already have children will also be concerned about how older brothers or sisters will adjust — will they like the new baby or try to smother him?

It's a world of worry that you only really fully understand when you become a parent — at least that's how it seems to me. During that first night at home with my baby, after another feed, I should have been heading back into a deep sleep, when instead I lay there in terror. What if anything happened to my baby? I realised I'd fallen in love with my daughter and nothing would ever change that. It had finally sunk in. I was a mum and it was all down to me — with a little help from my husband.

Once you are at home, you might be forgiven for thinking that everything will slot into place. Think again. Expect everything in your life to feel upside down, including your relationships, as your little bundle of joy takes up all your energies. It is like a bomb going off in your life, upending everything you thought was important.

It's perfectly normal to feel a little scared and useless at the beginning — you can't predict how your baby will act and right now you don't really know what he is saying. Seasoned parents with several children will tell you that every baby is different and it takes time to work out what he wants. Your baby, meanwhile, will keep communicating with you using the only language he knows — crying — until you do the one thing he wants — feed him, change his nappy, put him down for a sleep or hold him close. In other words, babies are parent-proof — you will work it out and it gets easier, promise. Within the next few days and weeks you will grow to understand your baby better.

In the meantime, getting anything done, including going to the loo, having a shower and eating can be a serious challenge, as baby demands every bit of your time and energy. And yet it's really important to eat properly at the moment as you will be up day and night and will need added energy reserves to cope with the huge demands made on you.

If you're breastfeeding you will need to eat more calories every day, although they shouldn't all come from chocolate and it's a good idea not to go back on the alcohol just yet. Every baby is different and you will become aware of things you eat that don't agree with him — a friend of mine cut out peas while breastfeeding because they made her baby especially windy, for example.

Getting enough rest is essential if you're going to survive this stage. Try to sleep when the baby does, which will probably not be during the night, and don't worry about the outside world — it will carry on without you, and your partner can look after anything practical that needs doing.

One thing you will notice straight away is that you will start to develop muscles you didn't know you had in your upper arms. This is down to carrying your baby everywhere you go. Holding him close will comfort him when he can hear your heartbeat, a sound he is familiar with from being *in utero*.

Your baby's head is big in comparison with the rest of his body, and you will need to support it and his neck until he is strong enough to do it himself — most babies can sit up at around six months and try to hold their wobbling heads before that. When you can't hold your baby he will be happy to lie on his back in a baby gym with safe dangly toys above his head, or you may prefer to carry him around in a sling.

If you need to do something, including going to the loo, take your baby with you. He is light and portable, and can lie on the floor or in a tilted baby chair (as long it is suitable for newborns). He will not be able to sit up in a small fold-down buggy for several months, although some bigger prams and travel systems come with a carry cot inserted which allows your baby to lie flat. Your new baby will not be able to see very far in the early weeks, but the sound of your voice will calm him, so chat and sing away, even if it makes you feel silly.

Women who have just had babies can find that their back is a bit sore due to weakened abdominal muscles, so it's really important to avoid any activities that put strain on this area. If you're breastfeeding ask your partner to help you position the baby so that you are not hunching over, as this can lead to back strain. If you are finding it difficult to get the position right and there is no one around to help you, lie down on your side to feed your baby.

Walk as upright as you possibly can and don't hunch over your baby's pram, ask for help with lifting shopping out of the car and bend your knees when doing any lifting. One sure way to strain your back is to bend over a changing table when changing your baby's nappy — if your back is feeling delicate put your baby on a mat on the floor and change him there while on your knees.

Accept that you simply cannot do everything yourself — on the plus side, there will be people who are willing to help you. So accept their offers and suggest ways in which they could really help — if your mum or sister is willing to come round and cook, buy food, do the washing, or hoover the house — say yes please! You might prefer your mum to do practical things so that you can concentrate on your baby, but don't expect her to magically know this: you will need to talk about your needs. If you don't have family support, you might consider hiring a cleaner or asking a good friend to come and stay. These days dads tend to take some time off when their baby is born, which is the perfect time for them to bond while you get some rest.

Beware of Visitors

People will want to congratulate you and bring presents, which is nice, but if you are inundated with visitors who expect tea or food you can quickly feel that it is just too much. Ask your partner to help you schedule visitors so that you don't feel so overwhelmed that you just want to disappear into the bedroom with your baby and never come out again. Ask visitors to text you or your partner first, rather than just turning up on your doorstep when you might be sleeping, dealing with a smelly nappy, puke-fest or sitting breastfeeding and unable to move.

You can call them back at a good time for you, and arrange a brief visit at a time that suits you and your baby, i.e. when your partner is there. Most visitors would rather come for half an hour and see you and your baby when you are awake rather than sit making small talk while you both sleep because they have just turned up unannounced. Putting a time limit on their visit is also a good idea too — it's not rude, it's all about survival, and they should understand.

It's also important to avoid others over-handling your baby as you are still getting to know each other as a family and your smell and touch is important to your little baby. Being passed about too much can upset a small baby who is looking for reassurance from Mum or Dad.

In my daughter's early weeks we found that she was much more likely to settle against her dad's chest than mine — whenever I picked her up she could smell my milk, even if I couldn't, and turned her little head to my breast with her mouth wide open (called 'rooting'). Mind you, she sometimes did this with her granny, too, which caused a smile.

Take Each Day at a Time

Try to view getting through every day as an achievement — looking after a new baby is the toughest job you will ever do and as the days and weeks go by your baby will start to breastfeed for longer, or drink more formula, will put on weight and sleep for longer periods. At times looking after a baby can feel like a thankless task — he cannot talk to you or say thanks, but it's important to look at the big picture. You have a beautiful baby who will play a major part in the rest of your life, so congratulate yourself. It's easy to wish these days over because they are so tough, but in years to come you will find yourself looking back with tears in your eyes as you remember those early weeks — honest!

A good way to survive this time is to make the effort to meet up with other mums of new babies. I found my local health centre breastfeeding group was great, but it can be any get-together with other mums. Getting washed and dressed and out the door, being able to talk to other shell-shocked new mums, and having your baby weighed, all help to keep you sane.

Finally, don't feel bad if you need some time to yourself — being a mum is exhausting and will push you to the absolute limit. Give Dad the bottle of expressed milk and get in the bath, go to the cinema, to the shops or out to dinner with friends — you are a person, too, and need to do something for yourself occasionally. You might think it's too early for that, which is fine, but it's surprising how a small break can give you a lift.

Whether you had your baby in hospital or at home, your midwife or a public health nurse will visit to check on you and your baby in the early days — she (it's usually a woman) will weigh your baby and ask you how feeding is going. She might also check your stitches or c-section scar if you have one. Use this visit as an opportunity to ask any questions.

Finally, please try not to compare yourself to other mums. We're all different, and beating yourself up about how you look and so on is only torturing yourself, because right now you are doing a wonderful job, despite extreme sleep deprivation. There will be plenty of time for getting back into shape and easing your baby into a routine — but no matter what anyone else says, the first six weeks is not the time. Instead, give yourself a pat on the back and enjoy your lovely baby.

PRACTICAL CONSIDERATIONS

Registering your Baby's Birth

If your baby was born in hospital you may be given information on registering her birth during your stay there. All babies must be registered no later than three months after their birth in order to be issued with a birth certificate, which is essential for applying for child benefit, a passport or even enrolling at school.

For the most up-to-date information on this, check out *www.citizensinformation.ie*.

Child Benefit

If your baby is born in Ireland, when you register the birth of your baby, the Department of Social Protection will begin a Child Benefit Claim for your child. If your baby is born in Ireland, the Child Benefit section will send you either an application form or a letter confirming payment.

Twins and More

At the time of writing, according to *www.citizensinformation.ie*, 'The rate of child benefit paid for twins will be 1.5 times the normal monthly rate for each child. Where the multiple birth involves three or more children, the rate of benefit paid is double the monthly rate, provided at least three of the children remain qualified.'

In addition, a special 'once-off' grant is paid on all multiple births. 'Further once-off grants... are paid when the children are 4 years of age and 12 years of age.'

For further information on child benefit, check out *www.citizensinformation.ie*; or the Department of Social Protection at *www.welfare.ie*. See Chapter 11.

BABY EQUIPMENT — WHAT YOU WILL NEED

Cut the Cost

You could easily be forgiven for thinking that babies and small children don't need much — other than to be fed, clothed and loved. That's true, but what comes as a shock to most new parents is that the smallest person in the house has the most stuff. In these financially straightened times it can be sobering to discover that some prams and travel systems can cost nearly €1,000, and that's before you've bought a moses basket, cot, high chair, bouncy chair, sling, clothes or a single toy.

So before you buy a thing, get clever and check out the following websites:

- *www.dublinwaste.ie* Good for big items like cots and buggies.

- *www.freecycle.org* The Freecycle Network has groups in various Irish cities and counties and aims to keep good stuff out of landfills.

- *www.jumbletown.ie* A good source of free stuff and somewhere to pass on things you no longer need.

- Start dropping into charity shops — you'd be surprised by what you can find there. Some of them won't accept buggies, but they can be a good source of baby gyms and travel cots for a fraction of the new cost.

- Don't be shy — tell everyone you know that you are looking for something well in advance, and see whether the jungle drums can find a match with someone who wants to pass on something that's taking up valuable space in their home that they no longer need. Friends with older children will be only too glad to pass things on.

A Note on Safety Standards

Most baby equipment you buy in good baby shops will comply with either British or European safety standards, but if you are concerned, ask around until you are satisfied.

My first antenatal class covered baby-equipment safety. We were given fact sheets, but just in case you are not given this information, here are the main points:

- Carrycots should be at least 7.5 inches deep.

- Any child in a pram or buggy should be clipped into a five-point harness, even if they are lying down.

- Never leave your baby in a car seat for more than two hours.

- Make sure your buggy has swivel wheels and a link brake — it locks to the two back wheels.

- Look for flame retardancy in all equipment.

- There should be a 2.36-inch gap between the bars of a cot.

- There should be a one-inch gap between the mattress and sides of the cot.

- There are three types of mattress for babies:
  Foam — tends to sag
  Fibre — denser
  Interior sprung — cooler to sleep on

- Make sure your baby's mattress has holes running straight through it. Follow the advice for preventing SIDS, or Sudden Infant Death Syndrome (page 223).

- Choose a mattress with zip-off covers for washing.

Pram or Buggy?

Believe it or not, a pram or travel system can be the most expensive thing you buy your baby (apart from their education) and you will use it more than you think.

The chances are that you will be pushing your baby around in his pram for up to a couple of years, even if you buy a smaller, more lightweight one for travelling. You'll be carrying shopping, a nappy bag, your handbag and toys in it too, so it's important to make sure that you can bear to look at it every day and that it suits all your needs.

Assuming you don't want to visit every baby equipment shop in your county, choose one with a wide range of prams where the staff are happy for you to wheel them around the shop and try collapsing and putting them back up again. Ask your partner to be there so that he can try pushing them, too — many tall men can find that pushing a pram is hard on their back, and these days many models come with extendable handlebars and in numerous different designs.

Things to Consider when Buying a Pram or Buggy:

- Ask yourself — will I be able to fold it down and put it up on my own? Will it fit easily into the boot of our car? Some prams, while beautiful, can be huge and I'm assuming you won't want to have to buy a bigger car too. Think about where you're going to store it at home too — is your hallway big enough?

- Your pristine pram, with all its padded covers and accessories, may be clean now, but you'd be surprised how mucky it can become once baby moves in, so find out whether everything can be wiped clean or go through the washing machine.

- If you have a summer baby you can buy a clip-on parasol to keep the sun off his face, and you will definitely need a good rain cover. Buying the specific one that fits your pram is important and you will be glad of it in a downpour as your baby smiles up at you from his cosy den (you'll be soaked, of course, but if he's not screaming, then who's complaining?).

- Many travel systems give you the choice of having your baby facing either you or the outside world. Make sure your pram will allow your baby to sleep comfortably.

Once your baby is big enough to sit upright and you don't want to knock all the clothes off the rails with your huge pram when you go shopping, you may want to switch to a buggy. Buggies are great because they are much smaller than prams when they fold down and you can hang your shopping bags on the handles. Don't overload them, though, or you could end up with your baby being tipped backwards due to the weight (Never happened to me, honest!).

Car Seat

Many Irish hospitals will not discharge you until your baby is safely fitted into a car seat. This can be tricky at first because newborns have wobbly heads, but many seats now come with an insert designed to support their heads. Once you have secured your baby in his seat, it needs to be fitted into the back seat of your car, facing backwards. This can involve a bit of fiddling with seatbelts, but it is important to follow the instructions properly for safety's sake. You could also opt for a system where the baby car seat clicks into a base, fitted into the back seat of the car. Many prams these days come as 'travel systems', with car seats designed for 0–12 months, and people will often offer these to you second-hand, but it's important to buy a new car seat to ensure its safety, even if you choose to go with used for other baby equipment.

Moses Basket

It's debatable whether you need one of these, but many parents prefer to put babies into them until they are big enough for a cot at around eight weeks or so. Your baby will be sleeping in your room, and a moses basket will take up much less space. You won't get very much use out of one, though, so say yes if one is offered to you. My daughter's moses basket had seen dozens of babies sleep in it. You may want to buy a new mattress for a second-hand basket. Some moses baskets come with stands, but if yours is a bit wobbly then the safest place to put baby is on the floor beside your bed. We put ours on a large, sturdy coffee table which was a good solution in the short-term.

When you put baby down to sleep in his basket he will need to lie on his back with his feet to the bottom (see SIDS information on page 223).

Cot, Mattress, Sheets and Blankets

You probably don't need this now, but a wooden cot will, at some point, become important. As mentioned above, European standards state that the bars should be a certain width apart and high enough that baby cannot jump out. These standards are designed to stop your baby hurting himself, and believe me, some active little terrors can fling themselves around the cot once they are big enough. If you're offered a cot, check that it meets European standards and invest in a new mattress from a baby equipment shop.

You can buy fitted sheets for your cot, but these can be expensive — another option is to cut a single flat sheet in half. Hey presto, a cot sheet for a fraction of the cost.

You will no doubt hear a lot about 'cellular blankets' during your pregnancy, and they're not something we really consider before having a baby. Basically they are cotton blankets, knitted to let air in, that are ideal for newborns because they keep them warm and also allow them to breathe should they wriggle down underneath. Wrapping a baby in a blanket before putting him down to sleep can be comforting for him because he is not able to fling his arms and legs about. Some babies, like my daughter, however, will thrash about until they get their arms free, then fall asleep.

Travel Cot

Do you need one of these? Right now you might not think so and there's no need to go rushing out to buy one, but if someone offers you one, don't turn it down. These creations are clever because a child up to the age of three (at a squeeze) can sleep anywhere in them, making it easier to go away for the weekend, and they can be used as a safe playpen — so that you can have a shower. Brilliant invention.

Monitor

What did parents do before the invention of the monitor? I really can't imagine. Having a monitor can mean the difference between you being able to relax for a short time because you know your baby is safe, and having to go up and down stairs to check on him because you're worried he might not be breathing — a common occurrence before these miracle machines, so I'm told by my mum. The really great ones can be clipped onto your clothes so that you can walk from room to room without having to move the base from one socket to another. Hey presto! Your baby is asleep, it's a sunny day and you can hang washing out. Many monitors also have built-in nightlights so that you can check on your sleeping baby without waking him, and a room thermometer, too, and newer monitors have a video screen so that you can see your baby. Babies ideally should sleep in a room at around 18°C.

Changing Equipment

You might be dreading dirty nappies, but because your precious baby has produced them, they won't seem so bad — honest. Sometimes, however, you can be astonished by how much mucky stuff comes out of such a small person and it's important to be prepared in order to save your home from being ruined. Changing mats are cheap and many baby books will advise you to have one downstairs and one upstairs — they are right. Make sure the raised border is below baby's bottom to catch anything messy. These can be washed clean under the tap and air dried.

A changing bag is essential for outside excursions. In it you can put nappies, cotton wool or wipes, nappy cream, plastic bags for soiled nappies and clothes, a muslin cloth, a portable change mat, if needed, and a set of spare baby clothes. At home you may choose not to expose your baby to the chemicals in wipes, but they can be handy when out and about. (For more on choosing nappies see page 208.)

Muslins and Bibs

Some babies can be quite frankly, a bit pukey. The milk goes in and then minutes later, some of it comes out again. In the early days this can be over your shoulder if you are winding your baby and you may not even realise you have a trail of sick down your back until someone tells you. The good news about this is that it nearly always stops by about six months, when the muscle that holds food down in the baby's tummy has developed. In the meantime, keep a bib on your baby at all times and throw a muslin cloth over your shoulder for winding — these are sometimes called burping cloths and are available from any maternity shop.

Baby Sling

This invention is good for mums who do not suffer from back-ache, and often dads enjoy carrying their babies around. Your baby can face towards you or, when bigger, look outwards. They can be useful for babies who find it hard to settle because when facing you they get to hear your heartbeat. You will also be free of the big pram for a while. Don't, however, go on a hike with a sling — if you get tired you will have nowhere to safely put your baby.

Baby slings are also great for getting things done around the house if baby wants to be up in your arms. When using a sling, it's important to ensure that your baby's chin is not tucked into her chest, so that she can breathe properly. Make sure that you adjust the sling so that baby is free to breathe through her mouth and nose.

Baby Gym

You might think that it's impossible to 'entertain' your baby at this early stage, and indeed his needs are simple in the early weeks, but after the first six to eight weeks or so he may start to show signs of boredom. A baby gym is a fancy term for a padded mat with various baby-safe soft toys suspended across it. Baby lies on his back and can play with the toys — one guaranteed favourite with all babies is the toy with a mirror, they just love to look at themselves. Meanwhile, you can make a cup of tea — fantastic! Some of these baby gyms even play classical music, which many babies enjoy.

Bouncing Cradle

These semi-upright baby chairs, with a fabric 'sling' stretched over a wire frame, are designed for babies of 0–6 months. You strap baby in, he lies in a semi-upright state so that his back is supported and you can do something that requires two hands. Other types of baby chairs can clip into a frame and rock back and forth. The smaller ones are good because you can carry them around the house with you. Always keep your cradle on the floor and don't be tempted to put it on the counter while you make dinner: babies are experts at moving, even when tiny!

Bath Equipment

Bathing your baby is scary at first, but as he grows this can become a truly joyful experience. My daughter was bathed in the sink in the kitchen in her early weeks and this is great because it is at waist height and you won't hurt your back by leaning over. There's also space on the draining board to put your changing mat, a towel and clothes and nappy gear. Alternatively you could put a plastic baby bath on a table.

Even though you will be holding your baby firmly, he may be slippy and a baby-shaped sponge in the bath or little seat for him to lean on can help to make the whole experience feel that bit safer. You must never leave a baby unattended in water, and try to avoid using any lotions or products while his skin is so delicate.

Baby Clothes

You will receive a lot of these from friends and family, and be grateful for them, too, as your baby can get through as many outfits as feeds in the early days. If you receive anything with ribbons, drawstrings or long lace bits, pull all of these off, as your baby could try to eat them. Small babies are most comfortable in a vest that buttons over and below their nappy, a babygro and cardigan. There will be plenty of time for little jeans, dresses and the like.

One mum told me that she had great success taking clothes back to the shop, if she received too many of the same size, or two of something. After all, asking for an exchange is not like demanding a refund. You could also try asking people to give you gift receipts for baby clothes in case they don't fit.

In the first year of his life your baby will go through at least four clothes sizes, which comes to a lot of vests, t-shirts, babygros and so on. A good idea is to get together with other mums to swap and pass on clothes. Babies will get very little wear out of their clothes in the early months; after all, they are not painting and digging in sandpits, so worn clothes can be as good as new.

Nappies — Cloth or Disposable?

According to ENFO on *www.askaboutireland.ie*, Ireland's environmental information service, a child will use, on average, 5,850 nappies on his or her way to being potty trained. That's a lot of nappies, and they account for about 5% of landfill in Ireland.

Made with wood pulp from softwood trees such as spruce and pine and a number of chemicals to make them super absorbent, disposables are undoubtedly convenient and easy to use. But in an age when many parents are becoming increasingly environmentally aware and want to leave a healthy planet to future generations, it's a sobering thought that a disposable nappy dumped in landfill will take at least 300 years to decompose.

In recent years there has been a resurgence in the popularity of cloth or 'real' nappies in Ireland. New hi-tech fabrics reduce the risk of nappy rash and discomfort. Parents who use cloth nappies point out that the disposable liner that can be flushed down the toilet means that the nappies can be put in with a normal wash, saving on time and electricity. Obviously, if you choose to go with cloth nappies, you will need to wash and dry them, but even taking into account water, electricity and detergent they work out cheaper than disposables. They also have a long life expectancy and can be used for more than one baby.

A wide range of washable cloth nappies are now available in baby shops — they come in flat and pre-fold nappy systems, fitted nappies, pocket nappies and all-in-ones. Some shops run a nappy advisor service to introduce mums to cloth nappies and they can also be bought online. You may have heard of Napuccino public meetings where a nappy advisor introduces mums to cloth nappies and sometimes will offer a rental kit to help them choose what system to go with — these might include a range of different kinds of nappy along with the other bits you will need: cream, tea tree oil, nappy bucket, inserts and liners.

The reason why shops have introduced nappy advisors is that it's not like picking up a packet of disposables in the supermarket and choosing something different next time, if they don't suit. You may need to spend up to €250 at the outset, so it's important that you are happy with your choice. The good news is that you stand to make significant savings by using cloth nappies — see the price comparison below.

Of course, washing up to ten nappies a day in the early weeks, when you don't have time to brush your teeth, may seem like a daunting task, and many parents who eventually go for cloth nappies will use disposables for the first few weeks. Unfortunately there is currently no nappy-washing service in Ireland.

For parents who choose disposable nappies manufacturers point to the government-commissioned life-cycle assessment (LCA), co-ordinated by the UK Environment Agency in May 2005 which reviewed the environmental impacts of both reusable and disposable nappies. The study concluded that 'there is little-to-no difference in terms of environmental impacts between disposable and reusable nappies'. This is largely due to the fact that disposable nappies contribute to household waste, while washable nappies consume energy, water and detergents. A recent update to the LCA (published in October 2008, again by the Environment Agency, in conjunction with WRAP, the Waste Resources Action Programme, and DEFRA [UK Department of Environment, Food and Rural Affairs]), confirmed these findings.

Another option for mums and dads who are not keen on cloth nappies but feel guilty about disposables is the Moltex disposable nappy, termed an 'eco nappy' and made from recycled materials such as unbleached wood pulp, thinner plastic material and with no perfumes, brighteners or lotions. These nappies are sold in certain shops, online and delivered to your door by Eco Baby, *www.ecobaby.ie*. Eco Baby are based in Dublin and say eco nappies can be composted using worms. One mum who tried the wormery option told me that she found it time consuming and didn't stick with it — it's not for everyone.

Cost Comparison

A Women's Environmental Network cost comparison between cloth and disposable nappies concluded that home-laundered nappies could save parents over €1,000 on the cost of keeping a baby in nappies.

The comparison states that the average disposable nappy costs 31.7 cent. This equates to an average cost of €13.31 per week and an overall spend of €1,730.30 over 2.5 years.

'Real' nappies vary widely in their cost depending on the style chosen. According to the comparison, you can buy all the nappies, waterproof covers, and fastenings required for the 2.5 years on the high street for just under €75, although many parents spend more than this.

FEEDING YOUR BABY

Feeding Equipment

All babies need to be fed, and you'd be amazed how often. If you're considering breastfeeding, a small breast pump can be useful. Available from baby shops, these allow you to pump some milk to be stored in the fridge (up to 24 hours) or freezer (up to one month), so that your partner can feed your baby, too. Some of them come with small bottles with teats and it's wise to sterilise these before beginning pumping. These machines can feel strange once attached, but will bring out the milk faster than if you squeeze by hand. You can also buy or rent bigger single or double-pumps and these are often recommended for mums of premature babies, who want to give the baby their milk before they are able to suck. Your midwife or a lactation consultant can tell you about these.

If you're bottlefeeding, you will be using your steriliser all the time (they're also useful for cleaning soothers) and it's wise to buy one that can hold at least six 8 oz bottles in one go. You will also need to scrupulously wash bottles with a bottle brush and detergent as the steriliser or steamer will not actually clean bottles like a dishwasher, but more finish off the process. Practise using it before your baby is born so that you are not learning a brand new skill with one arm while holding a baby with the other. In the early weeks your baby may only manage 2–4 oz per feed, and you can use smaller bottles or only fill the bigger bottles up half-way. There's a dizzying array of teats available and many mums try a number before they find the best for their baby. At the beginning you will need newborn teats. In terms of formula, there are specific ones for different ages and you will be given advice on this by your midwife or health visitor.

BOTTLEFEEDING

The information in the bottlefeeding section comes from *Feed Your Child Well* by Valerie Kelly, Phyllis Farrell and Therese Dunne; €17.99; ISBN: 978-1-906353-02-5; A. & A. Farmar.

- With rare exceptions, cow's milk-based infant formula should be the first choice for feeding healthy babies who are not exclusively breastfed. These formulas are made from extensively modified cow's milk under strictly enforced guidelines.

- First milk, which best resembles breast milk, should be the formula of choice for most babies. There is no need to change to any other formula — your baby can drink first milk until starting on cow's milk at about 1 year old.

- Bottle-feeding is completely different to breastfeeding and no one brand is superior to another. Which brand to choose is simply a matter of personal choice, both yours and your baby's. Easy availability, durability and cost are three factors worth considering.

Cleaning and Sterilising Feed Equipment

- All bottle-feeding equipment (bottles, teats, lids) and any utensils (e.g. knife, whisk) used during the mixing of the feed should be thoroughly cleaned and then sterilised until your baby is 12 months old. This is to ensure that any harmful bacteria are removed to prevent them from growing and multiplying in the feed and making your baby ill.

- Teats and bottles should be checked regularly for signs of wear and damage. If you are unsure about the condition of a bottle or teat, it's safer to throw it away.

- Before handling any sterile items it is essential to wash your hands with hot soapy water and dry them with a fresh cloth or disposable paper towels. Hand-washing reduces the number of bacteria on the skin but does not get rid of them completely. For this reason, once equipment has been sterilised take great care not to touch the inside of bottles, sealing discs, caps etc. Ideally, use a sterile tongs to handle teats.

- Teats and caps should not be placed directly onto work surfaces and once bottles are assembled the cap should always be fitted tightly in place.

Hygiene

Babies' immune systems are immature and for this reason they are very susceptible to infections from bacteria and viruses. Milk is the perfect medium for bacteria to grow and multiply. Good hygiene is important to protect your baby from infection, particularly tummy bugs (gastroenteritis).

- You should use hot water with washing up liquid to clean feeding equipment. Scrub the inside and outside of bottles with a bottle brush. Wash teats inside out or use a teat brush and pay particular attention to the rim and screw top of the bottle.

- Try to wash bottles and teats straight away after a feed or at the very minimum rinse them in warm tap water immediately after use. Bacteria can multiply very quickly in any remaining milk and form a film on the bottle which can be very difficult to wash away. After rinsing, the bottles can be left to one side until you are ready to wash them.

- Ideally you should keep any utensils that you use to prepare your baby's feeds separate from the others and use them only for this purpose. Plastic utensils tend to be more durable and, unlike stainless steel, they can be sterilised using a chemical solution such as Milton or in a microwave steam steriliser (provided the plastic is microwave proof).

- Bottle and teat brushes do not need to be sterilised but should be stored in a clean place. Dishwashers can be used to clean equipment provided the equipment is dishwasher proof but dishwashers do not sterilise equipment. Follow the manufacturer's instructions on the stacking of the bottles, caps etc. and inspect the items after the wash to make sure that they are completely clean.

- If you hand wash equipment, be sure to rinse it thoroughly before sterilising.

Methods of Sterilising

- Steam sterilising is the best method. Both electric and microwave steam sterilisers are available. When buying a steriliser check whether it is compatible with any feeding equipment you want to use or have already.

- Once the bottlefeeding equipment has been thoroughly cleaned and rinsed it should be placed in the steriliser according to the manufacturer's instructions. The length of time required varies, but equipment is usually sterilised in less than ten minutes. Sterilisers also vary as to how long equipment remains sterile inside them. It's best to sterilise equipment just before you need it.

- Milton is probably the best-known cold-water chemical steriliser but there are other products available. They come in tablet or liquid forms. The sterilising solution should be made up according to the manufacturer's instructions. Special containers are available but any non-metallic container can be used to hold the solution, e.g. a plastic bowl or ice-cream container.

- Clean all the utensils thoroughly in hot water with washing-up liquid and rinse them before placing them in the sterilising solution. When placing bottles, teats etc. in the sterilising solution, make sure no air bubbles are trapped inside. All the surfaces of the feeding equipment need to be in contact with the sterilising liquid. Items are generally ready for use after 15–30 minutes — check the manufacturer's instructions. It is safe to leave items in the solution until you need them, for up to a maximum of 24 hours. After 24 hours a fresh solution should be prepared.

- Ideally items should only be removed from the sterilising solution as they are needed. There is no need to rinse them, simply shake off excess fluid. However, if you do choose to rinse items, you must use cooled boiled water.

- To sterilise by boiling, add feeding equipment to a pan full of cold water. Make sure that all items are fully covered with water and that no air bubbles are trapped inside bottles, teats etc.

- Cover the pan with a tight-fitting lid, bring to the boil and boil for at least 3 minutes, making sure the pan does not boil dry. The pan should then be kept covered until the feeding equipment is needed. Keep this saucepan for sterilising equipment only.

- While boiling water can be used to sterilise all feeding equipment, certain items, especially teats, tend to wear out faster using this method.

Making up Bottle Feeds
- Before starting to make up bottles you should thoroughly clean the work surfaces and thoroughly wash your hands in hot soapy water. Then boil the water for the feed and allow it to cool for 30 minutes,

but no longer. It is essential to use freshly boiled tap water to make up infant formula.

- Empty the kettle, run the cold tap for a few seconds and then fill the kettle. Don't boil the kettle more than once because this may increase the concentration of certain minerals. Boil the water and allow it to cool.

- Having boiled the water and allowed it to cool for 30 minutes but no longer, you are ready to prepare the feed. Pour the required amount of hot boiled water into a sterile bottle. Always pour the water in first. Add the infant formula powder following the manufacturer's instructions using the scoop provided. Level the powder off with a sterile knife — don't press down on the powder. Re-assemble the bottle tightly and carefully. Shake well to mix the powder with the water until it is fully dissolved.

- Once the bottles of formula have been made up it is important to cool them quickly.

- If you do not need to feed your baby immediately place all the bottles in the coolest part of the fridge. The temperature of the fridge must not exceed 5°c. Don't place bottles in the door of the fridge. Bottles can be stored in the fridge for up to 24 hours.

- If you are using a feed immediately after making it up, cool the milk as above and then check its temperature before feeding your baby. Shake the bottle and drip a little milk onto the inside of your wrist. It should feel lukewarm not hot. If it still feels hot, cool it some more before feeding. Discard any unused feed after 2 hours.

- You can warm the feed using a bottle warmer or by simply placing the bottle in a container e.g. a jug of warm water. To prevent contamination always make sure the water level is below the neck or lid of the bottle. Shake or swirl the bottle occasionally to make sure the milk heats evenly. To prevent growth of harmful bacteria it is important to re-warm feeds for no longer than 15 minutes. Never warm feeds on a radiator or near a fire as this will create the perfect conditions for bacteria to grow and multiply.

Feeding Patterns

Bottlefed babies, like breastfed babies, should be fed on demand. This does not mean that you can't establish a feeding routine for your baby e.g. 3–4 hourly feeds. What it does mean is that your baby should be allowed to decide how much formula to take at each feed, in other words to feed to appetite. It is normal for your baby to drink more formula at some feeds than at others. Feeding to appetite means that your baby learns to recognise when he or she feels full.

Initially, newborn babies may feed every 2–3 hours. By around 2 months many babies are feeding about every 4 hours and some even manage without a night feed. If you are lucky, from around 2 months your baby may start sleeping 6–7 hours overnight, obtaining all nutrition in 5–6 feeds a day.

For the first 6 months your baby should be taking 150–200 ml of formula per 1 kg (or 70–90 ml per lb). For example, a baby weighing 5 kg should take 750–1,000 ml (150/200 ml multiplied by 5) in 24 hours. It is normal for some babies to take slightly more than this, some a little less.

What position should my baby be in during a bottle feed?

You baby should be held in a supportive, semi-upright position which encourages eye contact and bonding. It is good to alternate the side you hold your baby for feeds — if you use your right arm for the first feed use the left arm for the next and so on.

How long should it take my baby to drink a bottle?

About 20 minutes is the right length of time for a feed but some babies are slow feeders and others fast. The flow of milk from the teat and wind are two factors that may affect your baby's feeding.

'How to Prepare your Baby's Bottle Feed' is a booklet produced by the Food Safety Promotion Board and the HSE. It is available to download from *www.safefood.eu* or phone 1850 404567 to order a free copy.

BREASTFEEDING

The Department of Health and Children is working to encourage breastfeeding and make it the natural choice for the vast majority of Irish parents.

Breastfeeding may be 'natural' but for most women it is a skill you and baby will need to learn — sometimes a mum and brand new baby can just get it together with no problems at all, but most mums report problems with latching on and getting the positioning right so that the baby is getting what they need without causing mum pain.

For the first couple of days in hospital it will feel like your baby is sucking on an empty breast (he is actually getting the wonder food colostrum), then on the third day or so your milk will 'come in'. All of a sudden your breasts are like footballs and positively bursting with milk. As I said in the previous chapter, this engorgement is not a permanent state (thank goodness, because it can hurt!) and it does pass once your supply and your baby's demand for milk has settled down into a natural balance.

The best way to recover quickly from engorgement is to feed your baby on demand for the first few days and offer both breasts at each feed. This will mean that you get relief from both breasts which will be stimulated to make milk and establish a good milk supply. If your breasts are extremely full, your tiny baby may find it hard to latch on, but expressing some milk first can help. Ask for help with this.

Wearing a nursing bra with a clip-open front 24 hours a day will also give your milk-producing boobs some support when they are three times their normal size.

If you choose to stay in hospital for a few days you may experience engorgement while you are still there, which will give you a chance to ask for help from midwives or a hospital lactation consultant. However, if you leave on an Early Transfer Home Scheme or have a home birth, your milk may come in after you go home. If this is the case, ask the visiting midwife for help and advice. Some women hire lactation consultants to help them get the hang of breastfeeding in the early days.

Although it may seem hard to believe, if you can get through the first few weeks of breastfeeding, your milk supply will balance out so that you are producing just the right amount for your baby and both of you will start to settle into something resembling a routine. Also it's comforting to know that a newborn baby who feeds 12 times a day in the first few weeks will settle down to five to seven feeds at three months, so having your boobs out at what seems like hourly intervals doesn't last all that long.

Many women worry they don't have enough milk for their baby because they cannot measure it, but if your baby seems contented and is putting on weight, everything is fine. For most mums it is about having confidence in their ability to feed their baby.

Most of the problems mums have with breastfeeding are caused by their baby not latching on properly. Don't be afraid to ask for help with breastfeeding — if it hurts then something must be wrong. Sore or cracked nipples are quite normal, but don't ignore them — try using a lanolin cream, putting cabbage leaves in your bra and ask your public health nurse or lactation consultant for help.

Attending a local breastfeeding group once you are settled back at home will introduce you to other breastfeeding mums, and you can talk about issues that may be worrying you. The nurse or counsellor can help you to get the technique right, overcome problems such as sore nipples and mastitis and will weigh your baby, too, which helps you to know that he is gaining weight and doing well on your milk. Oh, and you can feed your baby in the group, so no worries there.

Some good tips I got from my group were good discreet places to breastfeed in public, what kind of clothes to buy (long tops which can be lifted up), how to feed so no-one can see your breasts and your baby hides your belly and how to put the baby on the breast before she starts screaming for milk. If you are out and about hardly anyone will notice you are breastfeeding unless your baby is screaming his head off to get in your bra.

One issue we discussed quite a lot was leaky boobs — your breasts seem to have a life of their own and can catch you out. It's hard to believe but the cry of a baby (not even your own) can cause your breasts to leak milk, called the 'let-down' reflex. Sometimes if your baby comes off your breast during a feed, his little face can be sprayed with milk, or the breast you are not feeding from will leak milk, and other times your boobs can just drip, leaving milky stains on your clothes.

Breast pads that sit in your bra will catch leaks — you can buy disposable or washable ones. It's also a good idea to carry a spare top in case you are caught out and find you have two dark wet patches. Leaky boobs should settle down with time.

There has not been a strong tradition of breastfeeding in Ireland and many mothers (including, possibly, your own) do not know enough about it. If you want to breastfeed your baby, ask your partner for his support and don't be pressured by the opinions of others. This is your baby and you can feed him how you see best.

To get you started here are the basics of breastfeeding:

- Sit down on a hard-backed chair or upright against a firm headboard on your bed with your baby and a pillow. Lie your baby on the pillow and turn him onto his side so that his tummy is against yours. His nose should be in line with your nipple and you shouldn't have to lean over for him to latch on. If you do, you're in for backache and sore nipples as your baby will hang off your nipple.

- Support your breast by placing your hand underneath it, with your thumb up and put your other hand under your baby's head so that you can move him towards you at the right level. When you move the baby towards the breast his upper lip should touch your nipple first and he will automatically open his mouth wide. Now aim your nipple at the top of his mouth. Your baby should take all of your areola (the dark bit) into his mouth — if he only takes in your nipple, it will be painful. If you don't get the positioning right first time, you can take him off by putting your clean little finger into the edge of his mouth, breaking the suction. When you have the position right, he will suck in a rhythm and may take short rests while still latched on.

- Once you get the hang of breastfeeding you will find that you can do it lying down, especially good when you are exhausted, and use a variety of different positions. Feeding while lying down is also good after a c-section.

Because it can take a while to feed a new baby — many mums say a feed followed by winding and a new nappy takes about an hour — I'd like to make a few recommendations. Park yourself on the sofa with your favourite TV programme or DVD, have that newspaper or book you haven't found time to read at the ready, have a few healthy snacks in a bowl within reach, make sure you have the phone in case anyone rings and you can't move, and have a large glass of water available to sip. And go to the toilet before you start the whole process.

Breastfeeding Help

Check out the HSE breastfeeding website *www.breastfeeding.ie* for useful information about help in your local area, which is usually available from public health nurses, GPs, voluntary Cuidiú Breast-feeding Counsellors, La Leche League Leaders or lactation consultants.

Help during your hospital stay and after you have gone home is available from qualified lactation consultants working in the hospital or at drop-in clinics. Ask your hospital for information.

National Maternity Hospital, Breastfeeding support service Mon, Wed, Fri, 10 a.m–12.30 p.m. by appointment.
Phone 01 637 3251

Coombe Women and Infants University Hospital
For info, phone 408 5287 or 4085200 and bleep 199 Monday to Friday 7.30–9 p.m.
For info, phone 4085214 Monday to Friday 9 a.m.–12.30 p.m.

The Rotunda Hospital
Breastfeeding support group meets Thursday 11.30 a.m.–12.30 p.m.
Phone 01 817 1700

University College Hospital Galway
Breastfeeding helpline, phone 091 54551
Lactation consultant weekly drop in clinic Wednesday 2–4 p.m. in St Angela's lecture room. To book, phone 091 893470.

Cork University Maternity Hospital
Rebecca O'Donovan, Lactation Consultant, phone 087 662 3874

For advice on breastfeeding once you have been discharged from the hospital, or for those who had home births, check out *www.lalecheleagueireland.com*, the association for breastfeeding mums who have informal monthly meetings in 40 groups across the country as well as telephone and one-to-one advice.

www.cuidiu-ict.ie: The Irish Childbirth Trust (Cuidiú) run breast-feeding support groups co-ordinated by trained counsellors. 01 8724501 They can supply you with an up-to-date list of breastfeeding counsellors.

www.alcireland.ie: Association of Lactation Consultants Ireland
E-mail: *alci@ireland.com*

INFANT COLIC

Colic can be very worrying for parents. Your baby might cry for long periods of time, and you won't be able to soothe him and he may be restless and unable to settle. Colic can affect babies from as young as three weeks, before stopping after a few months. What causes colic is unknown, but it's certainly not down to anything you are doing wrong.

Your baby may have colic if he cries for long periods at a time, three or more days a week and this tends to happen in the early evening, if he arches his back, pulls his legs up to his stomach, clenches his hands, his face goes red and he looks in pain and passes wind.

Unfortunately, there is no known 'cure' for colic other than time, but there are a number of things you can do to help your baby. The first step is to take him to see your GP to make sure that he is in good health.

One cause of colic could be the amount of gas or air he is taking in. If you are bottlefeeding try using a curved bottle to limit the amount of air your baby is swallowing when feeding. If you are breastfeeding, try to avoid eating any foods that may produce wind, such as beans, cabbage or onions — you may want to discuss this with your public health nurse. Make sure you spend enough time burping your baby after a feed as he may still be full of wind.

As well as trying these ideas, your baby will need lots of reassurance during an episode of crying. Bring him into a quiet and semi-dark room to reduce stimulation, wrap him in a blanket and walk around slowly to calm him. Some colicky babies react well to a walk in their pram or the car, rocking in your arms in a rocking chair or being given a gentle tummy massage. Another tip is to let your baby listen to white noise (this trick works on many small babies who have difficulty settling) — the dishwasher or washing machine is a good one.

Your baby will grow out of colic, but this can be a difficult time, so please ask others for help. If you are worried about your baby's colic, talk to your public health nurse, midwife or GP. In certain cases, the GP may suggest a course of simethicone or lactase drops. However, if your baby's colic is not severe, time will make all the difference.

The Six-Week Check

When your baby is six weeks' old, you should both be seen by your GP, hospital doctor or midwife. I have to say that I dreaded this appointment as I feared my GP would want to look at me 'down there', but my fears were unfounded.

At this check your baby is weighed, measured and generally checked over. Your GP or the hospital doctor or midwife will also advise on vaccinations. Then he or she may do something alarming with your little baby's legs, rotating them in what looks like an uncomfortable movement. This is to check for 'congenital dislocation of the hip' (CDH). If your baby has CDH it can be corrected using a harness during the first three months before the hip joint fully develops.

Then your doctor will ask how you feel, whether your stitches have healed and if you have had sex yet. You might wonder if he is joking and most women I know have told me that this is totally unrealistic when they are getting no sleep, still recovering from the birth and breastfeeding, which can decrease libido too. Don't worry about this too much at the moment, it will sort itself out in time. Your doctor is simply ensuring that you realise you could get pregnant soon after birth.

Call your doctor straight away if your baby:

- Has a temperature
- Has diarrhoea
- Has a stiff neck
- Is vomiting much more than usual
- Has a temperature and rash
- Is limp and his skin feels cold
- Never give your baby medication other than a short course of Calpol for a cold etc., unless specifically instructed by your GP.

Sudden Infant Death Syndrome (SIDS, or Cot Death)

It's heartbreaking for parents to even think about losing their little baby to SIDS, let alone it actually happening. The rate of SIDS in Ireland has declined from 2.3 per 1,000 live births (134 deaths per year) in the 1980s to 0.55 per 1,000 live births (34 deaths) in 2004. This is a drop of 76% and can be largely put down to advice given to parents to place babies to sleep on their backs. These are the latest guidelines from the National Sudden Infant Death Register, Temple Street Children's Hospital. Helpline 1850 391 391/ *www.sidsireland.ie*.

1 Always place your baby to sleep on his back.

2 Keep your baby in a smoke-free zone at all times and do not smoke during pregnancy.

3 The safest place for your baby to sleep at night is in a cot in your room for the first six months.

4 Place your baby with his feet to the foot of the cot.

5 Do not let your baby get too hot and keep his/her head uncovered while sleeping.

6 Do not fall asleep in bed with your baby if you or your partner:

- are a smoker (even if you never smoke in bed);

- have drunk alcohol or taken drugs;

- are excessively tired or have taken medication that makes you sleep more heavily;

Or if your baby:

- is less than three months of age;

- was born prematurely (less than 37 weeks);

- was low birth weight (less than 2.5 kg).

7 Never fall asleep with a baby on a sofa or armchair.

8 If your baby is unwell, seek medical advice promptly.

Less than 1 in every 1,000 babies born die from cot death, so please don't let worrying about it stop you enjoying your baby's first few months.

The Irish Sudden Infant Death Association also run support groups. Phone 01 8732711
www.isida.ie

YOUR EMOTIONAL WELLBEING

Postnatal Depression

Life as you know it will change utterly after your baby is born, but the vast majority of women with new babies do not develop postnatal depression, even though the first few weeks and months can be tough.

While it's hard to pinpoint exactly what causes PND, it's not difficult to see how exhaustion and huge pressure can contribute to feelings of not coping. A sense of not being in control and a lack of routine can be distressing for many women, combined with being stuck at home with a crying baby while your partner goes out to work, a total loss of freedom and trying to establish breastfeeding — for many of us it's the toughest experience of our lives.

What doesn't help is when we see images of celebrities looking slim and glowing only days after birth, who seem to be able to pick up their lives where they left off. These unrealistic images of motherhood only make us feel inadequate and a failure. Having good support during this time can make a huge difference, and women who are isolated from their families can find it even tougher. Also, if you've suffered from depression in the past you are more likely to develop PND.

According to current evidence, your likelihood of developing PND is not related to complications at birth or hormonal changes afterwards. However, a woman may dwell on a difficult birth and develop post-traumatic stress. Postnatal depression affects 14–15% of mums in the western world and the main risk factors are a woman's coping mechanisms, her relationship with her partner and socio-economic factors.

Apart from the very real psychological symptoms of PND such as despair, feelings of inadequacy, chronic anxiety, lack of interest in life and suicidal thoughts, there are physical symptoms too. Feeling dizzy or faint, having pains in the chest and suffering headaches are all associated with PND, although a woman may feel they indicate something much more serious, like a life-threatening disease, due to her heightened sense of anxiety. Some women think they are going mad, have nightmares and panic attacks and feel there is something wrong with them because they cannot love their baby.

Many women who recover from PND worry about the effect their illness had or may have on their child, but quick recognition and treatment can help to re-establish the bond between mum and baby more quickly.

Postnatal Depression Ireland runs support groups in Cork Maternity Hospital and can put mums in touch with women around the country who have recovered from PND. They also have a support line and online forum.

PND is a medical illness — if you develop PND, it's not your fault. There are good treatments and support is hugely important.

The advice below comes from PND Ireland.

For further information contact them at *support@pnd.ie* or call 021 4923162.

DOS AND DON'TS

- Do take every opportunity to get your head down and sleep. Try to learn the knack of cat-napping.

- Don't blame yourself or your partner: life is tough at this time and tiredness and irritability on both sides can lead to quarrels.

- Do get enough nourishment and consider taking a multivitamin.

- Do find the time to have fun with your partner. Try to find a babysitter and get out together.

- Do let yourself and your partner be intimate, even if you don't yet feel like sex: at least kiss and cuddle.

- Do take life one day at a time. Try to find the positive in things.

- Do try to get some exercise every day, even if it is only a short walk around the block.

- Don't put yourself in situations that could be potentially stressful.

- Do talk to your GP and public health nurse — they are there to help you.

- Do keep a diary and write down how you feel — try to include some positive statements too.

- If things are really bad in the middle of the night and you have nobody to talk to, ring the Samaritans on 1850 609090.

- Consult your public health nurse, GP or support group for advice.

YOUR SEX LIFE

You may feel that once your baby has reached the six-week stage, you should start to have sex with your partner again, and some GPs will ask you whether you have 'done it' at your six-week check. However, many new mums will not have fully recovered from the birth yet, especially if you had a tear, an episiotomy or caesarean section, may feel too exhausted thanks to constant feeding, or simply not in the mood. This is all perfectly normal, and you shouldn't feel rushed into getting back to normal after such a life-changing event as having a baby.

The important thing right now is for you and your partner to keep talking and to continue to be loving towards one another. If you feel ready, then by all means try it, but don't feel bad if you just don't want to right now.

Couples wanting to get back in the saddle should take it very slowly, use a lubricant and not put themselves under any pressure to perform. Don't forget to use contraception as you could get pregnant now, even if you are breastfeeding. While it's important to try not to tense up with nerves, you may find that sex hurts the first few times you do it. Don't worry — this isn't permanent.

Many women find that doing pelvic floor exercises helps to tone up their vaginal area and makes sex more pleasurable after a baby.

Don't worry if first-time sex after the birth of your beautiful baby is less than amazing — it can take time for both of you to re-establish your physical connection, but as your baby settles into some sort of routine and you both get some well-needed rest you will get your sex lives back.

REAL STORIES

'When my daughter was two weeks old, I got mastitis in one breast and was very weepy, tired and sore. The infection cleared up after a week of antibiotics, but all my energy was drained for weeks afterwards. During the following six weeks, the breastfeeding established itself to meet baby's demand, so the initial engorgement calmed down.'
Nuala

'I found the recovery from the c-section quite difficult and my partner's help was invaluable. Luckily he had taken three weeks off work to be here when the baby was born. The first six weeks seemed to go by quite slowly, mainly because of the fact that I couldn't drive and do any difficult housework or cook. Within a couple of weeks I made it out to the weekly breastfeeding clinic run by the local public health nurses and found this of great benefit. I breastfed on demand and found this fine: she was a hungry baby in the first few weeks and fed every couple of hours. As I settled into it so did she and I found she naturally pushed her feeds out as the weeks passed.'
Ruth

'The first week at home was OK but tiring as I was run down from having a section. I thought I was superwoman and only I could look after the baby and do everything else. The third day at home my hormones got the better of me and I actually cried for a full day in bed. My partner took the baby out to let me get some rest — I was told it's normal to get weepy after birth and it was like a load off my chest and I felt much better. I stayed in for a week and after that started going out and about with the baby. It is overwhelming everyone calling to see the baby and I was very protective of people wanting to pick him up and touch him.'
Leanne

'At eight weeks I had a check-up with my consultant (with whom I had attended antenatal appointments as a private patient) and everything had healed very well, but I got the shock of my life when she asked me why had I not had intercourse yet? I was still very sore at this point — she did an internal and I was nearly glued to the wall with the pain! Thankfully all was normal.'
Nuala

'When my daughter was two weeks old and feeding about ten times a day my nipples were in agony — latching her on was excruciatingly painful. Soaking my breasts in warm water in the bath gave me some relief and I used a lanolin cream, which is safe for breastfeeding. I also sent my husband out to buy water-filled pads which can be put in the fridge for a while, then on your breasts. Then a neighbour suggested cabbage leaves, which amazingly did help. Saying that, I did use shields to get through that really difficult week to give my nipples a chance to heal, but after a few days was able to put them away. I was warned it could give my baby nipple confusion and she would reject the breast if I used them, but they worked out OK to get through a difficult patch.'
Lucy

Some Advice for Dad

You're a dad! And just as the thrill and relief of the birth starts to wear off and both you and your partner are struggling with a lack of sleep and non-stop baby demands, the daunting realisation that you are responsible for this little life hits you like a smack in the head. While new mums have told me that in the early weeks they worry about caring for their little baby down to the minute details of feeding, changing, bathing, sleep and so on, new dads seem to go around with a haunted look in their eyes, and they've told me it's all down to worry.

After all the worry throughout the pregnancy, you will most probably worry about whether you will be a good father, how your relationship with your partner will change, how you will cope with work, childcare, social lives and, the biggie — finances. It seems new dads worry about money most of all as they add up how much this small person is going to cost them over the next 20 years or so.

Stop! Try not to obsess about might-bes and enjoy these early weeks as much as you can. It's perfectly normal to worry, but the more you talk to your partner about how you will handle this time, the more you will be able to enjoy spending time with your baby. Talking to other dads about how they cope will also help you to realise that all of these feelings are normal and an important part of parenthood. Being concerned is not a sign of weakness, more about taking responsibility and growing into your role as a father.

Adam Brophy, in his book *The Bad Dad's Survival Guide,* says that new babies mean less sleep, more slavery, unsympathetic friends and that when a new mum comes home with your baby it can be something of a letdown.

My advice for all new dads is to knuckle down in the early weeks and months — it isn't going to be easy for either mum or dad. A new baby means upheaval and tons of work, so why not share it and still be on speaking terms at the end of the day. Here's what some new mums have told me they'd like their partner to do in the first few weeks:

- Don't just offer to help — pick the baby up and change his nappy, hang a load of washing, cook dinner, anything would be appreciated.

- Do not ask for sex, it's the last thing on our minds right now. Sorry about that one. It doesn't last forever — honest!

- Don't abandon us and head to the pub — we'll be reminding you of this crime for the rest of your life.

- Don't snore when we're breastfeeding in the middle of the night — it makes us want to kill you.

A FINAL NOTE FOR MUM

The first six weeks of your baby's life will pass in something of a blur, and then one day you will notice that things have somehow become a little easier. You have become more confident as a new mum and your baby has settled. Now is the time to give yourself a pat on the back — you've done it!

Chapter 9 ⟋

EXTRACTS FROM THE CUIDIÚ CONSUMER GUIDE TO MATERNITY SERVICES

The information in this chapter comes from the current *Cuidiú Consumer Guide to Maternity Services* and is reproduced with thanks to them.

'Cuidiú (The Irish Childbirth Trust) means "caring support" in Irish. It is a parent-to-parent community-based voluntary support group. On 18 December 2007 Cuidiú launched an updated *Consumer Guide to Maternity Services in Ireland* on its national website (*http://www.cuidiu-ict.ie/* and click on 'Consumer Guide'). The Guide provides comprehensive information on policies and practices alongside comparison tables for maternity units nationwide.

'The Guide is a user-friendly "one-stop shop", aimed at providing practical information and support for parents regarding all aspects of maternity services in the Republic and is an update to Cuidiú's 1999 *Consumer Guide*. Cuidiú has expanded this edition to provide very comprehensive hospital information and statistics. All hospital statistics relate to the year 2005 and the policies and practices documents, on the Cuidiú website, are relevant to 2007, so they may have changed since then.' (Cuidiú plans to update its consumer guide in spring/summer 2011.)

'Late in 2006 Cuidiú sent an e-mail questionnaire to all 22 hospital units and the two Midwifery-Led Units (MLUs) seeking details of their practices and policies. Cuidiú did not set out to find a best maternity unit or service. That depends so much on an individual woman's wishes, but to provide an overview of hospital policies and practices.

'All data was provided by the hospitals and percentages were calculated by Cuidiú. There are obvious differences in the data-collection systems in the maternity services across the State. Some units were able to provide very comprehensive statistics, whilst others could only provide the most basic figures.

'The next section comprises Cuidiú information on what you might typically experience going through the Irish maternity services and their analysis of the data provided by the hospitals and MLUs. Unless otherwise stated the information relates to what to expect with a straightforward pregnancy and birth — obviously complications may alter circumstances.'

ANTENATAL CARE

According to the Cuidiú research, 'You can book directly with some hospitals or clinics although some units require a letter of referral so you may need to visit your GP first. If your local maternity unit is busy, it is advisable to make contact with the hospital early in pregnancy.

'At around 12 to 14 weeks you will have your first clinic appointment at the hospital/unit, known as the Booking Clinic (although this changes depending on where you live and how busy the hospital is). The usual tests offered at this appointment include blood tests, blood pressure, urine tests and sometimes a weight check. Ultrasound scans are offered at different times and frequencies in different patterns of care and in different units. In general there is at least one scan offered early in pregnancy. At the booking clinic you can inform your carers whether or not you are opting for combined care with your GP.'

LABOUR

'When you arrive at the hospital in labour you will be met by a midwife who will take you through the admission procedure. This usually includes noting your account of how labour started, checking your temperature, pulse, blood pressure and urine. The midwife will offer to feel your abdomen to find out the baby's position and will listen to the baby's heart. You will probably be offered an internal examination to assess how labour is progressing. In many hospitals, but not all, it is still routine practice to monitor the baby's heart rate using an external electronic (belt) monitor for 20 to 30 minutes soon after arriving at the hospital. Alternatives include offering women intermittent monitoring (using hand-held devices) which is less restrictive in terms of positions and movement.

'In most busy units the accommodation in early labour is in a communal room with more than one bed. Your partner/birth companion will be welcome to stay with you but may be asked to leave occasionally when staff are carrying out rounds or procedures. This is to ensure the privacy of other women in the ward.

'For as long as you are comfortable, which may be throughout your entire labour, you will be encouraged to walk. This is because movement helps you cope with labour and gravity helps to keep your labour progressing when you are upright. You will have access to a bath or a shower for washing, but very few units have ensuite facilities.

'You may have the baby's father as your birth companion or you may choose someone else such as your mother, sister or friend. Many, but not all, hospitals restrict you to only one birth companion unless there are special circumstances and prior arrangements have been made. If you wish to have more than one person with you, for any reason, you should negotiate this with your caregivers before your labour.

'Once you are in established labour there may be restrictions in what you eat and drink depending on hospital policy. Hospitals differ quite a lot in this area. Policies range from 'whatever you want', through 'light diet', to 'fluids only' and even to 'ice only' in one unit. Remember, you don't have to comply with something that doesn't feel right to you.

'You may find that you can manage your labour with the support of your birth companion and the midwife. They can assist you with changes of position, breathing techniques, massage and psychological support. Methods of pain relief for labour vary from hospital to hospital but Transcutaneous Electrical Nerve Stimulation (TENS), Entonox (Gas and Air), Pethidine and Epidural anaesthesia appear to be widely available. Only a few units offer alternative therapies (e.g. reflexology, acupuncture, homeopathy, hypnotherapy, aromatherapy etc.) or facilitate an alternative therapy practitioner to accompany you.

'Figures provided for epidural usage appeared to have been recorded differently in different units. Some units did not appear to include women who used epidural in labour but who subsequently had a Caesarean birth. Other units appear to have reported all labouring women who used this form of pain relief regardless of how they ultimately gave birth. The graph shows the figures as reported and therefore direct comparisons may not be useful.

'Almost all hospitals stated that they facilitate a wide variety of labouring positions. However, not all of these units had the birthing aids (floor mats, bean bags, birth balls etc.) required to really make this possible.

'Birthing pools are available in two units for labouring only and two more units have pools but are not utilising them yet. Currently babies are not born underwater in Irish hospitals.

'If your labour is normal you will be offered intermittent monitoring of the baby's heartbeat by Pinard's Stethoscope or Sonicaid. The criteria for continuous monitoring depends on the hospital policy or the individual obstetrician. However, if you have an epidural, Pethidine, or if there is any other condition or complication, continuous electronic monitoring may be recommended.

'Many hospitals (but not all) set time limits for each stage of labour (Active Management of Labour). In order to meet these time limits, you may be offered the use of a Syntocinon drip to artificially speed up labour. You do not have to agree to this.'

BIRTH

'You usually give birth in the same single room where you and your birth companion spend the latter part of your labour. Birthing beds are available in some units and many hospitals stated a flexible approach to the position in which a mother gives birth.

'*Note: the figures given in the paragraphs below are based on data provided by the hospitals. Not every unit provided figures for all categories and averages were based on those that did respond. In particular, only about half of the units' surveys provided data for first-time mothers.*

'You are likely to have a normal (spontaneous vaginal) birth. In 2005 about 60% of women gave birth this way. The figures for first-time mothers was lower — 46%.

'In 2005 almost 15% of mothers had an assisted birth by vacuum or forceps. The figures for first-time mothers is quite a bit higher — just over 27%.

'Episiotomies are still very common in some units in Ireland.

'In 2005 over 25% of mothers gave birth via Caesarean Section. First-time mothers had a higher rate again in this category — 27%. Your partner usually accompanies you in the operating theatre if the

Caesarean Section is under an epidural or spinal anaesthetic, but usually not where a general anaesthetic is used.

'After your baby is born you will probably be offered an injection to speed up the delivery of the placenta, which necessitates that the cord is cut promptly (Active Management of the third stage of labour). Some units facilitate natural third-stage management (which means that they give the placenta time to come away naturally and the cord is not cut until it stops pulsating). In some hospitals the father cuts the umbilical cord if he requests to do so.

'Skin-to-skin contact has been shown to regulate a baby's breathing and temperature, help get breastfeeding off to a good start and to enhance bonding between mother and baby. Most units actively encourage it in the hour after birth. However, only six units stated that mothers and babies remain together in the recovery room if the birth has been by Caesarean Section.

'Hospital policies vary in relation to the administration of Vitamin K for the baby but it is your choice whether your baby receives it by injection (one dose) or orally (three doses) or not at all.'

POSTNATAL

'On the postnatal ward, you will be shown how to bathe your baby and change nappies, how to care for the umbilical cord and keep your baby warm. You will be encouraged to breastfeed and offered support, which will include assistance with early feeds and showing you positions for breastfeeding. (If you choose to formula feed, you will be shown how to safely make up and store bottles of formula. You may choose the brand of formula milk you prefer.)

'In most hospitals you can obtain something to eat between your evening meal and breakfast. In some hospitals a microwave is available for something more substantial to be prepared, which you may need, especially if you are breastfeeding.

'Usually a physiotherapist will see you on the postnatal ward and give you advice on suitable exercises to assist in postnatal recovery. (Most hospitals have a Stress Incontinence Programme for those women who have longer-term pelvic floor problems.)

'The heel-prick test for metabolic disorders (PKU/Guthrie Test) is done on your baby four or five days after birth either in hospital or in the community. Depending on where you live in the country you may be offered an opportunity to have your baby immunised against tuberculosis with the BCG vaccine in the hospital or in the community.

'Visiting arrangements vary widely and can be found in each unit's policies-and-practices document (on *www.cuidiu-ict.ie*). Generally speaking, partners can visit at any time during the day or evening.

'If this is your first baby you can opt to stay in hospital for around three days if you have had a vaginal birth and around five days if you have had a Caesarean birth. Your stay is typically shorter if you have had a baby before. Early-discharge schemes are available in some units.

AT HOME

'The hospital will notify your local Public Health Nurse of your baby's birth. She will visit you and your baby within a few days and will be able to offer you support and information. The Public Health Nurse, many of whom are also qualified midwives, will maintain contact with you throughout your baby's early childhood.

'When you leave the hospital your GP will usually have been informed, but you might like to let him/her know you and the baby are home. The community health care professionals — Public Health Nurse, Area Medical Officer, GP and sometimes a Practice Nurse — offer a number of services to the new mother and her baby, e.g. baby clinics, advice and encouragement with breastfeeding, immunisation. Voluntary organisations like Cuidiú — Irish Childbirth Trust and La Leche League also provide valuable breastfeeding support.

'Most hospitals stated that they continue to offer support for up to six weeks after your baby's birth. This may take the form of: emergency 24-hour mother-and-baby services, a drop-in baby clinic, breastfeeding clinic or telephone contact person/helpline.

'You will have a postnatal check-up when your baby is about six weeks old — done at the hospital or with your GP. This is done to assess your recovery from the pregnancy and childbirth. A cervical smear test is available three months after the birth or when breastfeeding has ceased.'

VAGINAL BIRTH AFTER CAESAREAN (VBAC)

'As there are varying policies in different units regarding VBAC (Vaginal Birth After Caesarean), if you wish to try for a normal labour after a previous birth by Caesarean Section, you should discuss your options fully with your caregiver. Few hospitals were able to provide figures for VBACS.

'The increasing rate of Caesarean birth (17.8% reported for 1998 in the last *Consumer Guide*, versus 25.4% for 2005 figures provided by hospitals for this *Guide*) and in particular the high rate of first-time mothers (average 28.5% for those units that provided figures, with one unit at 35.6%) who give birth this way means that more and more women will require VBAC services including support and encouragement to give birth vaginally subsequently.'

SPECIAL CARE FOR BABIES

'Many hospitals have intensive care facilities, known as NICU (Neonatal Intensive Care Unit) or SCBU (Special Care Baby Unit). These units care for very small, premature or ill babies. The number of special-care cots in the hospital and whether or not there is a full-time Paediatrician or Neonatologist is shown in the unit's policies-and-practices document on the Cuidiú website.

'Some hospitals have a room where parents may stay if the baby is in NICU and this may be important if you live a long way from the hospital. Every hospital has stated that a mother wishing to breastfeed her baby in NICU or SCBU will have the following: encouragement; additional support; training in hand expression; training in the use of pumps; storage facilities for milk; use of the hospital electric pump. Some hospitals have a quiet room available for expressing milk and/or the loan of a breast pump for home use.'

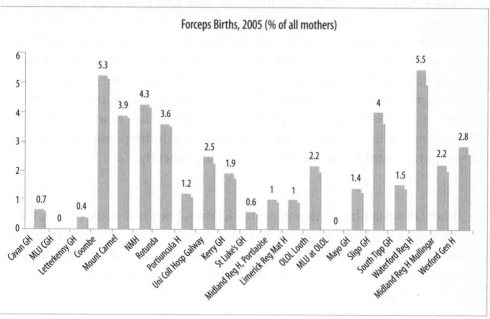

Forceps Births, 2005 (% of all mothers)

MLU CGH — Midwifery-led Unit, Cavan General Maternity Hospital
MLU at OLOL — Midwifery-led Unit, Our Lady of Lourdes, Drogheda

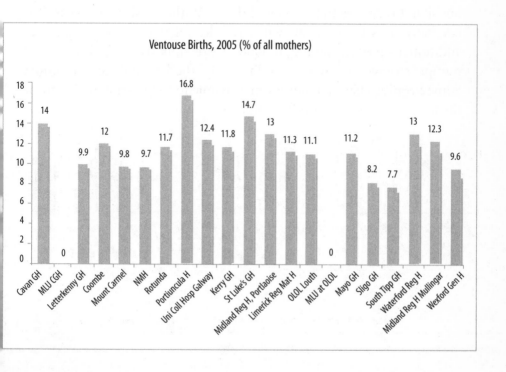

Ventouse Births, 2005 (% of all mothers)

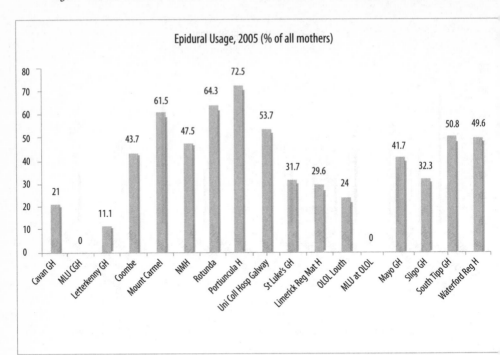

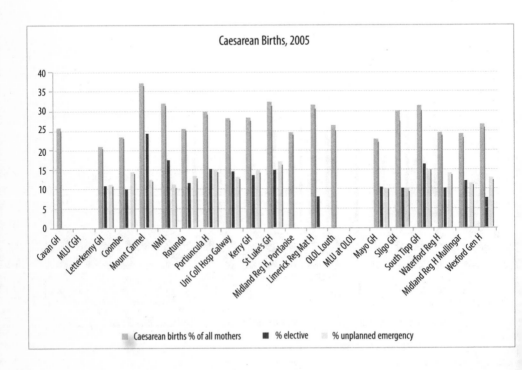

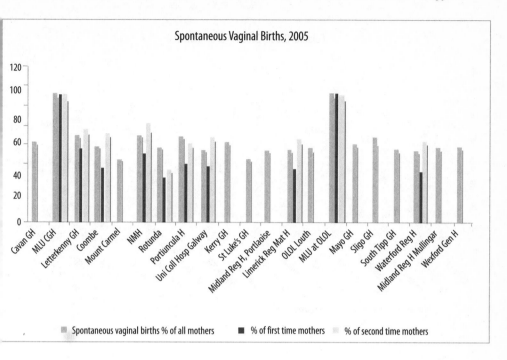

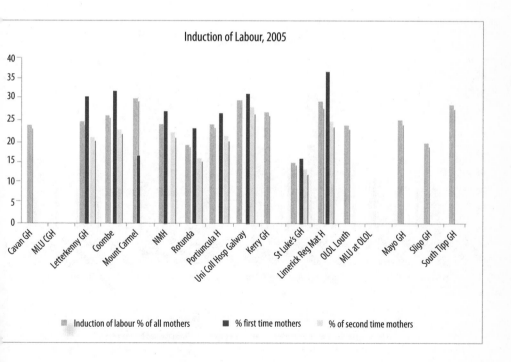

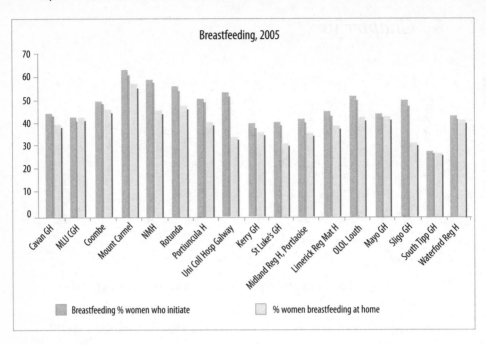

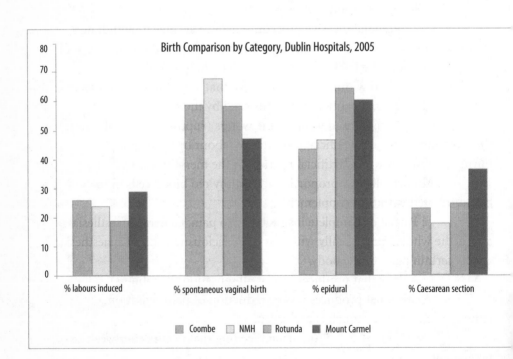

Chapter 10 ~

EUMOM GLOSSARY OF TERMS

A

Abruptio placentae: See *Placental separation*. Also known as placental abruption.

Adrenaline: Hormone that affects heart and circulation, metabolism and smooth muscles.

Afterbirth: The *placenta* and the membranes.

Amniocentesis: Prenatal invasive procedure using a syringe to withdraw a small amount of *amniotic fluid* through the abdominal and the uterine wall for examination of the fetal *chromosomes* or fetal lung maturity.

Amniotic fluid: Fluid within the amniotic sac that surrounds and protects the developing fetus; it contains fetal cells shed by the fetus.

Amniotomy: A method used to break the waters (rupture the membranes) that surround the baby, artificially, to induce labour or for diagnostic purposes. Also known as 'artificial rupture of the membranes' (AROM).

Anaemia: Abnormally low proportion of healthy red blood cells in the blood. Treated with iron supplements.

Anaesthesia: Partial or complete insensibility to pain. General anaesthesia affects the whole body, usually with loss of consciousness. Local anaesthesia affects certain parts of the body.

Anaesthetic: A drug that produces loss of all sensation (numbness).

Analgesic: A drug that produces loss or reduction of pain sensation, although sensitivity to touch is preserved.

Antepartum haemorrhaging: Antenatal bleeding that occurs after week 28 of pregnancy.

Anticardiolipin: Antibodies that can cause pregnancy losses and blood-clotting problems.

Apgar scores: See *Apgar test*.

Apgar test: A test carried out on a newborn at one and five minutes after birth to check heart rate/beat, breathing, muscle tone/movements, skin colour/tone and reflexes.

Artificial rupture of the membranes: See *Amniotomy*.

Augmentation: Acceleration of labour, usually by an *oxytocin* drip and AROM.

B

Baby blues: A condition characterised mainly by feeling down after giving birth and which passes days or a week or so later.

Basal body temperature: Temperature taken each morning at the same time. During the second part of the cycle (after ovulation), the basal body temperature is slightly higher than during the first part of the cycle.

Bilirubin: Breakdown product of haemoglobin in the red blood cells, metabolised by the liver. Increased amounts of bilirubin lead to *jaundice*.

Braxton Hicks contractions: 'Rehearsal' contractions. Contractions of the uterus occurring throughout gestation, in most cases only noticed in the ninth month.

Breech position: Presentation of the baby in the uterus with bottom down instead of head down.

C

Caesarean section: An operation where a cut is made through the abdomen and uterus to deliver the baby.

Candida albicans: Fungus that causes a yeast infection in the mucous membranes of the mouth or genitals.

Cardiotocogram: Electronic device to monitor the baby's heartbeat and uterine contractions, placed externally on the abdomen.

Cardiotocograph: See *Cardiotocogram*.

Carpal tunnel syndrome: Accumulation of fluid in the hands, causing pressure on the nerves in the wrist and thus numbness and tingling in the fingers.

Cephalic position: Presentation of the baby in the uterus with the head down.

Cephalopelvic disproportion: State in which the baby's head is larger than the maternal pelvic cavity. Delivery has to be performed by *caesarean section*.

Cerebral palsy: Spastic paralysis caused by a wide variety of damage to the baby's brain, either before or during birth.

Cervical erosion: Redness of the cervix around the lower opening due to injured surface.

Cervical incompetence: Abnormal weakness of the cervix.

Chloasma: Discoloration of the skin, often facial.

Chorion: Outer membraneous tissue enveloping the developing placenta.

Chorionic villus sampling: Prenatal invasive procedure to sample a small amount of chorionic villi (developing into the placenta) to analyse the fetal *chromosomes.*

Chromosomal disorder: A disorder caused by a faulty chromosome.

Chromosomes: Rod-like structures containing *genes* occurring in pairs within the nucleus of each cell. Human cells carry 23 pairs of chromosomes.

Cleft lip or palate: Congenital malformation, 'hare lip'. Treatment by plastic surgery.

Colic (infantile): A condition characterised by severe spasmodic pain in the intestines.

Colostrum: The first milk secreted by the breasts in late pregnancy; changes into mature milk a few days after delivery. Very rich in nutrients and antibodies.

Congenital disorder: A disorder that is present at birth.

Contraction: The regular painful spasms of the muscles of the uterus that occur during labour.

Convulsions: Convulsive seizure or fit.

Cord prolapse: Dangerous situation in which the *umbilical cord* falls into the birth canal and is subsequently compressed by the baby's head so that the oxygen supply is interrupted.

Cot death: *Sudden infant death syndrome (SIDS)*; cause is unknown in at least 50% of cases.

CTG: See *cardiotocogram.*

Cystic fibrosis: Genetic disease, in which changes of the function of various internal enzymes lead to bronchial and digestive problems.

Cystitis: Inflammation of the bladder and the urinary tract, often producing a stinging sensation when urine is passed.

D

D and C: Surgical dilatation (opening) of the cervix, and curettage (removal of the contents) of the uterus.

Decelerations: Slow-down of fetal heartrate measured by *cardiotocograph* or Pinard; can indicate *fetal distress.*

Dehydration: Insufficient water or fluid.

Diabetes: *Diabetes mellitus.* Failure of the body to metabolise glucose, traced by excess sugar in the blood and urine.

Diagnostic test: A test used to detect problems with the baby during pregnancy.

Dichorionic: Multiples having chorions of their own. Dichorionic/dizygotic twins (fraternal twins) are produced by the fertilisation of two different eggs by two different sperm and are no more similar genetically than brothers and sisters.

Dislocated hips: Congenital malformation of the hip joint.

Doppler: The Doppler effect, used to convert the fetal heart rate into sound.

Down's syndrome: Congenital abnormality caused by an additional chromosome 21 (trisomy 21), resulting in distinctly recognisable features.

E

Eclampsia: A condition characterised by symptoms of severe *pre-eclampsia*, followed by fits.

Ectopic pregnancy: A pregnancy that develops outside the uterus.

ECV: See *External cephalic version.*

Endorphins: Substances produced naturally in the body to relieve pain.

Engorgement: Occurs when breasts are congested with milk.

Entonox: Mixture of gas and oxygen, a short-term inhalation *analgesic.*

Epidural: An injection of a local anaesthetic into the epidural space around the spinal cord to provide pain relief during labour.

Epidural block: See *Epidural.*

Episiotomy: A cut at the vaginal opening away from the anus to make it bigger.

External cephalic version: Gentle movement of a body to help to change the presentation of the baby from breech to a head-down position.

External monitor: Device to check fetal well-being through an *external transducer* placed on the mother's abdomen over the area of the fetal heart.

External transducer: Device placed on the mother's abdomen over the area of the fetal heart to monitor fetal heartbeat and the strength of the contractions.

F

Fallopian tube: Tube into which the ripe egg is expelled from the ovary, and through which it travels on to the uterus.

Fetal abnormalities: Structural defects of the unborn child.

Fetal alcohol syndrome: Congenital disorder with mild to moderate intellectual disability and distinct facial features as well as a wide range of malformations, found in babies of mothers who are alcoholic or drink large amounts of alcohol during pregnancy.

Fetal distress: A condition characterised by an abnormal heart rate or the presence of meconium (the baby's first bowel movement) in the amniotic fluid, due to the lack of oxygen supply.

Fetal heart rate (FHR): Frequency of fetal heart beats per minute (normal range is 120–160).

Fetal tissue: Formation of cells derived from the developing fetus.

Fontanelle: A soft area on the baby's head where the skull bones do not fully join together until about 18 months.

Forceps delivery: A method used to assist and ease the baby's head out of the vagina using curved metal tongs.

G

General anaesthesia: Method of achieving complete insensibility to pain, usually causing loss of consciousness.

General anaesthetic: Anaesthetic drug that affects the whole body, usually causing loss of consciousness.

Gene: Segment of the DNA molecule that codes for a single protein, thus carrying genetic information.

Genetic disorder: A disorder caused by a faulty gene.

Gestational diabetes: A type of *diabetes mellitus* occurring during pregnancy. In most cases symptoms disappear after delivery.

Guthrie/heel-prick test: A test carried out on a newborn about a week after birth, where blood is taken from the heel to test for various inherited metabolic disorders including PKU.

H

Habitual abortion: Three or more consecutive *miscarriages* at around the same time during pregnancy for the same reason.

Haemorrhage: Bleeding.

Haemorrhaging: See *Haemorrhage*.

Haemorrhoids: Piles, swelling of the veins around the rectum.

hCG: See *Human chorionic gonadotrophin*.

Heart defect: Congenital malformation of the baby's heart.

Homeopathy: System of alternative medicine that treats disease by prescribing extremely small doses of substances that produce symptoms similar to the disease itself.

Human chorionic gonadotrophin (hCG): A hormone released into the woman's blood by the developing placenta from about 6 days after the last menstrual period was due. Detection in urine is a reliable pregnancy test.

Hydrocephalus: Congenital abnormality of the baby's brain.

Hyperbilirubinaemia: A condition characterised by *jaundice* due to excessive amounts of bilirubin in the blood (bilirubin is a waste product of broken-down red blood cells).

Hyperemesis gravidarum: Very frequent vomiting during pregnancy; can result in dehydration and metabolic imbalance. Hospital treatment is required.

Hypertension: High blood pressure.

Hypnotherapy: Hypnosis. Method of pain relief inducing a mental state of passivity, with a marked susceptibility to suggestion.

I

In-vitro fertilisation: Artificial fertilisation (fusion of sperm and egg) outside of the womb.

Incubator: Closed unit for keeping preterm babies in a warm, moist and — if necessary — oxygen-enriched environment.

Induction: Artificial initiation of labour.

Internal monitor: Device to check fetal well-being through an electrode inserted through the cervix and clipped to the baby's scalp.

Intrapartum haemorrhage: Bleeding that occurs during labour.

Intrauterine death: See *Stillbirth.*

Intrauterine growth restriction: Retarded growth of the baby in the uterus, usually because of placental insufficiency.

Intravenous drip: Infusion of fluids directly into the bloodstream by means of a fine catheter induced into a vein.

J

Jaundice: A condition characterised by yellowing of the skin and whites of the eyes due to the accumulation of bilirubin in the blood (bilirubin is a waste product of broken-down red blood cells).

L

Labour: Three distinct stages of childbirth. The first stage includes the onset of labour to full cervical dilation; the second stage is until delivery of the baby; and the third stage is delivery of the placenta.

Lactation: Production and secretion of breast milk.

Lanugo: Primitive fine hair on the body of the fetus.

Light therapy: See *Phototherapy.*

Linea nigra: Darkened vertical line on the abdomen.

Local anaesthesia: Anaesthetic drug that affects limited parts of the body (like caudal, epidural or paracervical anaesthesia).

Local anaesthetic: See *Local anaesthesia.*

Lochia: Postnatal vaginal discharge of the lining of the womb.

Longitudinal position: Presentation of the fetus in the uterus, where the spine of the fetus and of the mother are parallel.

Low birthweight: A birthweight below 5½ lb (2.5 kg).

Lumbar epidural: See *Epidural.*

M

Meconium: First contents of the bowel, present in the fetus before birth and passed during the first days after birth. The presence of meconium in the *amniotic fluid* can be a sign of fetal distress.

Meningitis: Infection of the cerebral membranes.

Metabolism: Process by which the body uses food to grow, to keep warm and for energy.

Miscarriage: Loss of the baby before week 28 of pregnancy. Also known as spontaneous abortion.

Monochorionic: Multiples sharing the same chorion. Monochorionic/monozygotic twins are derived from one single fertilised egg and are genetically identical.

N

Nappy rash: Sore, red rash in the genital area, caused by bacteria which break down urine and produce ammonia, burning the skin.

Neural tube defects: Abnormalities of the spinal cord, including anencephaly and *spina bifida.*

Nuchal translucency: Fluid accumulation in the area of the fetal neck. Can indicate a chromosome disorder or other fetal abnormalities.

O

Oblique position: Presentation of the fetus, where the spine of the fetus lies at an angle across the uterus.

Obstetric cholestasis: A rare liver condition characterised mainly by a rash and severe itching, and possibly *jaundice*, which occurs during late-stage pregnancy.

Occipitotransverse: Position of the baby in the uterus where the back of its head is towards the side of the pelvis.

Oedema: Fluid retention in tissue, swelling under the skin.

Oestrogen: Hormone produced by the ovaries.

Oxytocin: Hormone secreted by the pituitary gland that stimulates uterine contractions, and also stimulates the milk glands in the breasts to produce milk.

P

Palpitations: Increased heart activity.

Perineum: Area between the vagina and the rectum.

Pethidine: Narcotic *analgesic.*

Phenylalanine: See *Phenylketonuria (PKU)*

Phenylketonuria (PKU): Hereditary metabolic disorder in which a baby cannot break down a protein called phenylalanine; untreated, it builds up in the brain and affects brain development. Can be effectively treated by a phenylalanine-low diet. Is detected with a Guthrie (heel prick) test.

Phototherapy: A method using ultraviolet light to treat *jaundice.* Also known as light therapy.

Pica: Craving for non-edible substances.

Piles: Haemorrhoids — swelling of the veins around the rectum.

Placenta: Organ which develops on the inner wall of the uterus and supplies the fetus with all its life-supporting requirements and carries fetal waste products to the mother's system.

Placenta praevia: A condition characterised by the placenta partially or completely covering the cervix.

Placental abruption: See *Placental separation.* Also known as *abruptio placentae.*

Placental insufficiency: A condition that occurs when the placenta is unable to support the baby adequately.

Placental separation: A condition characterised by the placenta partially or completely separating from the wall of the uterus. Also known as placental abruption or *abruptio placentae.*

Polycystic ovaries: Multiple cysts in the ovaries, often combined with *amenorrhoea* and infertility.

Postepidural: After an *epidural* anaesthesia.

Postmaturity: A pregnancy that lasts more than 42 weeks.

Postnatal depression: A condition characterised by fairly severe depression after giving birth.

Postpartum haemorrhage: Bleeding that occurs after the baby is born.

Pre-eclampsia: A condition characterised mainly by hypertension, protein in the urine and swelling. Also known as pre-eclamptic toxaemia or pregnancy-induced hypertension.

Pre-eclamptic toxaemia: See *Pre-eclampsia.* Also known as pregnancy-induced hypertension.

Pregnancy-induced hypertension: See *Pre-eclampsia.* Also known as pre-eclamptic toxaemia.

Premature labour: Labour that occurs before week 37 of pregnancy.

Premature membrane rupturing: A condition characterised by the waters breaking (membranes rupturing) before time, potentially leading to premature labour and delivery.

Prematurity: Birth of the baby before week 37 of pregnancy.

Prolactin: Hormone which induces milk secretion in the breasts, also usually prevents ovulation.

Prolapsed umbilical cord: A condition characterised by a loop of the umbilical cord bulging out of the vagina.

Prostaglandins: Natural substances which can stimulate the onset of labour contractions. Prostaglandins in gel or tablet form can be used to soften the cervix and to induce labour.

R

Rhesus incompatibility: Rhesus disease in the fetus or newborn, caused by the fact that the mother is Rhesus negative and the fetus Rhesus positive. Prevention is by injection of anti-D gamma globulin after birth.

Rooting reflex: An automatic reflex of a newborn where the baby will turn towards a touch on the cheek with an open mouth.

S

Sciatica: Pain in the area of the sciatic nerve, leading down from the lower back to the legs.

Screening test: A test used to determine the risk of a woman having a baby with an abnormality.

Sex chromosomes: x and y chromosomes. The 23rd pair of chromosomes in females consists of two x chromosomes (xx). The 23rd pair of chromosomes in males consists of one x chromosome and one Y chromosome (xY).

Small-for-dates babies: Babies born with a much lower birthweight than would be appropriate for the given week of pregnancy.

Sonic aid: See *Doppler*.

Spina bifida: Congenital neural tube defect below the brain, in which the fetal spinal cord forms incorrectly.

Spinal anaesthesia: similar to Epidural anaesthesia, but the onset of analgesia is very rapid and a top-up dose cannot easily be given. Used mainly for Caesarean sections.

Stillbirth: Delivery of a dead baby after week 28 of pregnancy. Also known as intrauterine death.

Stress incontinence: Involuntary leakage of urine resulting from weakness in the pelvic floor muscles when abdominal pressure increases.

Suction: Method of extraction or removal of the baby from the birth canal using vacuum.

Sudden infant death syndrome (sIDS): See *Cot death*.

Synthetic oxytocin: Artificial hormone given to stimulate uterine contractions and the milk glands in the breast to produce milk.

Syntocinon: See *Synthetic oxytocin*.

Syntometrine: A combination of synthetic oxytocin and *ergometrine*.

T

Thrombosis: Blood clot in the heart or blood vessels.

Thrush: Fungal infection caused by Candida albicans, usually affecting the mouth and genitals.

Transcutaneous Electrical Nerve Stimulation (TENS): A method of relieving pain during childbirth, using non-painful nerve stimulation.

Trimester: A period of pregnancy lasting roughly three months, with pregnancy being divided into three trimesters.

Trisomy 21: See *Down's syndrome*.

U

Ultrasound scan: A test using sound waves to check the baby and his/her progress during pregnancy, and to guide certain diagnostic tests or operations.

Umbilical cord: Connects the placenta and the fetus. Contains two arteries and one vein.

Urge incontinence: Involuntary leakage of urine caused by a sudden urge to urinate not related to abdominal pressure.

Uterine contractions: See *Contractions*.

Uterine wall: Wall of the uterus.

V

Vacuum extraction: See *Ventouse delivery*.

Ventouse delivery: A method used to ease the baby's head out of the vagina using a rubber cap or metal plate and a vacuum extractor. Also known as vacuum extraction.

Vernix caseosa: White cheese-like substance that covers the fetus in the uterus to protect it in the *amniotic fluid* towards the end of the pregnancy.

Vertex position: See *Cephalic position*.

Villi: Chorionic villi. Layer of tiny fronds out of the outermost fetal membrane which forms around the fertilised egg when it implants into the *uterine wall*, and which later develops into the placenta.

Chapter 11 ～

SUPPORT GROUPS AND USEFUL ADDRESSES

GOVERNMENT WEBSITES

Department of Social Protection
Phone 1890 400 400
http://www.welfare.ie

www.citizensinformation.ie

Equality Authority
Clonmel Street, Dublin 2
Phone 1890 245545
www.equality.ie

Maternity Benefit Section, **Department of Social Protection,**
Inner Relief Road, Ardarvan, Buncrana, Co. Donegal
Phone 1890 690690
www.welfare.ie

Parental Equality (Shared parenting and custody support)
Social Services Building, 15a Clanbrassil Street, Dundalk, Co. Louth
Phone 042 933 3163

SUPPORT GROUPS AND ORGANISATIONS

Cuidiú — Irish Childbirth Trust
Carmichael Centre, North Brunswick Street, Dublin 7
Phone 01 8724501
www.cuidiu-ict.ie

Irish Association for Improvements in Maternity Services (AIMS)
AIMS Ireland, 18 Shantalla Place, Rahoon Road, Co. Galway
www.aimsireland.com; info@aimsireland.com

The Homebirth Association of Ireland
30 Cushla Downs, Monkslands, Athlone, Co. Roscommon
Phone 090-6493596
www.homebirth.ie; enquiries@homebirth.ie

Doula Ireland
www.doulaireland.com
TracyDonegan@DoulaIreland.com

Tiny Life (Premature and Vulnerable Baby Charity)
33 Ballynahinch Road
Carryduff
BT8 8EH
Phone 048 90815050
www.tinylife.org.uk

The Preeclampsia Foundation
www.preeclampsia.org

La Leche League of Ireland
Look in your local telephone directory
www.lalecheleagureireland.com

HOSPITALS

Cavan General Maternity Hospital
Phone 049 4376000

Coombe Women and Infants University Hospital
Phone 01 408 5200
www.coombe.ie

Cork University Maternity Hospital (CUMH)
Phone 021 492 0500

Galway University Hospital
Phone 091 524222
Maternity outpatients: 091 544 527

Kerry General Hospital
Phone 066 718 4000

Letterkenny Hospital
Phone 074 912 5888

Limerick Regional Hospital
Phone 061 301 111

Mayo General Hospital
Phone 094 902 1733

Midland Regional Hospital, Portlaoise
Phone 057 862 1364

Midland Regional Hospital, Mullingar
Phone 044 934 0221

Mount Carmel Hospital
Phone 01 492 2211/406 3400

National Maternity Hospital, Holles Street
Phone 01 637 3100
www.nmh.ie

Our Lady of Lourdes Hospital, Drogheda
Phone 041 983 7601

Portiuncula Hospital
Phone 090 964 8200

Rotunda Hospital **01 817 1700**
www.rotunda.ie

Sligo General Hospital
Phone 071 917 1111

South Tipperary General Hospital, Clonmel
Phone 052 612 1900

St Luke's General Hospital, Kilkenny
Phone 056 778 5000

Waterford Regional Hospital
Phone 051 848 000

Wexford General Hospital
Phone 053 915 3000

MULTIPLE BIRTHS

Irish Multiple Births Association
Carmichael House, North Brunswick Street, Dublin 7
Phone 01 874 9056
www.imba.ie

www.twinsandmultiples.org

OLDER MUMS

www.mothersover40.com

www.mothers35plus.co.uk

FERTILITY

National Infertility Support and Information Group
Phone 1890 647 444 (Lo-call)
Lo-call telephone line open from 7.15–9.15 p.m. (Mon–Fri)
Mobile Phone 087 797 5058
E-mail: *nisig@eircom.net*
www.nisig.ie

www.fertilityfriend.com

TTC: Trying to Conceive: The Irish Couple's Guide
Fiona McPhillips, Liberties Press, 2008.

Sims Clinic, Dublin
Fertility treatments
Phone 01 299 3920
www.sims.ie

Merrion Fertility Clinic
20 Holles Street, Dublin 2
Phone 01 678 8688
info@merrionfertility.ie
www.merrionfertility.ie

The Kilkenny Clinic
Phone 056 775 1420
info@thekilkennyclinic.com
www.thekilkennyclinic.com

Cork Fertility Centre
Phone 021 486 5764
info@corkfertilitycentre.com
www.corkfertilitycentre.com

Assisted Conception Unit at Clane Hospital
Clane General Hospital, Prosperous Road, Clane, Co. Kildare
Assisted Conception Unit
Phone 045 989 500
info@clanefertility.ie
www.claneacu.ie

HARI
Human Assisted Reproduction Ireland
Rotunda
Phone 01 807 2732
www.hari.ie

Galway Fertility Unit
Phone 091 515 600

Miscarriage and Pregnancy Loss

Miscarriage Association of Ireland
Carmichael Centre, North Brunswick Street, Dublin 7
Phone 01 873 5702 (the Centre will give you a support number for that month)
info@miscarriage.ie
www.miscarriage.ie

www.babyloss.com
UK-based resource of information and support for bereaved parents and their families who have lost a baby at any stage of pregnancy, at birth, or due to neonatal death.

Irish Stillbirth and Neonatal Death Society (ISANDS)
Carmichael House, North Brunswick Street, Dublin 7
Phone 01 872 6996
www.isands.ie

Irish Sudden Infant Death Association
Carmichael House, North Brunswick Street, Dublin 7
Phone 1850 391391; 01 873 2711
www.isida.ie

National Sudden Infant Death Register
Helpline Phone 01 878 8455
www.sidsireland.ie

Birth Websites

www.yogabirth.org
www.birthingfromwithin.com
www.sheilakitzinger.com
www.hypnobirthing.com
www.caesarean.org.uk
www.DoulaIreland.com
www.waterbirth.org
www.madeinwater.co.uk

LONE PARENTS

www.solo.ie A site for lone parents run by a lone parent.

Treoir, the National Federation for Unmarried Parents and their Children
14 Gandon House, Custom House Square, IFSC, Dublin 1
Phone 1890 252 084
www.treoir.ie

OPEN One Parent Exchange and Network
7 Red Cow Lane, Smithfield, Dublin 7
Phone 01 814 8860
www.oneparent.ie

One Family
Phone 1890 662 212
www.onefamily.ie

Citizen's Information Phone Service
Phone 1890 777 12

Money Advice and Budgeting Service (MABS)
Helpline: 1890 283 438 (Mon–Fri, 9 a.m.–8 p.m.)
www.mabs.ie

STEM-CELL PRESERVATION

Medicare Health & Living Ltd
Glencormack Business Park, Kilmacanogue, Co. Wicklow
Phone 01 201 4900
E-mail: info@medicare.ie
www.medicare.ie

PARENTING WEBSITES

www.eumom.ie
www.parentline.ie
www.netmums.com

www.babycentre.co.uk
www.helpme2parent.ie
www.rollercoaster.ie

Useful Reading

Babycentre Pregnancy Questions and Answers, 2009, Rodale.
Ian Banks, *The Dad's Survival Guide: the Early Years*, 2001, The Blackstaff Press.
Daniel Blythe, *Dadlands, The Alternative Handbook for New Fathers*, 2006, Capstone.
Dr Peter Boylan, *The Irish Pregnancy Book*, 2005, A&A Farmar.
Adam Brophy, *The Bad Dad's Survival Guide*, 2009, Gill & Macmillan.
Kaz Cooke, *The Rough Guide to Pregnancy and Birth*, 2006, Rough Guides.
Tracy Donegan, *The Better Birth Book, Taking the Mystery (and Fear) out of Childbirth*, 2006, The Liffey Press.
Pam England and Rob Horowitz, *Birthing from Within: An ExtraOrdinary Guide to Childbirth Preparation*, 1998, Partera Press.
Sheila Kitzinger, *The New Pregnancy and Childbirth*, 2003, Dorling Kindersley.
Mary Maher, *You and Your Baby*, 1973, Torc Books, published by Gill & Macmillan (no longer in print).
Ina May Gaskin, *Ina May's Guide to Childbirth*, 2008, Vermilion.
Heidi E. Murkoff, Arlene Eisenberg and Sandee E. Hathaway, *What to Expect When You're Expecting*, 2002, Simon and Schuster.
Jenny Smith, *Your Body, Your Baby, Your Birth*, 2009, Rodale.
Dr Miriam Stoppard, *Conception, Pregnancy and Birth*, 2008, Dorling Kindersley.
Juju Sundin, with Sarah Murdoch, *Juju Sundin's Birth Skills*, 2007, Vermilion.
Heather Welford, *The Complete Guide to Pregnancy and Birth*, 1998, Apple Press.
Toni Weschler, *Taking Charge of your Fertility*, 2006, HarperCollins.

Re-usable/Eco Nappies

The Natural Baby Resource
1 Flurrybridge Centre, Jonesborough, Newry BT 8SQ
'Napuccinos' — cloth nappy demonstrations — are run in south
Dublin, Bettystown, Dundrum and Stillorgan.
www.thenaturalbabyresource.com/

www.ecobaby.ie
Phone CallSave 1850 52-52-53 (Republic of Ireland)

www.bambinomio.com

Women's Environmental Network cost comparison
http://www.wen.org.uk

www.nappyinformationservice.co.uk/

www.realnappycampaign.com

ENFO
Phone 01 6761167
www.askaboutireland.ie

Depression

Postnatal Depression Ireland
Support line 021 4923162
www.pnd.ie

Aware
72 Lower Leeson Street, Dublin 2
Phone 01 661 7211
www.aware.ie

Pets

Anne Rogers — Pet Central
Phone 086 8765267

INDEX